# SECONDARY SCHOOL JOURNALISM

By Judith Ann Isaacs

Illustrations by
Greg Doud
Marcia Repaci

Butterfly and Bear Press
Seattle, Washington

Copyright ©1991 Butterfly and Bear Press

All Rights Reserved

1818 Fourth Avenue West
Seattle, Washington 98119


No part of this book may be reproduced in any form or by any means without permission in writing from Butterfly and Bear Press.

Printed in the United States of America


ISBN 0-9629645-0-6


**About the Author:** Judith Ann Isaacs, a writer and writing teacher, has taught language arts and journalism in middle school. She has a Bachelor of Journalism degree from the University of Missouri and a Master of Arts degree in Educational Administration from Seattle University. She is on the adjunct faculty of Seattle Pacific University.


**Acknowledgments:** Many thanks to Pat Welch, a skilled proofreader, and John Cook, whose encouragement never wavered.


All inquiries for volume purchases of this book should be addressed to Butterfly and Bear Press at the above address. Telephone inquiries may be made by calling 206/284-1691.

# SECONDARY SCHOOL JOURNALISM
# Table of Contents

**Chapter 1**  **Introduction to Mass Media**  1

1. Why study the media?
2. Definition of media.
3. Purposes of mass media.
4. Purposes of school media.
5. Your textbook.
6. Review for quiz.

**Chapter 2**  **All About Newspapers**  7

1. News.
2. Sources of news.
3. Opinion/Editorial.
4. Features.
5. Photos.
6. Business/Economy.
7. Sports.
8. Comics.
9. Other standard features.
10. Other types of newspapers.
11. Advertising.
12. Newspaper production.
13. Review for quiz.

**Chapter 3**  **Writing News Stories**  26

1. What is news?
2. Writing news stories.
3. Types of news stories.
4. Review for quiz.

**Chapter 4**  **Editing A Newspaper**  36

1. Style book.
2. Copyreading symbols.
3. Page layout.
4. Headlines.
5. Proofreading.
6. Review for quiz.

| **Chapter 5** | **Getting the Information** | **55** |

      1.    Interviews.
      2.    Polls.
      3.    Press conferences and speeches.
      4.    Research.
      5.    Review for quiz.

| **Chapter 6** | **Writing Features, Editorials, Sports** | **70** |

      1.    Features.
      2.    Editorials and editorial cartoons.
      3.    Sports writing.
      4.    Review for quiz.

| **Chapter 7** | **Advertising** | **85** |

      1.    Drawbacks and benefits.
      2.    Market research.
      3.    Advertising techniques.
      4.    Product identification.
      5.    Advertising appeals.
      6.    Principles of advertising.
      7.    Advertising in each medium.
      8.    Review for quiz.

| **Chapter 8** | **Magazines** | **107** |

      1.    Categories of magazines.
      2.    Magazine structure.
      3.    Editing magazines.
      4.    Advertising and research.
      5.    Production.
      6.    Review for quiz.

| **Chapter 9** | **Radio** | **120** |

      1.    Types of radio programming.
      2.    Advertising.
      3.    Writing broadcast news.
      4.    Production/Technology.
      5.    Review for quiz.

| | | | |
|---|---|---|---|
| **Chapter 10** | **Television** | | **130** |

        1.     Controversy and praise.
        2.     Types of programming.
        3.     Kinds of television.
        4.     Advertising.
        5.     Writing and producing for television.
        6.     Technology and production.
        7.     Review for quiz.

| | | | |
|---|---|---|---|
| **Chapter 11** | **Media and Society** | | **143** |

        1.     Freedom of speech vs. government control.
        2.     Right to privacy vs. right to know.
        3.     Individual rights vs. free enterprise.
        4.     Propaganda.
        5.     Review for quiz.

| | | | |
|---|---|---|---|
| **Chapter 12** | **History and Future of the Mass Media** | | **154** |

        1.     Newspapers.
        2.     Magazines.
        3.     Radio.
        4.     Television.
        5.     Advertising.
        6.     The next era -- computers.
        7.     Review for quiz.

| | | | |
|---|---|---|---|
| **Chapter 13** | **Careers in Journalism** | | **163** |

        1.     Types of jobs.
        2.     Is journalism the career for you?
        3.     Review for quiz.

# School Publications Handbook

| | | |
|---|---|---|
| **Chapter 1** | **School Newspapers** | **169** |

        1.   Structure.
        2.   Writing news stories.
        3.   Writing features.
        4.   Editing your school newspaper.

| | | |
|---|---|---|
| **Chapter 2** | **Yearbooks** | **191** |

        1.   Planning.
        2.   Writing for the yearbook.
        3.   Photography.
        4.   Editing.
        5.   Yearbook staff.

| | | |
|---|---|---|
| **Chapter 3** | **School Magazines** | **204** |

        1.   Structure.
        2.   Editing.
        3.   Production.

| | | |
|---|---|---|
| **Chapter 4** | **Advertising** | **209** |

        1.   Prospects.
        2.   Sales.
        3.   Layout.

| | | |
|---|---|---|
| **Chapter 5** | **Rights and Responsibilities of the Student Press** | **213** |

        1.   Student publications and the law.
        2.   Advertising and propaganda.
        3.   Editorial policy.

# Chapter 1

# Introduction to Mass Media

This is a course in mass media, a form of communication which has a tremendous influence on your life and the lives of everyone you know. In this chapter, you will learn (a) the importance of studying the mass media; (b) definition and purposes of mass media and school media; (c) what is in this textbook.

### Section 1. Why study the media?

We're living in a media-saturated world, in an age of instant media communication. Studies show the average person is exposed to more than 1,000 media messages each day! These messages come mostly from television, radio, movies, tapes, magazines and newspapers. Many people are tuned into stereo or television every waking minute. The average child in America by age 18 will have spent more hours in front of the TV set than in school, and teenagers are the biggest spenders in the music industry. The U.S. has approximately 2,000 daily and 7,000 weekly newspapers, plus thousands of magazines devoted to any topic you can imagine. Unless we want to live like hermits in the wilderness, we cannot escape this media bombardment. It is sending us messages whether we like it or not and even if we aren't conscious of receiving them. By learning about the influence of mass media, we can make better choices about how it affects thinking and behavior.

Because media messages are sometimes distorted or deceptive, it is necessary to develop an internal "lie detector" with which to analyze them. Advertisers may present their products in misleading ways or use psychological techniques to make you want something you don't need. Writers can slant news stories so a reader may not get all the facts and come to a mistaken conclusion. Through a study of the mass media, you will learn to separate fact from opinion and know when someone is trying to mislead the public.

As a child of the media age, you also need to be aware of hidden or indirect messages. What does seeing 5,000 advertisements showing women upset about dingy laundry contribute to stereotypes of men's and women's roles? What do children learn about respect for the law when the most popular television shows feature police officers who break laws and resolve every problem by shooting as a first resort? The best-selling news is bad news, so disasters and horrifying crimes are featured most prominently in newspapers, TV and radio. What kind of opinion does this give us of our neighbors, at home and around the world?

Some experts believe the course of history has been changed by the media explosion of the 70s and 80s. Mass media has created what has been termed a "global village." We learn about people and events in other hemispheres as quickly as people used to learn about occurrences in their home town. Events in recent history illustrate this idea.

Wars fought in foreign lands come into our living rooms on a minute-by-minute basis. Public opinion on the U.S. role in such wars is heavily influenced by what is broadcast on television and printed in the newspaper.

Candidates for public office must spend millions in media campaigns. Those who can't raise huge sums of money for advertising, no matter how outstanding their qualifications, have no chance of election.

The increased threat of terrorism has often been attributed to easy access to the media. Those who commit murder by bombing or who take hostages can count on worldwide media distribution of their messages.

The mass media play an important role in shaping society. American citizens have a constitutional right to a free press, which means journalists are able to report facts and opinions on all topics without restraint. This is not true in many countries, where no one can criticize the government or report any wrongdoing by those in power. Through studying the mass media, with all its flaws, you will understand that we could not be the same kind of people or live in a democracy without this freedom.

The mass media will continue to expand and exert its influence on our lives. We cannot stop it, but we can learn to understand it. Our best chance to control it is to become sensible, aware viewers and readers.

> ☆ *REVIEW: Restate the reasons to study the mass media and give an example of each. Suppose we had no television or newspapers. How would our lives be different?*

> ❏ *MEASURE YOUR INVOLVEMENT with the mass media by completing Homework #1.*

## Section 2. Definition of media.

***Communication*** means to transmit a message from a sender to a receiver. People communicate in many ways, verbal and non-verbal. Some means of verbal communication are telephone conversations, speeches, lectures, singing and screaming. Non-verbal communication includes sign language, writing, computer transmissions, dance, music and drawing.

Except for when a small number of persons speak face-to-face, communication requires a *medium*, which is singular for *media*. A medium which allows a single person to communicate with large numbers of people is one of the *mass media*. The forms of mass media you will study in this course are newspapers, magazines, radio, and television. Other forms of mass media are films, recordings (videos, compact discs, tapes), books, performing arts, and computers.

Media produced by students are newspapers and magazines, and, in a few schools, radio and television programs. Yearbooks are unique to schools. The school media are, of course, mass media, since they reach many more students than one person could communicate with individually.

☆ *REVIEW: Using your own words, define communication, medium, mass media.*

✔ *CHECK YOUR UNDERSTANDING of the terms introduced in this section by completing Worksheet #1.*

## Section 3. Purposes of mass media.

Generally, the purposes of mass media are to inform, to entertain, or to persuade. Some media emphasize one purpose and others mix all three. When considering fine arts, like sculpture or musical composition, an additional purpose may be the artist's desire for self-expression.

Newspapers' primary goal is to keep readers up-to-date on the latest news developments, and that's why people read them -- to obtain *information*. Newspapers also provide entertainment through non-news items like comics, puzzles and amusing stories. Other sources of information messages are newscasts and documentaries on radio and television.

Magazines for general audiences include a little of everything: fiction, humor, information and opinion. Others have only one intent, such as information *(U.S. News & World Report)* or entertainment *(Mad)*.

No matter how entertaining or informative it may be, advertising always has the purpose of *persuading* you to part with your money. Except for public radio and television stations, which are supported mainly by government subsidies and private donations, advertising pays the costs of print and electronic media.

Another form of persuasion is newspaper, radio or television editorials, which attempt to convince the audience of a certain opinion. In some magazines, all articles are presented with a specific political or social slant, and their purpose is more to persuade than to inform.

Television is above all an *entertainment* medium. Think of the most common television shows: sports, soaps, situation comedies, action/adventure, cartoons -- each designed to entertain people of all ages. Radio, too, is a medium of entertainment. Most stations play music all day -- music selected to entertain a specific group of listeners. People tune in to the station that plays "their kind of music."

Ninety-nine percent of the multi-million dollar recording industry is made to entertain, by selling music that suits everyone's taste. Videotapes for the home market have emerged as a previously untapped source of entertainment, capturing business from movie theaters, television networks and cable companies.

Computers may either inform or amuse. Some programs are for enjoyment, like games; others for education, like a spelling tutor. A subscriber to an information service can get stock market prices or an encyclopedic report on Afghanistan.

✔ *CHECK YOUR UNDERSTANDING of the purposes of mass media by completing Worksheet #2.*

## Section 4. Purposes of school media.

School media exist for the same purposes of *information, entertainment* and *persuasion*. School newspapers contain factual stories and amusing stories, editorials, and sometimes advertising. Yearbooks are extremely entertaining; nothing is more fun than looking at pictures of yourself and your classmates.

School media, however, have other reasons to exist. They are a form of expression for the students who participate and a means for those students to learn new skills and increase their knowledge. School media promote school spirit and create for students a sense of belonging. Because school newspapers and yearbooks are read in detail by nearly everyone in a school, they offer a common shared experience. Also, school media are a way for the school to communicate with the larger community. They say, "Look at this. Here's who we are."

## Section 5. Your textbook.

**Secondary School Journalism** is based on the idea that you understand any subject better when you have a chance to try doing it yourself. During this course, you will have many opportunities to practice the writing and production skills necessary to produce each medium studied. Worksheets, homework assignments, and projects will help you to improve your abilities.

Part One is a general study of mass media; Part Two gives specific instructions for writing, editing and producing media in your school. The following five chapters are devoted to studying newspapers, with emphasis on writing and information-gathering skills. Much of the vocabulary you learn in these chapters will be repeated in later chapters about other media. New skills you acquire in newspaper writing will be useful in writing for magazines, radio and television. Since you need no special equipment or facilities for publishing a school newspaper, you can start one this semester if your school lacks one now.

Some words used in the text may be unfamiliar to you. Journalism vocabulary is explained; you must take responsibility for learning the meanings of other new words so you gain the most from your reading.

When you come to a *REVIEW*, your teacher will instruct you to review silently to yourself or to participate orally with a partner or with the whole class.

Some students who take journalism want to start "working" on the newspaper and yearbook right away. However, it is important to master basic journalism skills through reading and practice before you can produce well-written and good-looking school publications.

> ☆ *REVIEW: Turn to the Table of Contents and read the list of topics you will study in* **Secondary School Journalism.**

## Section 6. Review for quiz.

1. The purposes of the mass media are to (a) inform, (b) entertain, and (c) persuade. In addition, school media increase school spirit and offer students a chance to learn new skills and express themselves.

2. The mass media you will study in this course are (a) newspapers, (b) magazines, (c) radio, (d) television.

3. Reasons to study the mass media are (a) to understand how inescapable they are in today's world; (b) to recognize deceptive and hidden messages; (c) to understand the impact the media has on our society; (d) to be better-informed media consumers; (e) to produce school media.

4. New vocabulary in this chapter:

   communication        mass media
   entertain            medium
   inform               persuade

# Chapter 2
# All About Newspapers

Most pages in a newspaper are devoted to news stories, which are reports about recent events at home and around the world. However, in addition to reporting "hard" news, newspapers inform readers about a variety of subjects from trekking in Tibet to changing the spark plugs in a car. Some newspaper readers want only to be entertained and turn directly to the horoscope or Dear Abby or the comic page. Others read nothing but sports news or only check the ads for sales. Newspapers try to provide something for everyone in order to increase their sales and to compete successfully with other newspapers, as well as other media, such as radio and TV.

In this chapter, you will learn the answers to these questions:

What can you find in a daily newspaper?
Where do newspaper stories come from?
Who decides what to print?
How does a newspaper get on the street?

You will be using copies of daily newspapers to complete classroom and homework assignments in this chapter.

Generally, daily newspapers have sections for the following categories, although some "sections" may be only two or three pages.

General news
Local news
Sports
Business
Arts and entertainment
Home and lifestyle
Editorial and opinion

Look for each of these sections in your newspaper.

Newspapers have three different kinds of writing: *news*, *feature*, and *editorial*. Some sections of the newspaper have only news, only editorial opinion, or only features, and some have all three. These three styles of writing fulfill the purposes of information, entertainment and persuasion.

*News writing* reports only verified facts about an event. Reporters make every effort to obtain the facts and to eliminate expressions of personal opinion in a story so it will be impartial. The first section of a newspaper contains the major stories of the day.

***Feature stories*** are entertaining as well as informative and may include the writer's opinions. Reviews of movies, restaurants, the latest fashions or new cars are definitely opinionated. In contrast to news stories, features don't have to be about the latest, up-to-the-minute happenings; for example, how to get the stains out of your clothes. Two of the sections in your newspaper, Arts/Entertainment and Lifestyle, are filled with features.

***Editorials and opinion columns*** are entirely for the purpose of stating opinions and persuading readers to adopt a specific point of view. Editorials are in the first section.

> ☆ *REVIEW: In your own words, explain the difference between news, features and editorials. Find examples of each in your newspaper. Analyze news stories to see if they include opinions.*

## Section 1. News.

You will find four levels of news in the paper: local, state, national and international.

***Local*** news covers events that happen in the city where the paper is published, and ***state*** news covers events that happen in the same state. ***National*** news occurs someplace in the United States, while ***international*** or world news involves countries other than the U.S. Although stories of national and international origin usually dominate the front page, readers frequently are more interested in state and local news, because it is more likely to affect their lives.

Following are examples of the four kinds of news stories:

*Local:* A teacher from your school successfully completes a 5,000-mile cross-country bicycle trip.

*State:* The governor announces the receipt of an additional $2 billion in highway construction funds.

*National:* Members of the United States Senate begin the fifth day of debate on the budget.

*International:* Six people were killed in a bombing during a parade in Londonderry, Northern Ireland.

> ☆ *REVIEW: Find an example of each kind of news story in your newspaper.*

✔ CHECK YOUR UNDERSTANDING of the four levels of news stories by completing Worksheet #3 and Homework #2.

## Section 2. Sources of news.

Good newspapers inform readers about the *sources* of each story, or where the information came from. A reporter's sources are the people s/he talks to or the documents s/he reads. Newspapers' major sources of news are their local staff, wire services, correspondents and press releases.

A newspaper has a staff of reporters, each of whom is assigned a *beat*. A beat is the place or type of story which the reporter checks on regularly. For example, a reporter may have the police beat. S/he goes to police headquarters and reads the police log each day to find out what has occurred in the past 24 hours. The reporter gets to know the officers and administrators so they will feel comfortable sharing information. Other local beats typically include major city and county offices, sports, teams, arts organizations, business leaders, and schools. Large newspapers have reporters assigned to cover the state capital and Washington, D.C. A reporter follows up on any *leads*, or bits of information from any source, that may develop into a news story.

Here's what a reporter might do who has the school district beat.

Chris Hollins covers the school beat. Tonight is a regular school board meeting, and the board is going to vote on increasing the budget for athletics. Chris calls all the board members in the morning to ask how they plan to vote and get any comments they have on the issue. Most say they won't comment in advance. One had mailed out a press release explaining why he opposes the increase, and Chris asks some questions about his statement. Chris has become good friends with the superintendent's secretary and has received several reports about athletics. In addition, Chris has a good quote from an interview yesterday with the superintendent.

The story for tomorrow's paper will report on the vote, what the board members said, either in the public meeting or in the phone interviews, and reports of other people's testimony at the board meeting. It will include the quote from the superintendent and background information learned from reading the reports. A followup story might be interviews with principals, parents, and students about their opinions on the issue, either way the vote goes.

☆ REVIEW: Define beat. Look through a newspaper and list what beats might be represented by the stories you read.

***Foreign correspondents*** in the truest sense are a thing of the past. In the 19th century, papers would pay an adventuresome writer to go to a remote or dangerous place and send back dispatches. A famous example of this is Henry Stanley, hired by the *New York Herald Tribune* to find the African explorer David Livingston, who had disappeared during his search for the headwaters of the Nile. His understated greeting, after the remarkable coincidence of locating Livingston in the unmapped African interior, has become an English cliche: "Dr. Livingston, I presume." Today, reporters from metropolitan dailies around the world cover the international "hot spots" and write stories for their papers.

Another type of correspondent is a writer for a small town paper who sells interesting local stories to a metropolitan daily. These writers are sometimes called ***stringers***.

All but the biggest papers depend on ***wire services*** to provide them with news from around the world. Wire services maintain bureaus, or offices, in all major cities. Their reporters submit, or file, stories from Johannesburg, Cairo, Manila, London, or Los Angeles. The stories, and photos, then are transmitted by telephone lines (the wire) to terminals in the newsrooms of the newspapers who subscribe to their service. The terminals print out stories and pictures twenty-four hours per day; editors use as much as they want. The two American wire services are Associated Press (AP) and United Press International (UPI). Two important foreign wire services are Reuters, based in Great Britain, and Tass in Russia.

Stories from wire services are identified in the ***dateline***. A dateline appears at the beginning of a story and names the city where it originated and the initials of the wire service. For example, BUENOS AIRES, Argentina (UPI) or WICHITA, Kansas (AP). In the early days, datelines included the date a story was written because it took days or even weeks for a paper to be delivered across the country. Therefore, the reader needed to know how old the news was.

> ☆ REVIEW: Define stringer, wire service, dateline. Look in your newspaper to find national and international datelines from both wire services. See if you can find a story that might have been submitted by a stringer.

***Press releases*** are written by any person or group which wishes to gain publicity by having its activities mentioned in the newspaper. Among those who consistently use press releases are political candidates, entertainers, social and charitable organizations and businesses. Press releases are written like a news story and mailed to all media. Editors choose whether or not to use the information. If it is used, it will usually be rewritten by a reporter. Often the job of rewriting press releases goes to an intern or beginning reporter.

Stories about new products, changes in a business organization, fund-raising functions, new construction, and celebrity appearances are examples of items that originate with press releases.

*SAMPLE PRESS RELEASE*

> LAX FORMAN COSMETICS
> SYLVIA LA GRANDE, (503) 543-6870
>
>
> FOR IMMEDIATE RELEASE
>
>
> Twenty-nine shades of green are featured in the new line of Lax Forman edible lipsticks unveiled today. The public will have a chance to see and taste the latest lipstick fashions at a show from 4-6 p.m. Thursday in the Royal Room at the Sheraton Hotel.
>
> The show will feature videos, live models, displays, and samples. Door prizes include free makeup kits and free facials. Company representatives will be present to answer questions about Lax Forman products.
>
> "The ingredients in the Green Goddess Lipsticks are a scientific breakthrough," stated laboratory supervisor Gloria Bilt. "They are, of course, edible, but the greatest benefit is that one lipstick tube has only one calorie."

Some stories in the newspaper state the writer's name at the beginning; i.e., By Lynn Scott. This is called a **byline**. Bylines appear on stories that involved exceptional work by a reporter, and it is considered an honor when an editor gives a reporter a byline. Bylines always appear on feature stories which may include an opinion, because the reader has the right to know whose opinion is being presented.

☆ *REVIEW: Define press release and byline. Look in your newspaper to find an example of a byline. See if you can find a story that sounds like it was based on a press release.*

✔ *CHECK YOUR UNDERSTANDING of sources of news by completing Worksheet #4 and Homework #3.*

## Section 3. Opinion/Editorial.

The opinion and editorial section of a newspaper (op-ed) is the place designated for expressing opinions and offering analysis and explanation of current events. You will find these items on the op-ed pages: staff (or house) editorials, editorial columnists, editorial cartoons, and letters to the editor.

House editorials appear on the left side of the first page of the op-ed section, usually set apart by a different style or size of type and different column width. They do not have a byline because they represent the newspaper's opinion, as agreed to by its editors and publishers, and not that of an individual writer. Common topics for editorials are proposed legislation, endorsements of candidates, court decisions, U.S. foreign or domestic policy, and outrageous or outstanding acts by individuals.

Many of the writers appearing on the op-ed pages are *syndicated* columnists who have a specific political viewpoint. Companies called syndicates employ these writers, and sell their columns to newspapers across the country. The same syndicated column can appear in papers in San Francisco, Dallas, Wichita, and Roanoke. Newspapers try to purchase columnists with different viewpoints, so readers can learn about all sides of an issue. Syndicated columns will be identified by a line at the end of the story.

Editorial cartoons are not cartoons in the sense that they are meant to be funny; some are funny, but not all. They express an opinion through pictures instead of words. Newspapers have staff cartoonists but also use the work of syndicated cartoonists. A cartoonist's subject must be something that is currently receiving a lot of attention in the press, because a reader often needs some background information in order to understand editorial cartoons. A frequent device in cartoons is to caricature a famous person by picking a unique physical feature of that person and drawing it in an exaggerated way. Cartoonists must couple a talent for drawing with a shrewd understanding of world and local news events.

In the past few years, comic strip writers have confused editors and readers alike by emphasizing political issues in their strips. A good example is Gary Trudeau, author of "Doonesbury," who in 1985 was moved from the comic pages to the editorial pages in some newspapers because of his controversial portrayal of public figures.

Every newspaper has a Letters to the Editor section. Here it prints letters in which readers respond to stories and editorials or letters which may call attention to an issue the letter writer thinks has been overlooked. Newspapers have a specific policy about printing letters, and the policy is printed on the op-ed pages. In general, these policies state that all letters must be signed, even if the person requests to have his/her name withheld, and the editor reserves the right to edit, or omit parts of, the letter. Letters to the editor can be a good indicator of public opinion on an issue, and metropolitan daily newspapers print only the most well-written of the hundreds of letters they receive.

Traditionally, a newspaper's *masthead* is printed in the editorial section. The masthead names the publisher and chief editors.

> ☆ REVIEW: Explain in your own words the differences among house editorials, syndicated columnists, editorial cartoons, and letters to the editor. Look at the op-ed pages in your newspaper for examples of each. Find one that especially interests you and discuss why you agree or disagree with the opinions expressed. Define masthead and find it in your newspaper.

> ✔ CHECK YOUR UNDERSTANDING of the op/ed section by completing Homework #4.

## Section 4. Features.

> It is funny what you remember in the end. His mother remembers being on her knees, scrubbing the bathroom floor, when her son, Paul, came in and sat on her bed and asked through the open door how long he had to live.
> He knew he had cancer. He knew that, at age 17, he had it bad. . . .
> "When you told me before about the prognosis, I thought that meant I might live until I was 30 or 40," he said. "Will I live that long?"
> She shook her head. . . .

These are a few paragraphs from a feature story that ran in *The Seattle Times*. Feature stories differ from news stories in that they are not necessarily tied to news events and do not follow the rules for news writing. Since the primary purpose is not to relate a set of facts, the style is more like a narrative.

One definition of a feature is to say it's everything in the newspaper that isn't a news story or an editorial. Features can be classified by type of story and by the subject covered.

Regular features usually are syndicated and run on a daily or weekly schedule. Advice columnists, Dear Abby and Ann Landers, for example, are syndicated feature writers which most newspapers run daily. Other syndicated how-to features run weekly. They discuss such diverse topics as pet care, sewing tips, stock market analysis or purchase of computers and software. These features are entertaining and informative to readers, and they help sell newspapers by appealing to a broad range of interests.

Feature stories can be identified by the focus or purpose of the story. The following discusses seven types of features.

***Personality.*** The purpose of a personality story (often called a profile) is to draw a word picture of a person who is well known or whose life is interesting in some way. Newspapers always try to get interviews with famous people when they come to town in order to run a personality feature.

***How-to.*** Americans are known for their do-it-yourself spirit. How-to topics are endless -- how to build a fence, how to rid your house of insects, how to select the right colors to wear, how to choose a ripe cantaloupe, how to be accepted at the right college, etc., etc., etc.

***Historical.*** Historical features describe an episode or period of time that has passed, but they may be prompted by a news event. Anniversaries of important events stimulate historical features; i.e., the Kennedy assassination, the Hiroshima bombing, the first moon landing. Others describe some aspect of local history.

***Humorous.*** Some features, usually written regularly by the same columnist, are simply funny. They may make a point about a current issue, but the primary intent is to amuse. Art Buchwald, Dave Barry and Erma Bombeck are humorists whose syndicated columns are widely used.

***Background or informative.*** The intent of background or informative features is to give the reader an in-depth understanding of an event or issue. Generally, they are prompted by current news, but some are interesting because they discuss something readers are curious about. Examples are stories on social problems such as child abuse, illiteracy, poverty and euthansia or environmental problems such as nuclear waste or acid rain.

***Human interest.*** Features that appeal to emotions, causing readers to laugh, feel sad, or have empathy for the person in the story, are called human interest. The story quoted at the beginning of this chapter, about the teenage boy learning his death was imminent, is a human interest story.

***Reviews*** are a type of feature that fill a category of their own. Newspapers have staff writers, also called ***critics,*** who regularly review movies, plays, art shows, concerts, dance performances, books, and restaurants. Reviewers can have a lot of influence on the success of those enterprises. In New York City, the American center of live theater, acting companies stay up all night on opening night to read the reviews in the morning papers. If the critics say the play is bad (if it is "panned"), no one will buy tickets and it will fold immediately. However, if the reviews are mostly favorable, their success is assured.

In other arts, noticeably movies, reviewers are not so influential. Many movies which have had huge commercial success have been routinely panned by the critics. If reviews are both positive and negative, a production has a "mixed" review.

Features add spice and liveliness to newspapers. Unfortunately, straight news is often bad news, and features offer readers a balance of information presented in an entertaining manner.

☆ *REVIEW: Before you go on, share what you recall about the seven types of features. See how many you can find in your newspaper.*

✔ *CHECK YOUR UNDERSTANDING of features by completing Worksheet #5, Homework #5 and Homework #6.*

## Section 5. Photos.

Many photojournalists have justifiably become famous, not only for the quality of their photos, but for their courage in obtaining photos in life-threatening situations. A reporter can send back a good story about a battle or a natural disaster based on interviewing people away from the scene. A photographer, however, has to be where the action is to get a memorable photo.

It is essential to have photos to run with major news stories. Sources are staff photographers, wire services, correspondents and press releases. Photos that accompany feature stories are often posed or selected with the purpose of illustrating the subject of that specific story.

The sentence of explanation under a photograph is referred to as the **cutline**. The term comes from the early days of printing when an engraving, called a cut, was made of an illustration before it could be printed. With new technology, the term no longer is descriptive. However, like much of the vocabulary of journalism, the old words still are used.

☆ *REVIEW: Look at the photos in your paper. Decide if they are news or feature photos. Discuss what the photographer might have had to do to get the photo. Read at least one cutline. What is the source of the photo?*

✔ *CHECK YOUR UNDERSTANDING of newspaper photos, by completing Homework #7.*

## Section 6. Business/Economy.

News of business and economy is important to many people. The life of a city or community is directly affected by the health of the businesses located there. Most adults depend on a business enterprise for their paychecks, and some people follow business news for leads on investments.

One famous daily newspaper, *The Wall Street Journal*, has nothing but business news or stories about how other events affect the nation's economy.

A regular feature in the Business Section of the daily newspapers is the stock market report. It covers several pages and gives a daily report on the price of thousands of stocks listed on the New York Stock Exchange and, in some papers, other stock exchanges. People who own stock like to check on whether the price is rising or falling.

> ☆ *REVIEW: Find the business section in your newspaper. What are the topics of the stories? Read a few listings in the stock market report.*

> ❑ *IF YOU WOULD LIKE to follow a listing on the stock exchange, complete Worksheet #6.*

## Section 7. Sports.

You may be one of the people who read only the sports section of the newspaper. Good sports writing is a must for a successful newspaper. Sports sections contain news stories, features, lots of photos, and, sometimes, opinion columns and letters to the editor. Most of the space is given to the major college and professional sports of football, basketball and baseball. However, all other sports get some attention, including hunting and fishing.

Sports sections always have a page of box scores, which cover all athletic activities of interest to readers. This includes high school (prep) scores and amateur leagues.

> ☆ *REVIEW: Find the page of box scores in your newspaper and make a listing of every different sport represented. Locate examples of news and feature stories and an opinion column.*

> ✔ *CHECK YOUR UNDERSTANDING of the sports section by completing Homework #8.*

## Section 8. Comics.

Readers develop intense loyalty to their favorite comic strips. For some readers, the comic pages are THE most important part of the newspaper. As you know, comic strips are not always comical. Some are like soap operas, some are adventure, and some are fantasy. Newspapers buy the strips from a syndicate and discontinue those which are not popular with a majority of readers. Each strip is signed by the writer and dated, so the paper will run them in the correct order.

Whole books have been written about single comic strips and the art of cartooning. Many popular strips are reprinted in books, and adults love to recall fondly the strips that were favorites when they were young. In the 1940s and 1950s (before TV), the Sunday comics were read aloud on the radio, and kids followed along in their living rooms.

If you have tried drawing cartoons, you know it takes special skill. A comic writer must provide clear, detailed drawing that will reproduce in a small format, and the story must be told with just a few words of dialogue in a "balloon."

☆ *REVIEW: Find the comics page in your newspaper and note the signature and date in each strip.*

❑ *TO CONTINUE this look at the comics, complete Homework #9.*

## Section 9. Other standard features.

***Weather.*** The weather is always news, as our personal correspondence frequently demonstrates. The weather column may include a weather map, tide tables, humidity index, air pollution index, and high and low temperatures around the world.

***Obituaries.*** "Obits" are announcements of deaths. They are full-fledged news stories when a well-known person dies; however, brief listings of all deaths in the city or county are carried in the newspaper. An obituary mentions the person's accomplishments and names surviving family members.

Newspapers keep pre-written obituaries of famous people on file, so if that person dies, the story will be ready with the addition of the circumstances of death. Writing and updating obits is a common assignment for a beginning reporter.

***Vital Statistics.*** Information on births, deaths, marriages and divorces is called vital statistics. Since they are a matter of public record, they are available to reporters and are listed in the daily newspaper. As with obituaries, it is generally only well-known persons whose divorces or children's births are made the subject of a news story. Some newspapers use wedding information if the story and photo are furnished by the family and if space is available.

***Horoscope.*** Most newspapers now print a syndicated horoscope column, and, like comics and sports, this is the only item some people read.

***Crossword Puzzle.*** All newspapers carry a crossword puzzle, and some now have added other types of puzzles as well. *The New York Times* Sunday Crossword is legendary for its difficulty and is now syndicated.

☆ *REVIEW: Find examples of each of these standard features in your newspaper.*

## Section 10. Other types of newspapers.

In this chapter so far you have studied a metropolitan daily newspaper. Your community also may have weekly or ethnic newspapers. They generally have the same types of stories and reporting standards, but they target a more specific audience or have a smaller distribution area. Tabloid newspapers are available nationwide.

**Weekly Newspapers.** Weekly newspapers serve small towns or neighborhoods within large cities. Stories emphasize the names of residents in their distribution area. They report on happenings that are of interest to people in that neighborhood but are not important to the general readership of the citywide newspaper. If you win a spelling prize at school, a big newspaper considers that too trivial to print, but a weekly newspaper is happy to use it.

❑ *ACTIVITY: To study weekly newspapers, read some from your area. Compare and contrast them to the daily newspaper you have been examining.*

**Ethnic Newspapers.** Ethnic newspapers are printed for a particular ethnic group and may be in a language other than English. Newspapers for Jewish and black communities are fairly common. Non-English newspapers are published in cities with large concentrations of residents who read another language; i.e., Spanish or Chinese.

❑ *ACTIVITY: If your city has an ethnic newspaper, obtain copies and compare and contrast it to the daily newspaper you have been examining.*

**Tabloids**. Tabloid newspapers, such as *The National Enquirer* and *The Star*, are in a class by themselves. The headlines are sensational and startling, and photos of film or music stars are displayed on the front page. They make no attempt to cover the news of the day, but tend to use the same type of stories and same celebrity names over and over.

Tabloids have become the objects of satire because of their repetitious stories on amazing miracle diets, encounters with aliens, bizarre natural phenomena, and scandalous behavior of famous people. These newspapers do not follow the strict journalistic standards of other newspapers. They often are subject to lawsuits by the people whom they write about, and the writers are accused of submitting stories without verifying the facts.

❑ *ACTIVITY: To study tabloid newspapers, read a copy, then compare and contrast it to the daily newspaper you have examined. If you wish to get into a discussion of libel at this point, study Section 2 in Chapter 11.*

## Section 11. Advertising.

Without question, newspapers offer an extremely valuable service to their communities. However, they do not do so out of the goodness of their hearts. Newspapers, and other media, are profit-making businesses. They strive for good reporting, entertaining features, and stimulating editorial opinions so they can attract many readers which will, in turn, attract many advertisers. The more advertising a newspaper can sell, the more money it can make. **Subscribers** (readers who pay to have the paper delivered each day) contribute only 25 percent of a newspaper's income.

Advertisers, in newspapers, are for the most part retail businesses in the paper's **circulation area**. Circulation area refers to the geographical boundaries in which subscribers live, and circulation is the number of people who subscribe. The cost of advertising is based on circulation, because the more people who read the newspaper, the more the advertising is worth.

Newspapers sell two kinds of ads: **display** and **classified**. Display ads are the ones distributed throughout the pages, in various sizes, usually with line borders. Some take up a whole page. Classified ads, the "want ads," are printed in small type and listed together in a separate section at the back of the newspaper.

Display advertising is sold by the ***column inch***, with special half-page and full-page ***rates***. The rate is the price the newspaper charges the advertiser for the space used by the ad. A column inch is one column wide and one inch high. Therefore, an ad that extends across three columns and is fourteen inches high has 42 column inches. The advertisers would be charged for 42 column inches; i.e., the rate for one column inch multiplied by 42.

A third category of newspaper advertising is ***preprints*** or stuffers. Those of you who have been paper carriers have had the job of inserting the preprints before delivering on your route. For example, a large furniture store may have four pages of color advertising printed and then stuffed inside the newspaper, instead of buying four pages of advertising.

The biggest advantage of newspaper advertising is its timeliness. A store can advertise sales and specials that have a time limit, and readers expect to get this kind of "news" about prices and bargains.

Classified advertising has dozens of categories, listed in an index. The largest categories are real estate, rentals, help wanted, and car sales. Rates are printed in the classified section and vary according to the number of words or lines and the number of days the ad will appear; for example, five cents per word or $2 per line.

☆ *REVIEW: Define circulation, display, classified, column inch, rate, preprint, subscription. Look in your newspaper for the cost of a subscription. Note the various sizes of display ads. Find the classified section.*

✔ *CHECK YOUR UNDERSTANDING of newspaper advertising by completing Worksheet #7.*

## Section 12. Newspaper production.

Producing a daily newspaper, like a daily broadcast, is something of a miracle. If you think of the time it takes you to write a one-page school assignment, you may begin to appreciate what is involved to write, edit, set into type, print and distribute EACH DAY a newspaper of between 60-100 pages. That's approximately 3,000 words per page!

Technological advances have speeded up production in the newspaper field as in many others. Today's newspapers have more pages, with more photos, make fewer errors, and print more copies faster than those of even 25 years ago.

Let's follow a news story from the time it is written until you read it in your home.

Remember a story is written from several sources. A reporter may sit at a desk and write from notes, or s/he may rewrite it from wire service stories. If *deadline* is close, a reporter may phone in the story and another reporter in the office will write it. Each newspaper has a deadline, a time by which all stories must be written and the editors have made all decisions about placement. Deadlines are approximately six hours before the paper hits the streets.

Newspapers today use *word processors* instead of typewriters. Word processors, as used in a newspaper, are computer terminals, or desktop computers, often linked together to a main computer that stores data. The reporter types on a keyboard and the words appear on a screen, the video display terminal (VDT).

Using word processors saves time in two ways. It eliminates handling hard copy, or stories typed on paper. The editor can read the reporter's story by calling it up on his/her VDT and either accept it or ask for changes. Formerly, the reporter typed a story and it was carried to the editor who read it, marked it with pencil, and had it carried back. A second important benefit is that word processing eliminates typesetting. The reporter's story is stored in the computer. When it is finished and approved by the editor, the computer prints it out in the format used in the newspaper; i.e., in column width with the right margin *justified*, or adjusted to print evenly. The computer eliminates the need for another person to retype the reporter's words on some form of typesetting machine.

☆ *REVIEW: Explain how word processors are used at a newspaper. Define deadline and justify.*

In addition to approving the reporter's work, editors decide what is printed and on which page to run it. Editors for local, national and international news, business news, and photos will meet with the *managing editor* to go over the news *budget* each day. The budget is a list of all news items they have ready. The front page is most important, and the editors decide not only what goes on the front page but WHERE on the front page.

The most important stories go **above the fold**, either across the top of the page or in the upper right-hand corner. Other stories they think are important will go up front, or in the first few pages of the newspaper. News days are "light" or "heavy," depending on how many important stories have come in. On heavy days, the editors must negotiate for which stories will make the front page. On light days, editors may have to scramble to fill the first few pages. These are the days when you see photos of cute kids or dogs on the front page.

Of course, the name of the newspaper must always appear on the front page, usually in very large, distinctive type. This nameplate is also called the **flag**, and it is always placed above the fold.

Written stories are referred to as **copy**, whether on paper or on computer. After the news editors have finished deciding what to use and where to use it, the reporter's copy goes to the copy editors. Their job is to check for errors of fact, spelling, punctuation, paragraphing and grammar. Copy editors write **headlines**, the titles above each story, and decide what size type to print them in. They memorize how many letters of each size type will fill a column so the headlines they write will fit. They also memorize the newspaper's **style book**, a guide to the usage preferred by the paper in all situations where there is more than one way to write something. For example, the style book will instruct reporters and editors whether to use 10 or ten; whether to use Ms., Mrs., or Miss; whether or not to put a comma before the "and" in a series.

After the copy editors finish with the copy, it goes to the layout editors. Deciding where to place all the elements on a page is called making a **layout**. The layout editors must know the size of each ad, the length of each news story or feature, the size of each photo and headline, and what page and section each must go on. This process, also, is computerized in large daily newspapers.

The stories provided by the editors must fit into the spaces left after the ads are placed, or into what is called the **news hole**. As you look at your newspaper, you will notice there are no blank spaces, or "holes," left. Every inch of every column has something in it. To accomplish this, layout editors cut off the end of a story if it is too long to fit the hole. If the stories are too short, they use **fillers**. Fillers are little items of no real importance that are used to fill space. If stories are to be continued on another page (jumped), the layout editors must keep track of the end of the story and be sure it is included.

Layout is also called composition, and layout editors follow certain rules of composition in arranging the elements on each page. For example, advertising always goes at the bottom; the larger headlines go at the top. Many other rules guide layout editors, and with minor variations, they are followed by all major newspapers in the U.S.

☆ REVIEW: Explain the jobs of news editor, copy editor and layout editor. Define these words: budget, flag, deadline, copy, style book, news hole, filler, headline. Find the following in your newspaper: flag, a filler, a headline. What stories are above the fold? Do you agree with the editor's placement?

After the final version of each page is ready, one copy is printed. A ***proofreader*** reads every inch of the page, looking for mistakes. All errors are noted and sent back for correction. Then the page is ready to be made into a plate.

Through a photographic process, a ***plate*** which fits onto the ***press*** is made of each page. The press is a machine which actually prints on the paper. In simplified terms, making a plate is like taking a picture of each page, and the plate is like a negative. It is treated so ink adheres to the type and photos.

Photos must go through a special process before they are ready to be printed. They are ***screened***. A microscopically fine screen is laid over the original photograph, and it is photographed again through the screen. The effect is to break up the dark parts in the picture, which would be difficult to print if solid. If you look at a newspaper photo under a magnifying glass, you will be able to see the screen.

After the plates are made, they are attached to high speed web presses. The presses are so named because the paper runs through on a long continuous roll. It is cut into pages after the pages are printed.

The papers come off the press folded and ready to be bundled. They are trucked to distribution points throughout the circulation area. Some of you have been paper carriers and are familiar with the routine of going to a pick-up point, counting out your papers, inserting the preprints, and making your rounds. Trucks also deliver to stores and fill the self-service newspaper boxes on sidewalks. Newspapers rely on their carriers for distribution, and the child labor laws specifically exempt paper carriers.

Some papers have several editions. The first edition of a morning paper is called the ***bulldog edition***. Minor changes will be made in subsequent editions to add the latest news developments. This means the whole process described above will be repeated for a few pages, which are substituted for those in the first edition. Such changes must be limited because of the time involved.

☆ REVIEW: Define proofreader, plate, press, screen, bulldog.

✔ CHECK YOUR UNDERSTANDING of newspaper production by completing Worksheet #8.

## STEPS IN NEWSPAPER PRODUCTION

Stories, based on reporters' notes or wire service reports, are keyed in on word processors. An editor goes over each story and approves it or requests changes.

News editors decide which stories will go on each page. Layout editors decide how to arrange stories, photos and ads on each page. Much of this process is computerized on a large newspaper.

Everything -- headlines, stories, cutlines, ads -- is read by a proofreader. Then, using a photographic process, completed pages are made into plates that fit onto a press.

Thousands of copies are printed on huge web presses, which also cut the paper and fold it into individual copies. Morning newspapers are delivered to distribution points during the night.

## Section 13. Review for quiz.

1. Most newspapers are divided into the following sections: News, Opinion/Editorial, Sports, Business, Entertainment/Living.

2. Newspapers have three types of writing: news, features, editorials.

3. Vocabulary words:

| | |
|---|---|
| beat | lead |
| bulldog | local news |
| byline | managing editor |
| circulation | masthead |
| classified ad | national news |
| column inch | news hole |
| copy | plate |
| critic | press |
| cutline | press release |
| dateline | proofreader |
| deadline | reporter |
| display ad | review |
| filler | source |
| flag | style book |
| headline | subscriber |
| international news | syndicated columnist |
| justify | wire service |
| layout | word processor |

# Chapter 3
# Writing News Stories

Newswriting has special requirements, which you will learn and practice in this chapter. You will study these aspects of writing news: (a) Recognizing news; (b) Using newswriting style; (c) Writing objectively; (d) Understanding different kinds of news stories.

## Section 1. What is news?

*News* is a report of a recent event or happening. News also is a report of a recent development in an ongoing event. For example, during a murder investigation, the news each day after the first report is about the latest developments such as clues, suspects, or arrests. News is based on *facts*, information which can be verified.

Now if you think about that definition, you realize that a newspaper uses other guidelines about what to print. A recent verifiable event was that you got out of bed, dressed and came to school. However, that hardly would interest a newspaper.

*The New York Times,* one of the world's great newspapers, has a slogan: "All the news that's fit to print." In order to decide what's fit to print, newspapers look at six criteria in addition to immediacy, or the fact that something just happened.

1. ***Nearness*** -- It's news because it happens in your town or your state. Often, when the same event occurs elsewhere, it isn't news. For example, your city council passes a dog leash law. That's news in your daily newspaper. However, it's not news if another town passes the same law, since you are unlikely to be walking your dog there.

2. ***Importance*** -- The more people affected by an event, the more important it becomes. Happenings that affect thousands are news, no matter where they occur. Scientific advances are news because they may save (or destroy) millions of lives.

3. ***Drama or conflict*** -- Stories that touch your emotions -- fear, sorrow, joy, anger -- are news. Items about crimes, fires, winning a lottery, lawsuits, or football games have drama or conflict. These are stories that readers can identify with and say to themselves, "That could be me."

4. ***Names*** -- Names are news because all of us love to see our names in the paper or to recognize the name of a friend or acquaintance. This is why newspapers print stories of weddings, scholarship winners, business promotions, high school sports, and newly elected club officers.

5. ***Famous people*** -- Famous people make news doing things that are of no interest if they happen to the average person. The divorce of a well-known entertainer is news; the divorce of your next-door neighbor is not. When the president has an operation, it's news; the same operation on the other 5,000 people that year did not get in the papers.

6. ***Amusing, entertaining or unusual happenings*** -- Something odd or unusual is news, and sometimes newspapers carry stories that are just amusing. Strange contests like slug races or raw oyster eating receive this kind of news attention, as well as weddings underwater, mass whale beachings, and growing a 300-pound zucchini squash.

Reporters analyze each bit of information they come across to see if it will lead to a news story; many carry notebooks to jot down story ideas. If an idea fits one of these criteria, an editor may assign a story.

> ☆ *REVIEW: Explain the six criteria for deciding what makes news. Look through copies of daily and weekly newspapers for examples of each.*

> ✔ *CHECK YOUR UNDERSTANDING of what makes news by completing Worksheet #9 and Homework #10.*

## Section 2. Writing news stories.

Newswriting has a style all its own -- one that is different from the writing styles you have learned in composition lessons or in creative writing. Learning newswriting is useful in school and on the job, even if you're not in journalism, because it is an excellent method of organizing information and presenting facts clearly. In this section, you will learn how to write news stories.

## THE LEAD

In news stories, the important facts are stated in the first paragraph, which is called the *lead* (leed). The most important facts are those which answer the questions: who, what, why, where, when and how -- ***the Big Six***.

Whatever the topic of a news story, you must always include the Big Six in the lead. The following leads show how this writing style applies to small, local stories, as well as national and international stories.

*EXAMPLE 1*

Daryl Evans, 15, yesterday received notice he had won a trip to Disneyland for raising the most money, $2,000, in the Walk-a-thon here last week.

who: Daryl Evans
what: won a trip to Disneyland
when: yesterday
where: here
why: raising the most money
how: in a Walk-a-thon

*EXAMPLE 2*

An American was killed yesterday when a terrorist bomb exploded in Frankfurt International Airport, wounding 22 people with shrapnel and falling debris.

who: an American
what: killed
when: yesterday
where: Frankfurt International Airport
why: wounded with shrapnel and falling debris
how: terrorist bomb

Not every story will have all six in the lead, and sometimes they will overlap, as in these examples:

*EXAMPLE 3*

Tryouts for high school pep squad will be held at 9:30 a.m. Saturday, Aug. 15, at the playing field at Third and W. Smith Street. All middle school students interested in trying out should register by 9 a.m. at the field house.

what: tryouts
when: 9:30 a.m. Saturday, Aug. 15
where: playing field at Third & W. Smith
why: (implied) to pick new pep squad members
how: (same as what)
who: (implied) students who want to be in pep squad

*EXAMPLE 4*

Four persons have died and at least 200 were injured when an office building collapsed during yesterday's earthquake in San Francisco.

> who: four who died and 200 injured
> what: building collapsed
> when: yesterday
> where: San Francisco
> why: earthquake
> how: (same as what)

By analyzing these leads, you will see that different facts receive emphasis depending on the story. Sometimes you will find the same facts answer two questions, such as "how" and "why" or "how" and "what".

☆ *REVIEW: Define lead and explain the Big Six. Explain how writing a news story is different from writing a short story.*

❑ *DEMONSTRATE YOUR UNDERSTANDING of news story leads by completing Worksheet #10 and Homework #11.*

## INVERTED PYRAMID

News stories are written in *inverted pyramid* style, which means to put the main facts in the lead. Less important facts go in the next one or two paragraphs. Other details that are not essential to understanding the story follow that paragraph, and so on until the least important facts are in the last paragraphs.

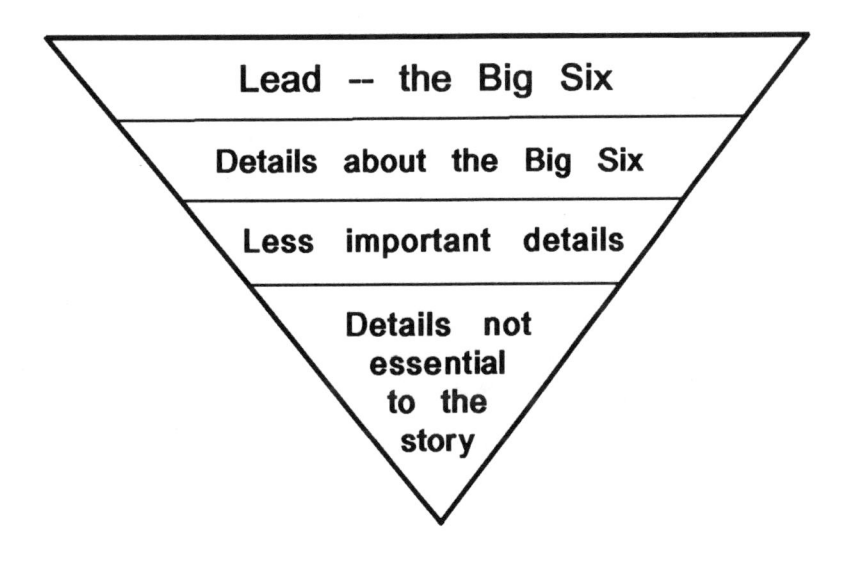

```
  _____
  \   Lead -- the Big Six   /
   _____/
    \ Details about the Big Six /
     _____/
      \ Less important details /
       _____/
        \   Details not    /
         \   essential    /
          \   to the     /
           \   story    /
            _____/
             \       /
              \     /
               \   /
                \ /
                 V
```

The inverted pyramid style is important for two reasons. First, newspaper readers rarely, if ever, read all of the words in a newspaper. They scan headlines to see what's happening and to decide which stories they wish to read. The average reader reads only the first few paragraphs of most stories. Therefore, the inverted pyramid writing style serves the needs of a newspaper's customers by allowing them to read the newspaper quickly and still get the most important information out of each story.

The second reason to use inverted pyramid style is to allow the editors to cut, or shorten, stories that are too long to fit in the space allocated. As you learned in Chapter 2, the amount of space in a newspaper is limited. Editors can't just order a couple of pages added if they have a large number of stories to run. Instead they must cut the stories to fit into the news holes. So, they cut from the bottom, eliminating the last paragraphs until the story is the right length. The inverted pyramid serves editors' needs by assuring that critical information is not lost if the last paragraphs in a story have to go.

Paragraphs in a news story are short, usually only two or three sentences. This makes them easier for the reader to scan quickly and gives an editor more places to cut if that is necessary.

Study the following news story as a model of inverted pyramid style.

| | |
|---|---|
| *Summary lead, includes The Big Six* | A North American Airlines jetliner with 322 people aboard caught fire and crashed into a wooded area of northern Wisconsin early this morning. No survivors of the Chicago-to-Quebec flight have been found so far. |
| *Details about "who"* | Flight #508 carried 310 passengers and a crew of 12. Most of the passengers are Chicago area residents, said a spokesperson for the airline. No names have been released. |
| *Details about "what"* | A pilot of a private aircraft in the area at the time of the crash reported seeing flames coming from an engine just before the crash. Firefighters reported the cabin was consumed by flames. |
| *Details about "where"* | The crash site is inside the Bad River Indian Reservation, approximately 15 miles south of the shore of Lake Superior. Ambulances and medical personnel from the nearest towns were on the scene within 45 minutes, according to Ashland hospital administrator Jan Sanders. |
| | Search parties continue to comb a 10-square-mile area for survivors, but have little hope of finding anyone alive. |

*Less important details*       Investigators from the Federal Aviation Administration and NAA expect to begin examining the wreckage tomorrow.

*Information not essential*       This disaster becomes the third worst airliner crash in U.S. history.

☆   REVIEW: *Study some of the stories in your newspaper and discuss whether they are written in inverted pyramid format. Examine the leads to see if they cover the Big Six.*

✔   CHECK YOUR UNDERSTANDING *of newswriting by completing Worksheets #11, #12, #13 and Homework #12 and #13.*

## FAIRNESS

A good news writer is **objective**, which means to be fair to all sides involved. Report the facts as fully and accurately as possible. Make an effort to get both sides of a controversial issue and report all the information, whether or not you agree. Never state a personal opinion, positive or negative, in a news story.

Writing **subjectively** (the opposite of objectively), a reporter can **slant** news in several ways: by leaving out facts to make one side of an issue look stronger, by not reporting quotations from an interview completely, or by inserting personal observations and opinions. A slanted story is unfair to the reader.

As a reporter, you may be assigned to write about a person or group you personally find disgusting--a child molester or the American Nazi Party, for example. Even in these extreme examples, the writing must remain objective and not reveal the reporter's bias. Controversial people and issues are what make news, so these situations are common to news writers.

Reporters are expected to go out of their way to get both sides of a story. This is why you will often see a small paragraph saying that a person declined to make a comment or to speak to reporters. Readers are thus informed that an attempt was made to report as fully as possible.

Following are examples of two stories on the same event. The first is subjective; the second is objective. Notice how even the reporter's observations about the subject's behavior have been eliminated in the second story.

*EXAMPLE 1 - SUBJECTIVE:*

In what seems to be a "mercy killing," Mary Alion is being held for investigation in the gunshot killing of her terminally ill husband, Fred. Neighbors are sure she did it because she loved her husband so much she couldn't bear to see him suffer.

After the murder, Alion did not call the police for several hours, although she quickly had an attorney ready to speak for her.

This past year, Mr. Alion became increasingly weak, and was often in excruciating pain, according to their neighbors.

It remains to be seen whether Alion will be prosecuted for this murder, as she clearly is not a common criminal. Her neighbors were eager to show what a devoted wife she had been.

When she left home with police after her arrest on Saturday, Alion did not look nervous or upset, even though her husband had been lying dead in the bedroom for several hours, blasted with a rifle found on the floor near the bed.

*EXAMPLE 2 - OBJECTIVE:*

Fred Alion, 70, who has been seriously ill for several years, died Saturday from a gunshot wound to the head.

Mary Alion, 59, his wife, is being held for investigation in the Queen County Jail. A hearing is scheduled this afternoon.

"They've been married for 40 years, and they always spent their spare time together -- shopping, gardening, everything," said neighbor Myrtle Blake.

This past year they rarely left the house as he became increasingly weakened by lung cancer.

Police arrested Alion at her home Saturday after Alion's attorney, Dudley Boren, called to report the man's death.

Police said they found him dead in a bedroom, shot in the head. He apparently had been dead for several hours. A rifle was found on the floor nearby.

☆ *REVIEW: Use these examples to illustrate the differences between subjective and objective writing.*

✔ CHECK YOUR UNDERSTANDING of objectivity, by completing Worksheet #14.

As with any new skill, you must practice newswriting to do it well. Study this list of reminders anytime you write a news story:

-- put the most important information in the lead,

-- check your lead to be sure you have included the Big Six,

-- use short sentences and short paragraphs,

-- keep writing in inverted pyramid style until you have used all relevant information,

-- be sure to write objectively.

✔ CHECK YOUR UNDERSTANDING of newswriting by completing Worksheet #15.

## Section 4. Types of news stories.

News stories fall generally into three categories: **advance**, **follow-up** and **spot news**. Advance stories are written before an event occurs and follow-up stories are written after it occurs. Spot news is written more or less on the spot about an event that was unexpected.

Advance stories usually are written about scheduled events such as sports contests, meetings, entertainment, or appearances by famous people. The purpose is to inform the public of what's coming up.

Follow-up stories are often written about the same events announced in an advance story, such as a report on the football game played last night or an account of what the president said at his scheduled press conference. Some follow-ups add details to a spot news story, such as names of survivors of an accident.

Spot news frequently is written about catastrophes, since these can't be predicted, or new developments in an ongoing event, such as the latest battle in a war zone.

Study these examples of leads for advance, follow-up and spot news -- all about the same event.

*Advance:*

Pitcher Wotan Jones is expected to start in tomorrow night's game between the Kansas City Chiefs and Chicago Cubs at 7 p.m. in Memorial Stadium.

*Spot:*

Two battles raged at once in Memorial Stadium last night as a fight in the stands erupted during a fight on the field. While umpires separated Chiefs and Cubs in the infield, police and stadium guards arrested three fans for assault.

*Follow-up:*

Chiefs' manager Martin Smith said he thinks their string of 14 losses contributed to tension during the game Tuesday with Chicago. With the score 9-1 in the eighth inning, emotions came to the boiling point after a close call at third base.

☆ *REVIEW: Use these examples to explain the three different types of news stories. Look in your newspaper for examples of each.*

✔ *CHECK YOUR UNDERSTANDING of the three types of news stories by completing Homework #14 and Worksheets #16 and #17.*

## Section 5. Review for quiz.

1. Six criteria are used to evaluate information to see if it is newsworthy. They are nearness, importance, drama or conflict, names, famous people, amusing or unusual.

2. The important points in newswriting are these:

   a. include the Big Six in the lead;

   b. write objectively in inverted pyramid style;

   c. write either an advance, spot, or follow-up.

3. These are the new vocabulary words introduced in this chapter:

advance
Big Six
facts
follow-up
inverted pyramid
lead

news
objective
slanted news
spot news
subjective

# Chapter 4
# Editing A Newspaper

A reporter's job is finished when a story is written and handed over to the editor. Editors follow a number of steps to turn that copy into a story on the printed page. In this chapter you will learn to (1) follow a style book and mark copy for the typesetter; (2) write headlines; (3) make a page layout; (4) proofread.

An editor will not accept copy from a reporter until it meets the requirements listed below. If a story fails to conform to these standards, it is handed back to the writer for rewriting.

1. The story is typed doublespaced.

2. Every word is legible.

3. Every word is spelled correctly.

4. The lead is complete and appropriate to the story.

5. No editorializing has slipped into a news story.

6. Facts have been double-checked for accuracy.

7. Usage conforms to the style book and rules of grammar.

8. Unnecessary words are omitted.

A copy editor's job is to insure accuracy and consistency in every story. The effect is to give readers confidence in the publication. If a newspaper has misspelled words or uses three or four different ways to write the time, it conveys an impression of carelessness. Readers may begin to wonder if the reporting and checking of facts are done with the same lack of care.

When in doubt about spelling, check a dictionary. Double- and triple-check names, especially those that have more than one spelling; i.e., Anderson or Andersen; Chris or Kris. Nothing upsets a reader more than seeing his/her name misspelled.

Next to your dictionary, have available a thesaurus and a guide to basic rules of grammar, abbreviations and punctuation. Your language arts text may be adequate or your teacher may suggest something else.

✔ *CHECK YOUR KNOWLEDGE of commonly misspelled words and commonly misused abbreviations by completing Worksheet #18.*

## Section 1. Style book.

Each newspaper has a style book that states how news stories are to be written. This is because editors want all stories to be consistent. Following are typical rules in a style book. If your school does not have a style book, use this as a guide when you write stories.

### UNNECESSARY WORDS

The journalism style of writing is economical. The goal is to use as few words as possible to make it easier for the reader and to make the best use of limited space. Following are five ways to omit unnecessary words in your stories. Unnecessary words are underlined.

1. Use active, not passive, verbs.

    *WRONG:* There was a program Wednesday to name the winners.

    *BETTER:* The winners were named at a program Wednesday.

    *WRONG:* His attorney will make a decision as to whether or not an appeal should be filed.

    *BETTER:* His attorney will decide whether to file an appeal.

2. Change prepositional phrases to modifiers.

    *WRONG:* Costumes worn by the band were white and gold.

    *BETTER:* The band wore white and gold costumes.

    *WRONG:* The team from the city of Des Moines arrived first.

    *BETTER:* The Des Moines team arrived first.

3. Make direct statements in which the subject is understood.

    *WRONG:* The way to measure your foot is to draw around it.

    *BETTER:* Measure your foot by drawing around it.

*WRONG:* <u>The</u> first <u>thing you do is</u> go to the corner of First and Bell.

*BETTER:* First, go to the corner of First and Bell.

4. Eliminate useless articles and prepositions.

*WRONG:* All <u>of the</u> girls are present.

*BETTER:* All girls are present.

*WRONG:* The semester begins <u>on</u> Jan. 15.

*BETTER:* The semester begins Jan. 15.

5. Eliminate useless clauses and phrases.

*WRONG:* <u>It is a fact that</u> real estate is a good investment.

*BETTER:* Real estate is a good investment.

*WRONG:* Use a T-square <u>for the purpose of</u> drawing a right angle.

*BETTER:* Use a T-square to draw a right angle.

✔ *CHECK YOUR UNDERSTANDING of unnecessary words by completing Worksheet #19.*

## TIME AND DATE

Write time and date as follows: 10 a.m. Thursday, Oct. 23, (time, day, date) or 4 p.m. June 3 (time and date). Don't write the year unless it is different from the current year.

*WRONG:* The race begins at 10:00 AM on Thursday, October 23rd.

*BETTER:* The race begins at 10 a.m. Thursday, Oct. 23.

If the event described is within a week of publication, refer to the day of the week. If the publication date is Monday, Dec. 12, refer to the next Wednesday, Dec. 14, as follows: "Another shipment is due Wednesday." Refer to the previous Friday, Dec. 9, as follows: "A third victim of the accident on Friday died today in a local hospital."

If the event is the day before or the day after publication, use "yesterday" and "tomorrow."

Use abbreviations for months when written with a date, as in Feb. 3, but not when the month is written alone.

Use noon and midnight; omit the 12.

## NAMES AND FORMS OF ADDRESS

When mentioning an adult for the first time in a story, write his/her full name. For subsequent references, use Ms., Mrs. or Mr. and the last name. The same rule applies to other forms of address which are substituted for Mr., Mrs. and Ms., such as Dr., Rev., Fr., Gen., Sen., or Rep.

*EXAMPLE:*

Joan Haynes and Donald O'Brien accepted the award. Ms. Haynes and Dr. O'Brien were the original sponsors of the project.

Identify persons mentioned in a story, but don't make up titles.

*WRONG:* According to Neighbor Wilma Smith

*BETTER:* According to Wilma Smith, neighbor

Usually children and youth are first referred to by their full name (Christine Brown) and thereafter, by first name only, as in "Christine was found safely by 6 p.m."

## NUMBERS

Write out all numbers below 11. Write out numbers that occur at the beginning of a sentence. Write out "percent."

*EXAMPLE:*

Two thousand runners entered the marathon, six of them in wheelchairs. Only 40 percent crossed the finish line.

Omit the decimal and zeroes in monetary figures; write $2 or $2,000. Omit the zeroes in figures above 999,000; write 1 million or $2 billion. Use cents for figures below $1, as in 97 cents or two cents.

*EXAMPLE:*

According to bank reports, most savings accounts amount to about $1,500. Some are as low as 97 cents and some as high as $1 million.

Avoid writing two numbers together; this can be easily misread.

*WRONG:* After saving 430, 100 were abandoned.

*BETTER:* Although 100 were abandoned, 430 were saved.

☆ *REVIEW: Look in your daily newspaper to see what style is used for names, times and dates, and numbers. Decide if their style book is the same as or different than this one.*

✔ *CHECK YOUR UNDERSTANDING of journalism style by completing Worksheet #20.*

## Section 2. Copyreading symbols.

An editor may make minor changes and corrections in a reporter's copy to make it conform to the style book. This is called *copyreading*. Following are the most common symbols a copy editor uses to *edit* a story, which means to make it ready to set into type. You can use copyreading symbols to edit any writing you do.

| Symbol | | Example |
|---|---|---|
| New paragraph | ⌐ | ⌐In December 1925, Scoutmaster |
| Transpose | ∩∪ | Fr(ed) Grinnell called the 29 |
| Insert | ∧ | memb^e rs of his Scout Troop 25 |
| Close up space | ⌒ | together and ⌒told them he |
| Leave in | stet | hadn't much longer ~~to live~~ stet |
| Change to upper case | ≡ | he handed them sealed |
| Change to lower case | / | /Envelopes and told the boys |
| Insert space | \| | not to\|open them until 1935. |
| Spell out | ◯ | He died in (Jan.) and was |
| Abbreviate | ◯ | buried in Boise, (Idaho.) |

☆ *REVIEW: What corrections are needed in the following copy?*

```
Much of the midwest was paralyzed by
Mon. by snow that drifted up to 6
feet high,clogged highways stranded
hundred of travelers and closed
schools.Blizzaed warnings issued were
for parts of Mich. where snow was
nearly 3 feet dep.
```

✔ *CHECK YOUR UNDERSTANDING of copy marking symbols by completing Worksheet #21.*

## Section 3. Page layout.

Layout guides the reader around the page and signals which are the most important stories. A layout editor must compose a page that is visually balanced and orderly, combining the elements of headlines, columns of type, photos, cutlines and ads in a way that eliminates confusion. Before a layout editor starts to compose a page, s/he knows the size of each element. Then it's somewhat like putting together a jigsaw puzzle.

Most metropolitan newspapers have six columns. Most school newspapers have four; some have three or even two. The fewer columns available to work in, the fewer options an editor has in layout.

An important rule in layout is to avoid **tombstone** headlines, where two or more adjacent headlines are set in the same size and style of type. Not only are tombstones less interesting to look at, they can be confusing if a reader reads straight across, as in this example:

### Man Shoots   Rare Horses
### Two Thieves   Have Colt

Eliminate tombstones by using stories of varying lengths and by using headlines of different column width. When headlines must be placed in adjacent columns, use different sizes and styles of type. Look at the following examples of layout and notice how tombstones have been avoided.

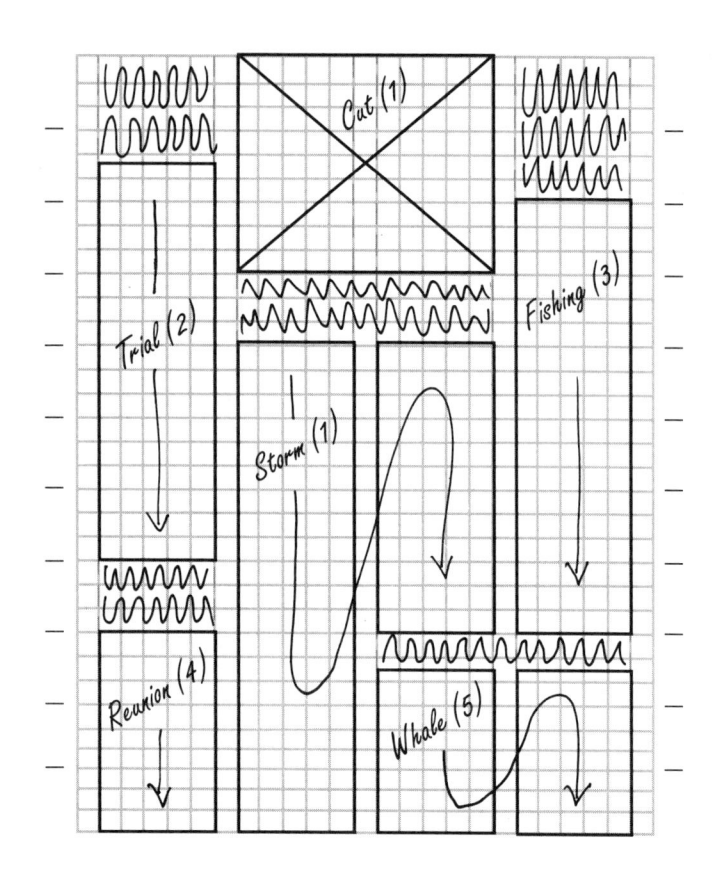

## EXAMPLE 1

Note the list of the various elements which must be fitted on the page. A layout editor starts with information on the size and length of each element. In this example, a photo is placed at the top of a column with the accompanying headline and story directly under it.

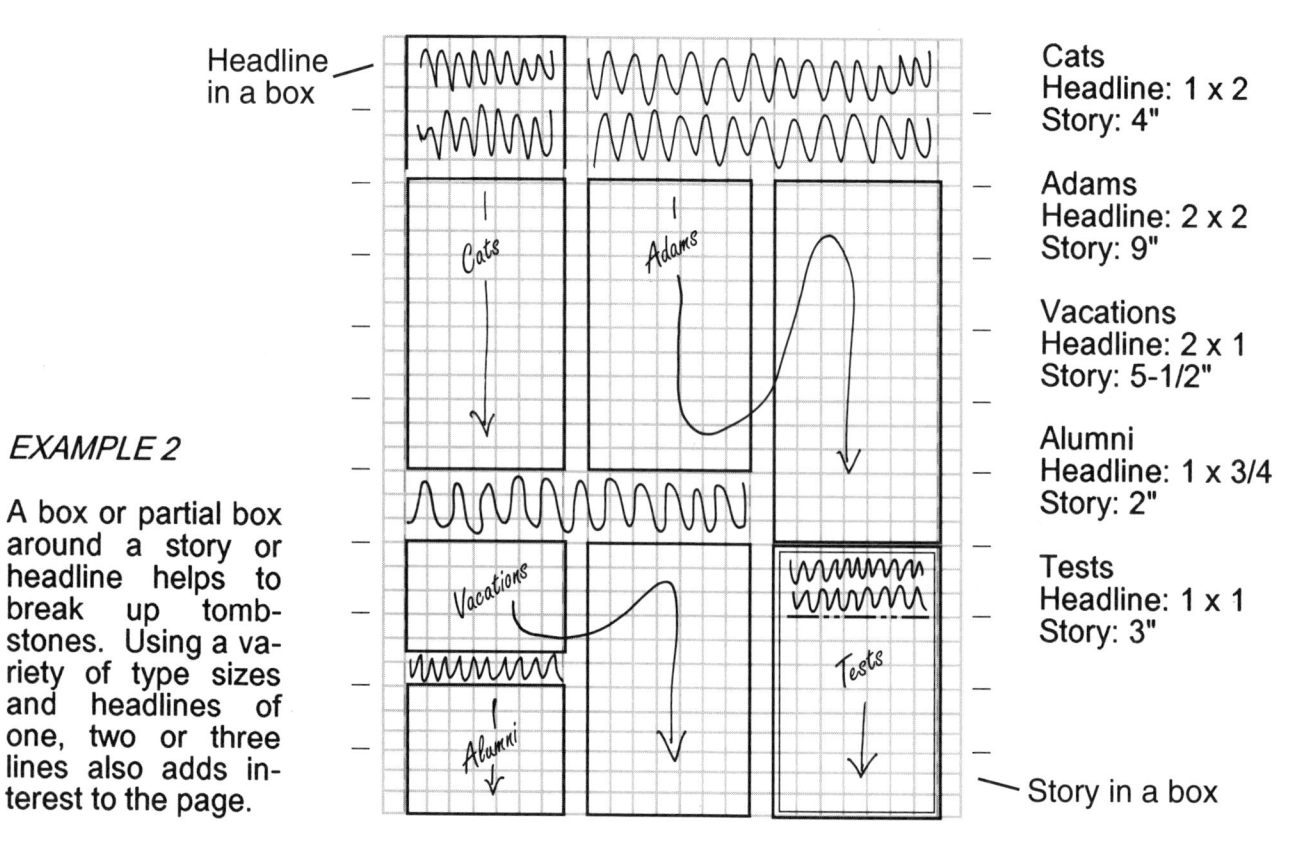

**Storm**
Cut: 2 x 3
Headline: 2 x 1
Story: 11"

**Trial**
Headline: 1 x 1-1/2
Story: 5-1/2

**Fishing**
Headline: 1 x 2
Story: 6"

**Reunion**
Headline: 1 x 1
Story: 3"

**Whale**
Headline: 2 x 1/2
Story: 6"

## EXAMPLE 2

A box or partial box around a story or headline helps to break up tombstones. Using a variety of type sizes and headlines of one, two or three lines also adds interest to the page.

**Cats**
Headline: 1 x 2
Story: 4"

**Adams**
Headline: 2 x 2
Story: 9"

**Vacations**
Headline: 2 x 1
Story: 5-1/2"

**Alumni**
Headline: 1 x 3/4
Story: 2"

**Tests**
Headline: 1 x 1
Story: 3"

Note that long stories are not run down one column; they are spread across two, three or four columns, depending on length. As you study newspapers, observe that every story is under a headline. No column starts with type.

You can see that a photo, also called a *cut*, is marked to size on the layout with an "X". Headlines are marked with zigzags, and stories are indicated by a line ending in an arrow. Inches are marked on the layout sheet. Stories and cuts are labeled on the layout with the slug on the story.

When describing an ad, cut, or headline like this -- 3x6 -- the first figure is the number of columns wide and the second figure is the number of inches high. The length of a story is shown in inches.

Balance the "heavy" elements equally top and bottom, right and left. These are large headlines and cuts, which are seen as dark areas when the page appears in print.

Pages can be varied by printing some stories two columns across or by putting a *box* around a story. A box is a thin line inside the column width. Three-sided boxes are sometimes used to set off headlines.

Place display ads on the page in a half-pyramid, with the largest ad on the bottom, then others, in order of size, stacked to the inside of the page. Ads, too, are marked on a layout with an "X" and one word from the advertiser's name. Ads can never be shortened or omitted to fit the space; cut the stories if space is tight.

The pyramid layout is intended to place some copy next to as many ads as possible, to draw the reader's eye to the ads. Avoid tombstones in arranging ads, and don't place photos next to ads. Traditionally, no ads are placed on the front page of a section or on the editorial pages.

Two examples of pages with ads placed in a half-pyramid appear on the following page.

An editor will try several different combinations before getting everything to go together on a layout. As you practice, be patient, and plan to use your eraser.

44 - Secondary School Journalism

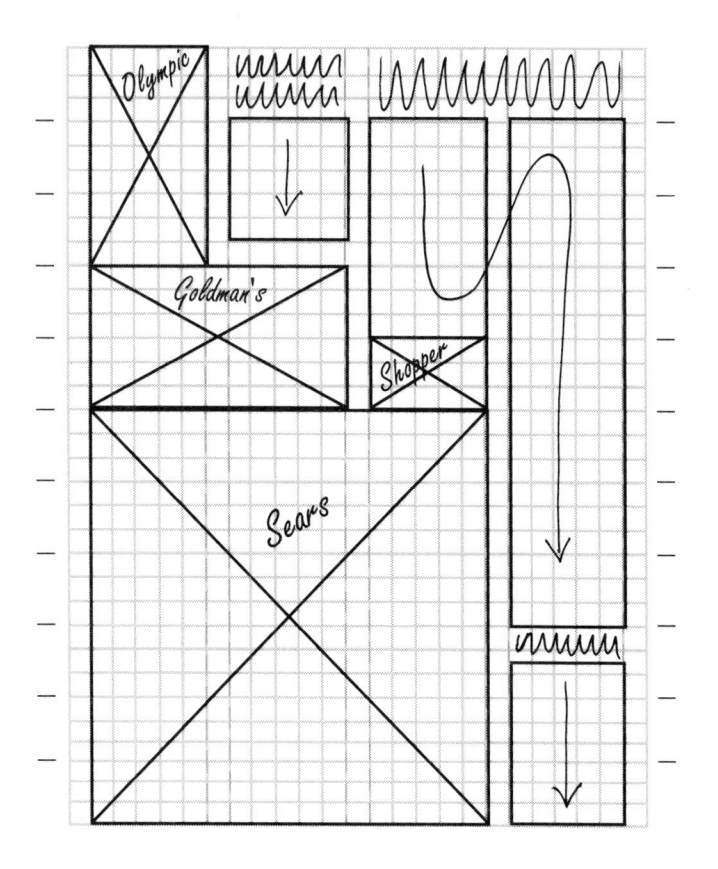

Ads for this page:

Sears: 3 x 6
Goldman's: 2 x 2
Shopper: 1 x 1
Olympic: 1 x 3

### EXAMPLE 1

The high point of the half pyramid is always toward the inside of the page.

### EXAMPLE 2

Avoid tombstones in ads by stacking them like blocks. If possible, each ad should have a bit of type next to it.

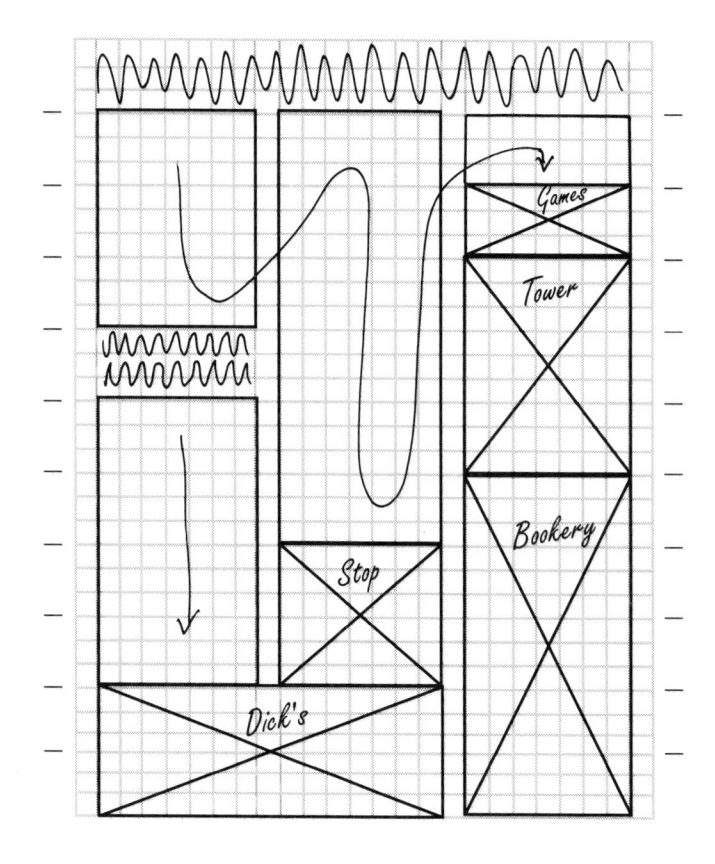

Ads for this page:

Bookery: 1 x 5
Dick's: 2 x 2
Tower: 1 x 3
Stop: 1 x 2
Games: 1 x 1

Chapter 4/Editing A Newspaper

Secondary School Journalism - 45

Following is an example of a poor layout, one which has violated all the rules. Tombstone headlines march across the top of the page. Ads are not in a pyramid. The effect is unbalanced and confusing.

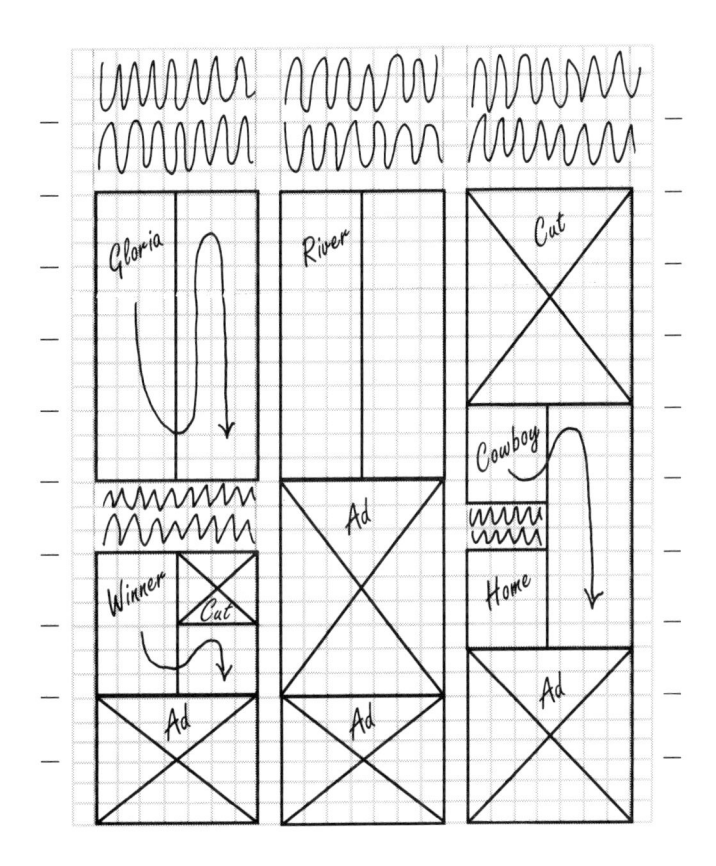

☆ REVIEW: By referring to the examples, explain how to avoid tombstones and how to place ads. Look at the daily newspaper to see how the principles of layout described here are applied. Do the pages look balanced? Do you see any tombstones? Are the ads stacked in a pyramid?

❏ PRACTICE drawing a six-column layout by completing Homework #15.

✔ CHECK YOUR UNDERSTANDING of composing a page layout by completing Worksheets #22 and #23.

Chapter 4/Editing A Newspaper

## Section 4. Headlines.

A headline, like a lead, summarizes the important facts of the story. However, headlines are limited by space to only a few words; rarely does a headline have more than ten words. Writing a headline is like writing a telegram. The message must be made clear in the fewest possible words. Look at the following example of a headline and the lead sentence it is drawn from.

### Congress Blasts Defense Firms For Cost Overruns

Members of Congress today strongly criticized defense companies which have submitted invoices for millions of dollars in cost overruns.

This headline expresses the main idea of the story in seven words, and illustrates the main points to remember:

1. Wherever possible, short words are substituted for longer ones, as in this example, where "blasts" substitutes for "strongly criticized" and "firms" for "companies";

2. No articles, like "a", "an", or "the" are used;

3. Even though the action is in the past (criticized), the headline verb is in the present (blasts);

4. It includes a subject (Congress) and a predicate (blasts).

☆ *REVIEW: Look at headlines in the news sections of your daily newspaper. Does each have a subject and predicate? Have they used any articles? Are the verbs in the present tense? List some short, expressive words which are substitutes for longer words or phrases. Some examples are: probe=investigation; meet=meeting or conference.*

An editor writes a headline by extracting the key words from the lead. The result is a brief "headline sentence," made up of the key words, sometimes rearranged.

*EXAMPLE:*

Ms. Anna Rosales, Spanish teacher, attended a six-week summer school session at the University of Mexico in Mexico City.

*Headline sentence:* Anna Rosales Attends School In Mexico City

> ✔ *CHECK YOUR UNDERSTANDING of picking key words for headlines by completing Worksheet #24.*

Some headlines have one line, also called a **deck**, some two lines, others three. Depending on type size and number of columns, some headlines contain more words than others. As you adjust headlines to fit the space, words may need to be omitted or changed.

Shorten or lengthen your brief sentence so that you have approximately the same number of words and letters in each line. Groups of words which should be read together are not divided between lines. These groups include verb phrases, prepositional phrases, proper names, and adjectives and the nouns they modify.

| | | |
|---|---|---|
| *WRONG:* | Hatton To<br>Be Executed | *(Divides<br>verb phrase)* |
| *WRONG:* | Judge Sentences Bob<br>Hatton to Execution | *(Divides<br>proper name)* |
| *WRONG:* | Leader Falls In<br>N.Y. Marathon | *(Divides<br>prepositional phrase)* |
| *WRONG:* | Runner Receives Serious<br>Injury During Marathon | *(Divides adjective and<br>the noun it modifies)* |

Study this example of changing a headline sentence into a two- and three-deck headline.

*Headline sentence:* Anna Rosales Attends School In Mexico City

*Two-deck headline:*             Anna Rosales Attends
                                         School In Mexico City

*Three-deck headline:*           Anna Rosales
                                         Attends School
                                         In Mexico City

✔ *CHECK YOUR UNDERSTANDING of dividing headlines into two or three decks by completing Worksheet #25.*

Choosing the correct verb is very important in writing good headlines. Something that has already happened is referred to in the present tense.

    *WRONG:*    Aviation Club Elected Officers

    *BETTER:*   Aviation Club Elects Officers

The helping verbs "is" and "are" usually are left out of headlines.

    *WRONG:*    Burglars Are Caught By Guard Dog

    *BETTER:*   Burglars Caught By Guard Dog

Future action in a headline may be shown by the future tense of a verb, with the helping verb "will". However, most newspapers prefer the infinitive, beginning with the word "to".

    *WRONG:*    Studio Shoots School Scene Here Tomorrow

    *ACCEPTABLE:* Studio Will Shoot School Scene Here

    *BETTER:*   Studio To Shoot School Scene Here

It is tempting to use abbreviations to fit headlines into a short space, but only commonly known and accepted abbreviations can be used.

    *WRONG:*    Decision To Be Announced Sun.
                  *(not good usage)*

    *BETTER:*   Decision To Be Announced Sunday

    *WRONG:*    GAA Convention Starts Today
                  *(not commonly understood)*

    *BETTER:*   Gardeners' Meet Starts Today

Use a comma in place of "and" in headlines.

    *WRONG:*    Houses and Highways
                  Damaged in Flood

    *BETTER:*   Houses, Highways
                  Damaged in Flood

✔ *CHECK YOUR UNDERSTANDING of correct headline writing, by completing Worksheet #26.*

As if writing headlines weren't difficult enough, they must also conform to a specific *count* or number of spaces, depending on the size and style of type. If a column is two inches wide, about nine letters and spaces will fit in type this size:

# 3 Honored

but about 19 letters and spaces will fit in the same space if the type is this size:

## 3 Honored at School

Therefore, the count for the first headline is nine, and the count for the second is 19. A headline writer must know the size of type specified for a headline, how many columns wide, and the number of decks. Then s/he counts each deck to be sure it will fit.

All type is counted in the same way, by assigning a value to each letter and space. While most numbers and letters and all spaces count for one, some thin letters, like "i" or "f" count for one-half and some wide letters, like "m" count for one and one-half. Following is a list of the counts for every letter and number, which applies to all type faces.

Each space and most small, or *lower case*, letters = 1
i,l,f,t,j and most punctuation = .5
--, ", ? = 1
m and w =1.5
Most capital, or *upper case* letters = 1.5
Upper case M and W = 2
Upper case I = 1
All numbers except one = 1
1 = .5

Study this example of counting a headline.

# 3  H o n o r e d  a t  S c h o o l

1  1  1.5  1  1  1  1  1  1  1  1  .5  1  1.5  1  1  1  1  .5

Total:   19

If the maximum count for one column is 19, this headline will fit. If the maximum count is 15, it must be changed; and if the count is 30, more words must be added to fill the space. A headline can be as much as three units under count, but never over.

For practice, count both lines of this headline:

# Student Makes
# Amazing Find

You are correct if you counted 13.5 in the top deck and 12.5 in the lower.

☆ *REVIEW: Pick several headlines of different sizes in the daily newspaper and count them.*

A copy editor will have a **headline schedule,** which is a list of all the type sizes and counts available for the newspaper. Usually, these are referred to by number; so the copy chief will say to an editor, "Write a No. 3 for this."

Each style of type, called a **type face,** has a name. This book uses Helvetica. The following headline is set in a type called Times Roman.

### Boy Bites Dog

The different sizes are designated by **points**. Six point type is the smallest generally used; this book is set in 12 point type. The largest headlines on most days are set in 60 point. Look at the samples of point sizes on the following page.

✔ *CHECK YOUR UNDERSTANDING of point size by completing Homework #16.*

*Illustration of Point Size:*

| | |
|---|---|
| *10 pt.* | Secondary School Journalism |
| *12 pt.* | Secondary School Journalism |
| *14 pt.* | Secondary School Journalism |
| *18 pt.* | Secondary School Journalism |
| *24 pt.* | Secondary School Journalism |
| *30 pt.* | Secondary School Journ |
| *36 pt.* | Secondary School J |
| *48 pt.* | Secondary Sch |
| *60 pt.* | Secondary |
| *72 pt.* | Secondar |

## Section 5. Proofreading.

The purpose of *proofreading* is to correct mistakes made by the typesetter. A proofreader does not change the copy in any way. Symbols for proofreading are similar to those for copyreading and used for the same kinds of errors, except they are marked in the margin. Study this list of proofreading symbols and note how the column is marked.

| Symbol name | Symbol | Example |
|---|---|---|
| paragraph | ¶ | ¶ — Start the paragraph here. |
| no paragraph | no ¶ | no ¶ ——— Start the next here. |
| insert period | ⊙ | Start the paragraph here — ⊙ |
| insert other punctuation | ∧ ∧ ∨ ⁽"⁾ ⁽"⁾ | He said) (Start the paragraph here." |
| insert space | # | # Start⌒the paragraph here. |
| close up space here | ⌒ | Start ⌒ the paragaraph ⌒ |
| upper case | ≡ | ≡start the paragraph here. |
| lower case | / | Start the Paragraph here. — lc |
| take out | ℓ | Start the} paragraph here. |
| spell out | sp out ○ | Start the (pp.) here. — sp out |
| abbreviate | abbr ○ | abbr — (Mister) Jones, start here. |
| transpose | ∽ tr | tr — Mr. J(o)(n)es, (here)(start). — tr |
| move to the left | ⊏ | ⊏ — Mr. Jones, start here. |
| move to the right | ⊐ | ⊐ — Mr. Jones, start here. |
| center | ⊐ ⊏ | ⊐Mr. Jones⊏ |
| leave in | stet | Mr. Jones, start ~~here~~. — stet |

☆ REVIEW: What corrections are indicated by the proofreader's marks in this copy?

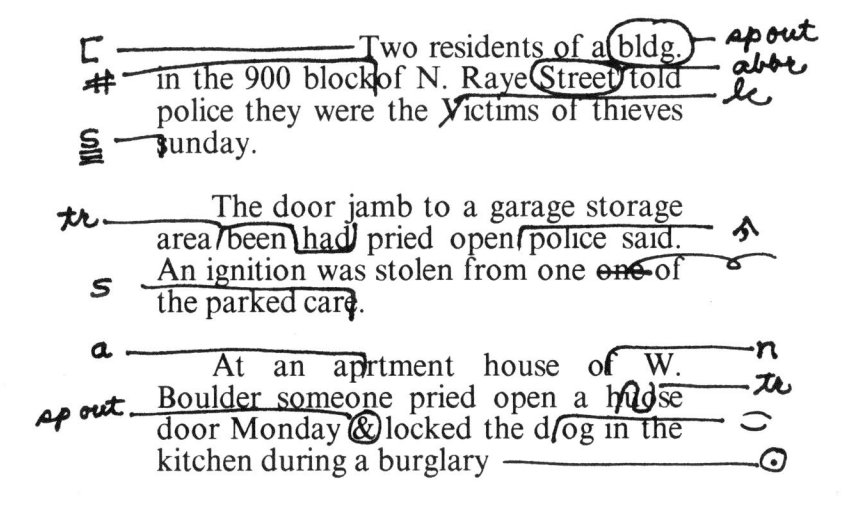

[example copy with proofreader's marks]

☆ REVIEW: Explain the different functions of a copy reader and a proofreader.

❑ PRACTICE using proofreading symbols by completing Worksheet #27.

## Section 6. Review for quiz.

1. If a reporter has not prepared his/her copy to meet an editor's standards, it must be rewritten.

2. A newspaper style book establishes a standard method of writing. It explains how to omit unnecessary words, and the preferred method of writing the time and date, names, numbers, and other words and phrases.

3. Copyreading symbols are used by an editor to prepare copy for the typesetter. Proofreading symbols are used by a proofreader to correct copy that has already been typed in justified columns.

4. A layout editor composes pages that are balanced and without tombstones.

5. Steps for writing headlines:

    a. Pick key words from the lead

    b. Use short, strong words

    c. Include a subject and predicate

    d. Write verbs in present or future tense

    e. Divide correctly into decks of nearly equal length

    f. Write to fit the headline count

6. New vocabulary in this chapter:

    | | |
    |---|---|
    | box | lower case |
    | copyreading | points |
    | cut | proofreading |
    | count | tombstone |
    | deck | type face |
    | edit | upper case |
    | headline schedule | |

# Chapter 5
# Getting the Information

A reporter usually gets information for a news or feature story by conducting an interview; that is, asking a person questions to get information. "Conducting" is a good word to use in this context, because you, the reporter, are going to plan your interview in advance and guide the conversation so you get the facts you need.

Other methods of gathering information are conducting surveys of groups of people, reading press releases or other printed material about an event or person, attending a press conference, listening to a speech, or doing library research.

In this chapter, you will have opportunities to practice all these methods of obtaining information, with the emphasis on interviewing skills.

## Section 1. Interviews.

To conduct an interview, you must plan carefully. Know exactly what you want to learn from the interview so you can keep to the point and not let the conversation wander. Write out at least ten questions in advance. Learn something about the subject or person before you do the interview by reading or talking informally with your teacher or others.

### Step 1. Make an Appointment

Call or see the person to make an appointment. State your name and the name of the publication you represent. Say you'd like to interview him/her and explain what the interview will be about. This allows the person to be better prepared to fully answer your questions. Write down and confirm the day and time before you hang up. Say thank you.

Of course, be on time for your appointment. Nothing will get you off on the wrong foot faster than rushing in ten or 15 minutes late when the other person is already impatient and you're flustered.

☆ *REVIEW: In triads, role play making an appointment by telephone. Take turns playing the role of reporter, secretary, and person to be interviewed.*

### Step 2. Prepare Your Questions

Probably the most important single rule is to NEVER ask a question that can be answered by "yes" or "no." Your interview will stop dead in its tracks, and you will have nothing to write if your notes consist only of "yes" and "no" answers. Instead, start questions with "what" or "why" or "how." Look at the difference in these examples:

*Reporter to a singer:* Do you like traveling so much?

*Singer:* Yes, it's great.

OR

*Reporter to a singer:* What are some things you like and dislike about traveling so much?

*Singer:* What I like most is the experience of different audiences in different cities. The atmosphere, the feeling, the responses are different and that's always a challenge. It always gets me up for a performance. I guess the worst part of it is being away from my family and missing important occasions like birthdays.

Another rule is to not waste your time or theirs by asking questions to which the answers are obvious. If you're interviewing a music celebrity, you're not going to ask the name of their group or of their latest release. You will have obtained that kind of information before you go. If you're going to ask questions about air pollution, read articles in newspapers and magazines to get some background on the subject.

Third, make sure all questions relate to the topic. Have the purpose of the interview clearly in mind; know exactly what information you want to get from this person. Then check to see that all your questions are directed toward that goal.

A common error of beginning reporters is to ask questions of a personal nature. This may be appropriate with some celebrities whose fans want every detail of their lives. If you're interviewing someone about how s/he developed revolutionary new software, however, you won't ask about his/her favorite breakfast cereal. The last point to remember as you prepare questions is to be sure they are appropriate for the story.

☆ *REVIEW: Explain the four rules to keep in mind when preparing interview questions. Think of an example to illustrate each rule.*

In some cases, the same person could be interviewed several different ways. An interview with the chief executive officer of General Motors could **focus** on the future of the auto industry, or the steps to becoming a successful executive, or the lifestyle of a wealthy and powerful corporate leader. A lengthy interview of the type published in magazines might touch on all these topics. A newspaper writer, however, concentrates the questions on one focus.

Following is an example of the preparation a reporter would undertake before an interview with a member of the crew on a recent space shuttle flight.

*State the focus:* The focus of the interview is the astronaut's experiences during the actual shuttle flight.

*Background research:* The astronaut, Susan Olway, 27, was responsible for two biomedical experiments during the flight. The nature of the experiments remains classified. She received a Ph.D. in Biology from the University of Chicago in 1982, and she has been employed as a researcher by Bioteck Corp. of Dallas for four years as head of a cancer research team.

*Sources of information:* Library copies of other newspaper and magazine articles about the shuttle flight. Press releases from Bioteck and NASA.

*Questions:*

1. What is your most vivid memory from the shuttle flight?

2. You have said there were no surprises. How did your training help to prepare you for the flight?

3. What was the most difficult aspect of the trip?

4. What would you do differently if you go again?

5. What qualities are important for a person who works as a team member under those conditions?

6. Your team encountered an emergency when it looked like James Ray might be stuck outside the shuttle. Describe your reactions and observations during that crisis.

7. Why have your experiments been kept secret?

8. Your work has been in cancer research. How do these experiments relate to your previous research?

9. How has this experience changed your perspective on your work or life in general?

10. Who has been your model or mentor during this phase of your career?

☆ *REVIEW: Find an interview story in your newspaper. Think of ten questions you think the reporter might have asked during the interview. Assume the reporter had some background information and knew how to prepare questions correctly.*

✔ *CHECK YOUR UNDERSTANDING of questions for an interview by completing Worksheet #28 and Homework #17.*

### Step 3. Ask Questions and Take Notes

Taking notes while simultaneously talking and listening requires years of practice. Following are five suggestions to make your interviews go smoothly. *First, don't try to write down every word.* Write a few key words that will remind you of the answer. When you go over your notes immediately after the interview, you will be surprised to find you remember most of the answers.

Many reporters use tape recorders, but you must always ask permission in advance before taping a conversation. If you wish to use a recorder, ask when you call for an appointment. Say, "Do you mind if I tape the interview?" When you record, you are free to focus entirely on the answers.

*Be sure to listen to the answers.* This may sound silly, but if you are nervous you will be worrying about your next question so much you may forget to listen. Frequently, the subject will answer one of your prepared questions before you ask it. If you're not listening carefully, you might go ahead and ask anyway. A good way to help you listen and remember is to paraphrase what was said: "So, what you're saying is . . ." or "If I understand correctly, you mean . . ."

*Follow up on any interesting comments that might lead to a good story, even the remarks don't relate to your prepared questions.* Don't be so eager to get through your list that you pass up a chance to get a good anecdote or more details. This, too, requires careful listening to each answer.

*Maintain eye contact,* and the subject will be more forthcoming. This isn't a staring contest, but it means frequently looking at the subject's eyes or face to show you are interested. Looking at your hands or out the window does not foster good communication.

*Finally, take a few minutes to go over your notes and clarify any parts that seem confusing.* Verify the spelling of any names.

In the following example, the reporter remembered to paraphrase and to follow up during the interview with Dr. Olway.

*Reporter:* What is your most persistent or vivid memory from the shuttle flight?

*Olway:* The mental picture that remains most clear is watching the earth recede and the features on the earth's surface diminish until I realized that it looks like a planet, one sphere among many others. That aroused some interesting feelings.

*Reporter:* What kind of feelings?

*Olway:* Well, feelings of insignificance, for one. It also started me speculating about life elsewhere in the universe. When you remove yourself from the earth, even that much, it starts to look less unique.

*Reporter:* So you're saying that once you viewed the earth as just one of many planets, intelligent life on other planets seemed more realistic.

*Olway:* Yes, that's it, although we certainly didn't find any kind of evidence to support that. It was just what came into my mind.

☆ *REVIEW: Explain the five points mentioned in Step 3 to keep in mind during an interview. Give examples that would help make each one clear.*

### Step 4. Write the Story

If you took notes during the interview, go over them immediately afterward and write out in detail everything you can remember. If you let your notes get "cold," you may not even remember what you meant when you wrote certain words or phrases. If you taped the interview, play it back to be sure everything is understandable.

It is appropriate to call back once to clarify any statements that seem confusing. Also, as you write your story, additional questions may occur to you. If you use a direct quotation, you may want to verify it with the person. Write a first draft of your story, leaving blanks for points to check, then make the call. This way, you can accurately complete your story without becoming a pest.

Following are four suggestions that will improve an interview story.

In writing a story based on an interview, use ***direct*** and ***indirect quotations***. Direct quotations are verbatim, that is, the exact words the person said, and are punctuated with quotation marks.

*Direct quotation:*

"This scandal is going to blow this department apart," said Assistant Police Chief Alice Smith. "The morale is dropping to zero."

Indirect quotations are explanations or paraphrases of a person's statements and are not punctuated with quotation marks.

*Indirect quotation:*

Assistant Police Chief Alice Smith said she thought the recent discovery of bribery was going to be a severe blow to the department's morale.

The reporter decides when to use direct and indirect quotations. Direct quotations are used most effectively when the statement is shocking or provocative in some way or is one that you want to be sure to get right. Indirect quotations are best used to summarize a long statement when it is not necessary to repeat every word.

When you write the story, alternate paragraphs consisting of indirect quotations with those containing direct quotations. The indirect quotations can be used as explanation to supplement the quotes.

✔ *CHECK YOUR UNDERSTANDING of writing direct and indirect quotes by completing Worksheet #29.*

Do not restate the questions when you write your story, and do not use "I asked . . . and he said . . ." or "when asked" to lead into the answers. The questions will be obvious by the way you write your story.

*Don't write:*

When asked to repeat his earlier statement, Mr. Collins said, "I have been misquoted. I did nothing wrong."

*Do write:*

Mr. Thomas refused to repeat his earlier statement, He said, "I have been misquoted. I did nothing wrong."

Because you are reporting what someone said in an interview story, it is easy to overuse the verb "said." To avoid repetition, substitute synonyms such as "commented," "stated," "announced," or "confessed." Dozens of synonyms exist, although not all of them are appropriate in newspaper writing.

Finally, an interview story is written in inverted pyramid form just as is a news story. However, a quotation may be used as a lead instead of a paragraph summarizing the Big Six. In that case, choose the most interesting or startling statement the person made to use as a lead. Remember you don't have to include everything the subject said in your story. Some of it probably just wasn't all that interesting.

Study the following story which demonstrates the guidelines for writing an interview story.

| | |
|---|---|
| *Interesting quote used in lead* | "Going into space is the strongest possible lesson in humility a person can have," said Dr. Susan Olway in discussing her recent flight aboard the space shuttle. "A person could feel like a real big shot to be a member of that club, but I feel only humbled by the vastness of space and the extent of human ignorance about the universe." |
| *Direct and indirect quotes are alternated* | Dr. Olway admitted that her secret experiments aboard the space shuttle related to her cancer research, but declined to be specific. Because cancer is such an emotional subject, she is reluctant to report any results for fear of starting some kind of cancer cure hysteria. |
| *Synonyms for "said" used in this story: "admitted," "asserted," "added," "emphasized"* | "When researchers work in an area that directly impacts so many lives, we have to be extremely careful not to make statements that could be exaggerated or taken out of context," she asserted. "I don't want to be responsible for the kind of media hype we saw with interferon, for example." |

*Written in inverted pyramid style*

Olway believes past experiences working as part of a team were extremely important on the shuttle. "A person who demands privacy and quiet time could not survive even one day," she said. "You just can't go into your room and shut the door when things get tough." She added that at times, the lack of privacy was very difficult to bear, even though she had mentally prepared for that problem.

The excitement that still lingers from the trip shines from Olway's eyes as she talks about its influence on her life.

"I feel it was a tremendous privilege to go," she emphasized. "It has inspired me to continue my research. It has also given me a new awareness of the value of life. I want to make every second count."

She has returned to her work at Bioteck in Dallas and has no plans to apply for another shuttle flight.

☆ *REVIEW: Explain the guidelines for writing an interview story. Give an example of each one.*

❑ *PRACTICE: Look in the newspaper and list all the synonyms for "said" you can find. Add to your list by brainstorming as many as you can. Finally, use a dictionary or thesaurus to list as many as possible.*

✔ *CHECK YOUR UNDERSTANDING of writing an interview story by completing Worksheets #30 and #31 and Homework #18.*

## Section 2. Polls.

Another type of interview story is a *poll* or survey, in which a reporter asks a number of people the same question or set of questions to measure public opinion on an issue. For example, a reporter may ask 50 people whom they plan to vote for in the next election. The story's lead depends on how the majority answers, as you can see in these examples:

> The field still is wide open in the mayor's race. A majority of citizens polled by the *Times* yesterday stated they were undecided.

> OR

> Incumbent Alan Jones has a strong lead in the mayor's race, according to a poll conducted yesterday by the *Times*.

Pollsters may ask yes-no questions or offer limited choices, such as "Which of the three candidates for mayor will you vote for?" The simplest way to keep track of responses from dozens of people is to make a tally sheet before starting to conduct the poll. Study the samples below. In the first, the pollster asks one yes-no question: "Do you own a personal computer?" and decides to keep track of answers from men and women.

*EXAMPLE 1*

| Do you own a personal computer? | Yes | No |
|---|---|---|
| Men | | |
| Women | | |

A tally sheet for a limited choice question would look like this one:

*EXAMPLE 2*

What is your favorite team sport?

| | Basketball | Football | Baseball | Soccer | Other |
|---|---|---|---|---|---|
| Adult | | | | | |
| Youth | | | | | |

For some stories, the questions may be open-ended. For example: "What advice do you have for parents who are worried about teenage drug abuse?"

The lead may be a summary of the advice given most often or a good quote from one or two of those interviewed.

*Summary lead:*

Parents who are worried about teenagers' drug abuse would do well to be sure they set a good example for their children. This was the advice most frequently given by those polled yesterday in a suburban shopping mall.

OR

*Quotation lead:*

"Any parent whose idea of a good time is to go out and get drunk has good reason to worry about their kids' drug use," declared Amy Hoffman, 42, mother of two teenagers.

A tally sheet will not work if the questions are open-ended, because each response may differ. If possible, use a tape recorder. If not, leave plenty of room in your notepad after each question to take notes. A reporter taking notes must decide at the time which answers to quote directly and take the time to write the words verbatim. Ask for each person's name and other identifying data, such as age or address, but remember they have the right to refuse.

Stories based on polls are written in inverted pyramid style, with the less interesting results at the end of the story.

It is important to include some information about the poll itself. Near the top of the story, state how many people were interviewed, where the interviews were conducted, and some breakdown on who responded, if relevant. In some cases, results make more sense when a reader knows the sex, age, ethnicity or employment of those who answered. A story that fails to substantiate data with this information can be highly misleading.

If only four people are asked their favorite ice cream flavor, and three say chocolate, a reporter could truthfully write that 75 percent of those interviewed prefer chocolate ice cream. But it is misleading, because so few were asked. In a poll on favorite radio stations, knowing the age of those interviewed helps the reader evaluate the results.

A good reporter will do library research and include some background information on the topic of the poll. S/he may also ask experts in the field to comment on the results. For instance, a drug counselor might be asked to comment on the results from the opinion poll on drug abuse.

As in other interview stories, it is not necessary to repeat the questions; they will be obvious by the way the story is written.

*WRONG:*

We asked people if they listen to the radio each day and 78 percent said "yes."

*ALSO WRONG:*

We wondered if people like to listen to the radio, so we did a poll to find out.

*BETTER:*

Seventy-eight percent of the students polled said they listened to the radio at least one hour per day.

Study the following story to see how it illustrates these points:

1. Don't repeat your questions in the story.
2. Substantiate your results.
3. Include background information.
4. Write the story in inverted pyramid style.

*EXAMPLE:*

*Summary lead*

Americans believe news media and find news reports more believable than they do the president, a new Gallup poll reports. But Americans also question press fairness and objectivity, according to a poll, which was released yesterday.

*Details on the first point in the lead*

Eighty-seven percent of those polled have the most faith in *The Wall Street Journal*. The next highest believability ratings went to TV network news, 79%; local TV news, 76%; *Newsweek*, 75%; *Time*, 75%; local newspapers, 71%; *USA Today*, 70%; *People*, 68%; *National Enquirer*, 14%.

*Details on the second point in the lead*

The news media get the facts straight, 55 percent said, but the same number also said the news media would try to cover up mistakes. Other criticisms were that the news media invade people's privacy (73%) and reports too much bad news (60%). More than half of those polled believed the news media tended to favor one side on issues and were influenced by the powerful. In contrast, more than 70% said journalists care about the quality of their work and are highly professional.

*Survey data*   The poll involved more than 5,000 interviews of more than 3,000 persons between July and December of last year (some were interviewed twice).

*Background*   The Gallup poll appears to conflict with the findings of a study done last year for the American Information Society of Newspaper Editors. The ASNE study concluded that "75 percent of all adults have some problem with the credibility of the news media" and that "20 percent of all adults deeply distrust their news media."

☆ *REVIEW: Look in the newspaper for stories based on polls. Decide whether or not the reporter followed the guidelines listed above.*

✔ *CHECK YOUR UNDERSTANDING of writing stories on polls by completing Worksheets #32 and #33.*

## Section 3. Press conferences and speeches.

Another way a reporter gets information is to attend a **press conference** or listen to a speech by a well-known person.

Reporters from all media are invited to cover a press conference, a meeting to which reporters come to ask questions. Press conferences may be called once or twice to announce news about a specific event or may be scheduled on a regular basis. Public officials often have weekly press briefings which the beat reporters attend.

When an important news story is breaking, someone in a position to have the latest information will meet with the press on a daily basis. For example, during the first heart transplant operations, surgeons in charge of the cases had daily meetings with reporters to give them the latest progress reports and answer questions.

A presidential press conference is televised live and provides an excellent opportunity to study how reporters phrase questions.

Reporters come with questions prepared, but they may ask follow-up questions on issues raised by another reporter. For this reason, they take notes on all questions and answers. Another reporter may have elicited the most interesting quotes.

Anyone who wants to make an announcement can call a press conference. An editor decides whether or not to send a reporter. Press conferences certainly are the most efficient way to handle the press on stories covered by hundreds of reporters.

Many political figures and celebrities distribute advance copies of their speeches. This allows a reporter to write much of the story in advance, but s/he still attends the speech. Often the lead comes from the speaker saying something surprising that was not in the printed speech, or questions from the audience may result in a good quote.

Take notes on a speech just as you would take notes in a class. A speech story should include some statements about the appearance and mannerisms of the speaker. Also important is information about the size and reaction of the audience. In some speech stories, members of the audience become the story either because they are heckling and fighting or they are wildly enthusiastic and adoring.

Study the following example of a speech story:

| | |
|---|---|
| *Name speaker and summarize speech in the lead* | Labor unions must pay their leaders more and find some way to stop the influx of illegal aliens into the United States, former Teamsters president Dave Beck told a labor gathering yesterday. |
| *Say something about the speaker* | In a rare public appearance, Beck, 92, said Teamsters President Jackie Presser now makes about $1 million "and he's earning that money." |
| *Use direct and indirect quotations* | "In my opinion, we have to get the finest kind of labor leadership we can, no matter what the cost," Beck said. "I am trying to emphasize that running a labor union is running a business." |
| *Say something about the audience* | Still a powerful and forceful speaker, Beck spoke for 33 minutes without notes to a meeting of about 100 business representatives of construction unions. Beck drew a standing ovation as he spoke on anti-communist and pro-labor themes. |

☆ *REVIEW: Look in the newspaper for examples of stories written from speeches and press conferences.*

## Section 4. Research.

Generally, you do library research to gain background information for a story or to prepare for an interview. Occasionally, a feature story can be based entirely on research; most often, these are historical features, such as the origin of Valentine's Day.

Do the research for a newspaper article in the same way you do research for a report in history or science class. Library resources that a reporter will find useful include *The Reader's Guide to Periodical Literature*, subject section of the card catalog, indexes to newspaper files, almanacs, *Who's Who* and various encyclopedias (general, biographical, or scientific).

## Section 5. Review for quiz.

1. Four rules for preparing interview questions:

    a. Never ask a question that can be answered yes or no.
    b. Don't ask questions to which the answers are obvious.
    c. Focus all questions on the purpose of the interview.
    d. Don't ask inappropriate personal questions.

2. Five points to keep in mind during an interview:

    a. Take notes or use a tape recorder.
    b. Listen carefully to the answers and paraphrase.
    c. Ask follow-up questions if an interesting point comes up.
    d. Maintain eye contact.
    e. Verify unclear statements and spelling of names.

3. Four guidelines for writing an interview story:

    a. Don't restate the questions in the story.
    b. Alternate direct and indirect quotations.
    c. Use synonyms for "said."
    d. Write in inverted pyramid format.

4. Four guidelines for writing a poll story:

    a. Don't restate the questions in the story.
    b. Substantiate your results with information about the poll.
    c. Include some background information about the topic.
    d. Write in inverted pyramid format.

5. Other ways to get information are by attending speeches and press conferences.

6. New vocabulary words in this chapter:

    direct quotation    interview
    focus    poll
    indirect quotation    press conference

# Chapter 6
# Writing Features, Editorials, Sports

In Chapters 3 and 5, you practiced news writing, interviewing and information gathering. Other types of newspaper writing are features, editorials, and sports reporting, which is a specialized type of news writing. In this chapter, you will study (a) writing four kinds of features: personality, historical, how-to, and reviews; (b) writing two kinds of editorials: criticism and appreciation; (c) writing and drawing comics and editorial cartoons; and (d) sports news. You will use much of the information you have already learned, but each of these requires additional skills and practice.

### Section 1. Features.

Features are written in a narrative style instead of the inverted pyramid. The first paragraph is the lead, the most important part of a feature story. Because a reader doesn't have any other reason to read a feature except that it looks interesting, the lead must hook the reader. The summary Big Six lead you learned to write for a news story is not often used in features.

The next few paragraphs, or body, of a feature relate the information in an entertaining way. All details are equally important to understanding the story and must be presented in logical order. Feature stories often contain more description than news stories, but still they are based on facts which have been carefully checked.

The last paragraph restates the main idea of the feature, either with a quotation or a summary sentence.

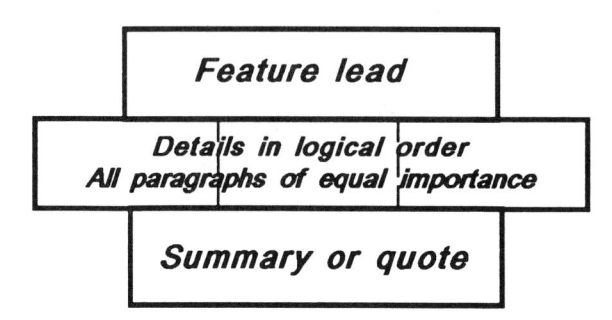

```
+----------------------------------+
|          Feature lead            |
+----------------------------------+
|     Details in logical order     |
|  All paragraphs of equal importance |
+----------------------------------+
|        Summary or quote          |
+----------------------------------+
```

## Three Kinds of Leads

In this section, you will learn to write three kinds of leads: question lead, quotation lead, and surprise lead.

A question lead, obviously, asks a question. The question must be one it is safe to assume a lot of readers will want to know the answer to. Otherwise, it will not tempt anyone to read further. Compare the following examples:

*QUESTION LEAD:* Students, have you ever wished you could get better grades without studying more?

*SUMMARY LEAD:* An exercise and diet program that improves brain functioning was described today by two former Olympic gold medalists.

It is safe to assume that most students want higher grades and less studying, so the first lead will attract more interest than the second.

A surprise or suspense lead makes an intriguing or outrageous statement and tempts the reader to continue in order to learn what it means.

*SURPRISE LEAD:* They came pushing strollers, carrying signs and wearing roller skates. They rode bicycles, carried balloons and were led by dogs.

The reader will be asking who, why, where are they going???, and read on to find the answers.

*SURPRISE LEAD:* The numbers sound terrible. Only 25.3 percent of Seattle's registered voters turned out for the Sept. 17 primary election.

You already have learned to write a quotation lead in Chapter 5. Remember to pick an interesting quote, one that will catch a reader's attention. "It's nice to be here today" is a quote, but not one that will encourage readership.

☆ *REVIEW: Look through several copies of your newspaper and find examples of quotation, question and suspense or surprise leads. Discuss whether or not they are appropriate to the rest of the story.*

✔ *CHECK YOUR UNDERSTANDING of feature leads by completing Worksheet #34.*

## Four Types of Features

In Chapter 2 you learned to recognize seven types of features. In this section, you will learn to write four: how-to, historical, personality and reviews. The pattern outlined at the beginning of this chapter can be followed for each one.

**How-to features** are used in many sections of the newspaper. They offer advice, such as how to get a summer job, or instructions on how to complete a specific task, such as building a bird house. Write your features in a logical sequence with enough detail that the reader can follow through, but remember you are not writing an instruction manual. Look at the following example:

| | |
|---|---|
| *Surprise lead* | While Halloween has been known to produce its share of ghosts and goblins, it can be a No. 1 nightmare for pet owners, too. |
| *Specific instructions on how to protect your pet* | But problems can be avoided by taking a simple precaution: Lock your dog or cat in a laundry room or den far from the front door. So your pet won't be bothered by a continually ringing doorbell, leave a radio playing in the room. |
| *Not inverted pyramid* | Absolutely nothing positive will result from allowing either a dog or cat to run loose Halloween night. Here are a few things to consider: |
| *All facts are equally important* | Even the most docile dog may become scared of costumed youngsters. Most dogs tend to be protective of their property, so when a little masked invader approaches, the animal may attack the child. |
| | Black cats are vulnerable to cruelty, probably because of age-old superstitions about this special day. |
| | The scare that parents of small children have faced in recent years about razor blades and tacks in candy and apples applies to dogs, too. Animals have died as a result of eating these supposed treats. |
| *Summary in concluding paragraph* | Make Halloween an enjoyable holiday for all of your household, including your pet. |

☆ *REVIEW: Look in a daily or weekly newspaper for an example of a how-to feature. Discuss how it is like or unlike the example here.*

✔ *CHECK YOUR UNDERSTANDING of writing how-to features by completing Worksheet #35.*

**Historical features** need to be tied to something in the present--a person or event or anniversary. For example, the death of an influential citizen may prompt a feature on the role s/he played in the civic or cultural development in your town.

Interviews with persons who remember incidents in the past can be successfully combined with library research in a history feature. Study the following example, prompted by Columbus Day:

*Question lead*

Who really discovered America? Weekend festivities around the nation honored Christopher Columbus, but experts are trying to determine if Basque whaling crews, not the famed Italian explorer, discovered America.

*Mentions current holiday that ties in to the story*

"We have 50 to 60 ships coming across every year to Newfoundland by the 1570s," archaeologist Susan A. Kaplan said. "The logical question is, 'How early were Basques in these waters?'"

*Story based on interview and research*

The Inuit, also known as Eskimos, may have come into contact with the Basques, who live along the Spanish-French border, in the first interaction between European and New World natives, Kaplan said.

The Basques did not consider themselves "explorers" and never tried to establish year-round colonies, as the Spanish, English, French and Dutch did, she said. They took down their encampments and headed home when winter made whaling too difficult.

Kaplan acknowledged that Vikings also crossed the Atlantic, but said it may never be known who arrived first.

*Closes with quote*

"People always love those questions of the first," she said. "That's a very difficult thing to pin down."

☆ *REVIEW: Look in a daily or weekly newspaper for an example of a historical feature. Discuss how closely it follows the example here.*

✔ *CHECK YOUR UNDERSTANDING of writing historical features by completing Worksheet #36.*

A **personality feature** captures the spirit and character of the person you are writing about. Use quotations and descriptions of his/her appearance and mannerisms to give the reader a picture of the person. It is more than a brief biography of someone's life. Let the subject's words describe his/her interests and beliefs. Study the following example of a personality feature:

*Surprise lead*

She's a drill sergeant, a den mother, a counselor and a friend to her ice skaters.

She's coached international champions like Olympic silver medalist Rosalynn Sumners; 1977 World Junior Champion Jill Sawyers; and the current second-ranked U.S. senior male skater, Scott Williams.

Skaters come from around the country to train with her; coaches judge her as one of their best. But there's a good chance that -- unless you're a skater -- you've never heard of Kathy Casey, head pro and skating director at Tacoma's Sprinker Recreation Center.

*Use quotations to reveal information about the person*

"You hear about the skaters, not the coaches," she says. "The skaters earn the headlines."

Tacoma has been Casey's hometown for almost 20 years. She arrived here at 26, eager to promote ice skating. Like most of her fellow coaches, she took up teaching after spending years competing on the ice.

"I was never much of a winner, but I had plenty of enthusiasm," she says. "I was always just as excited for other skaters who won as for myself, so that translated easily to coaching."

*Summary paragraph for conclusion*

What does it take to be a top coach? For starters: cold hands, a warm heart and a mind that can alternate between strict control and empathy. It takes a person who can accept the pain and rigors of skating six hours a day, six days a week for years on end, and understand the stress it places on her students.

☆ *REVIEW: Look through a daily or weekly newspaper for an example of a personality feature. Analyze it and see how well it portrays the person. What else would you have liked to know?*

✔ *CHECK YOUR UNDERSTANDING of writing personality features by completing Worksheet #37.*

The last category of feature writing you will practice is the **critical review**. As a beginning critic, follow this simple outline for all reviews:

1. State your opinion of the movie, concert, restaurant, book, or whatever, in the first paragraph.

2. The following paragraphs contain specifics about what was good and bad about the subject. Name specific items or persons that you want to praise or pan. It is appropriate to give a synopsis of the plot of a movie, play, or book, although it's not fair to give away an ending that is intended to be a surprise. Support your opinion by giving examples and details.

3. In the next to the last paragraphs include background information on the performers, director, playwright, or chef.

4. Close your review by restating your opinion and making a recommendation as to whether or not the reader should spend money on this.

Study the following example before writing a review:

| | |
|---|---|
| *State your opinion in the first paragraph* | "The Gods Must Be Crazy" is the best, brightest, and most popular work of art to come from South Africa in decades. It is the first widely released movie from that country and is enjoying richly-deserved acclaim. |
| *Be specific about what you liked and disliked* | Much of the humor is slapstick, charmingly innocent and hilariously funny. It is a refreshing change from the hip, slick comedy in so many contemporary films. The main character, a !Kung! bushman, portrays his culture and lifestyle in a simple, un-self-conscious way. |

*Include a synopsis of the story but don't ruin the ending*

Once upon a time in the Kalahari Desert, so the story goes, a Coke bottle was thrown from a small plane and landed in the midst of a !Kung! encampment. The strange object, obviously from the gods, caused so much trouble in the clan, that one member decided the only solution was to return it by throwing it off the edge of the earth. So he started walking, Coke bottle in hand, to the end of the earth. The rest of the story relates his adventures, and misadventures, in the "real" world, in which he continues to speak in the unusual clicking !Kung! language.

*Use example and detail to support your opinion*

He encounters a microbiologist whose research involves analyzing elephant dung. The scientist is smitten with the new school teacher, and the chance to watch his journey to meet her in a Land Rover with no brakes and doors that are stuck shut is worth the price of admission. Add a demented band of terrorists, an egotistical big-game guide, and a savvy assistant who is the only one of them who speaks !Kung!, and two hours later your ribs will be sore from laughing.

*Include background information*

None of the film's stars are big names in America; the bushman was discovered in the bush, so to speak, and had never acted before, which only enhances his impish performance.

*Restate your opinion; make a recommendation*

"The Gods Must Be Crazy" will be irresistible to movie fans of all ages and widely different tastes. Don't miss it!

☆ *REVIEW: Read a review in a daily or weekly newspaper. Explain how you are influenced by the review.*

✔ *CHECK YOUR UNDERSTANDING of reviews by completing Worksheet #38.*

## Comics

In most comic strips, the same characters appear each time. Readers get to know their personalities and habits. One way to approach drawing/writing a comic is to think of it as a story. Before you start to draw, answer these questions (which will sound very familiar by now):

Who -- are the main characters?
What -- are they doing or what will happen (plot)?
Where & When -- are they doing it (setting)?
Why -- are they acting this way (motivation)?
How -- will it end (conclusion or denouement)?

Pick the type of comic you will draw: humorous, drama, or fantasy/adventure. Humorous comics can be strips or single frames. The easiest way for a beginner to write a funny comic is to think of a familiar situation and add an unexpected twist or response. Some situations you may wish to use are sitting with the family at dinner, taking a test you're unprepared for, or being caught in a traffic jam. Dramatic comics are just like soap operas. The cast of characters is large, and the characters go through a series of significant life events such as illness, romance, divorce, or bankruptcy. Superheroes are the most popular characters in fantasy/adventure; other characters are detectives, spacecraft commanders, or war heroes.

It may help as you to draw a comic to pretend you are the eye of a camera. Draw your scene as though you were looking at it through an imaginary viewfinder. You may choose a long shot, close-up, wide-angle, telescopic, or, in a strip, some of each.

The best way to learn about comics is to study those in the newspaper. Pay attention to how the writers portray emotions through facial features and body positions. Recognize the use of comic strip "shorthand," such as drawing beads of sweat dripping off a face to indicate fear or anxiety.

❏ *DEMONSTRATE YOUR UNDERSTANDING of drawing comics by completing Worksheet #39.*

## Section 2. Editorials and editorial cartoons.

Editorials express opinions, but those opinions must be grounded in fact. Editorial writers need solid reasons behind their opinions if readers are to be persuaded to change their minds. Before you start to write, do interviews and research to get information on the topic. If it is a controversial issue, become familiar with both sides. You may already have your mind made up, but your readers deserve to hear the pros and cons before deciding. If you wish to write an editorial against a curfew for teens in your town, for example, find out why it has been proposed and who's in favor of it, what effect it will have on all those involved and what it will cost.

The two kinds of editorials you will learn to write are **editorial of criticism** and **editorial of appreciation**.

Writing an editorial of criticism is very much like writing an essay. Start with an introductory paragraph that states the issue or problem and give your opinion. If you have a solution to propose, put it at the beginning.

In the next few paragraphs, state the reasons for your opinion, supported by examples and explanations. Write at least one paragraph that summarizes the opposition to your position. You may concede that the other side has some valid points, even if you don't agree. Explain your proposal for change in more detail.

Close with a summary of the issue and a restatement of your opinion. Make a suggestion for specific action that can be taken immediately to implement your proposed solution.

Study the following example of an editorial of criticism to see how it follows this pattern.

*Explain the problem; state the editorial opinion; suggest a solution*

A tragedy of immense proportions is taking shape in the Amazon, where uncontrolled cutting and burning is destroying the rain forest at an alarming rate. If clearing continues at the present rate the entire forest, presently one-third of the forest remaining in the world, could be gone. It is an international crisis that demands a coordinated international response.

*Give more details; use examples*

No one can foresee with total accuracy the effect of losing the last great forest, but many scientists predict that the loss will cause a change in the world's climate. Without the great mass of trees and vegetation returning moisture to the earth's atmosphere, a global warming trend may occur. In some areas where the forest was cleared five years ago, the land has turned into a desert that sustains no life; where the tropical topsoil is without trees, it quickly erodes down to hard clay.

*Another reason, with examples and details*

Much of the Amazon remains unexplored; it contains thousands of plant and animal species unknown elsewhere on the planet. Researchers fear that species will be destroyed without having been discovered, and that holds potential for losing benefits those discoveries might bring. Rubber and latex are modern conveniences discovered in the Amazon, as well as several medicinal drugs. The native population has already been largely destroyed by white contact. Only about 200,000 Indians remain; four million existed only 50 years ago.

*Explain the other side of the controversy*

The Brazilian government, understandably, resents interference in its internal affairs and points out that Europeans and North Americans already ruined their own wilderness areas and native populations. Furthermore, Brazil has desperately overpopulated areas and its leaders wish to open up new land. They also need the rich mineral resources the jungle hides to improve their economic situation.

*Restate the problem; suggest action*

The uncontrolled destruction occurring now must be halted. Experts who are beginning to study the problem believe a way can be found to tap the mineral wealth and settle farmers in the Amazon, and not cause a drastic calamity. It is essential that other nations, many of whom are exploiting the resources themselves, join together to offer aid to Brazil and its neighbors and insist on a moratorium on cutting and burning until a safer plan can be tested and adopted.

The following four guidelines will help you to write good editorials.

1. As in news and feature writing, do not use the pronoun "I." Even though you are expressing an opinion, write in the third person. Occasionally, editorial writers use "we," but avoid this if possible.

2. Be brief and to the point. Editorials should be from 200-300 words long.

3. Do not use a preaching or scolding tone. It is tempting to do this in an editorial of criticism when you are trying to persuade readers to change their behavior; i.e., to stop the increase in smoking among teens. Think about how you feel when someone is attempting to change your mind by asserting you are stupid or by making you feel guilty. Your reader will respond to this style the same way you do -- by tuning out. Look at the difference in these examples:

    *WRONG:* Anyone who ignores the evidence that smoking causes lung cancer is just plain crazy!

    *BETTER:* Medical evidence that smoking increases the chance of lung cancer is overwhelming.

4. Avoid generalizations. This happens when you exaggerate in order to make your point stronger. Generalizations usually contain words like "all," "everybody," "never" or "always." Rarely can you document that "everybody knows better" or "all it will take is..." or "they never do their job." Your point will be made most strongly by good documentation to back up your opinion and proposals.

☆ *REVIEW: Reread the editorial of criticism to see how it illustrates the four guidelines listed above.*

☆ *REVIEW: Look in a daily or weekly newspaper for an editorial of criticism.*

✔ *CHECK YOUR UNDERSTANDING of the editorial of criticism by completing Worksheet #40.*

Editorials of appreciation are usually shorter than other kinds of editorials. In the introductory paragraph, state who is being recognized and why. The next paragraph mentions specific examples of the good work done by this person or group. In closing, state how the community or the world has benefited from these actions.

Study the following example of an editorial of appreciation:

*State who is being recognized and why*

Two giants of the acting world --Yul Brynner and Orson Welles -- have died within a day of each other. Their deaths are worth special notice because these two greats represented an era of excellence and depth in the movie world that is hard to find today.

*Specific examples of their good work*

For most of us, Mr. Brynner was and always will be the King of Siam, alternating willfulness with vision in the play and movie, *The King and I.* Known for his bald pate and dramatic acting style, he portrayed everyone from Pharaoh's jealous, scheming son in *The Ten Commandments* to the wise, tough gunslinger in *The Magnificent Seven.*

As for Mr. Welles, his name is synonymous with one of the all-time movie classics--*Citizen Kane*--based on the life of William Randolph Hearst. But the wonderful thing about Mr. Welles is that he will go down through history as the perpetrator of perhaps the greatest case of mass hysteria ever to hit this country. America panicked in 1938 when Mr. Welles' Mercury Theater of the Air presented a radio adaptation of *War of the Worlds* by H.G. Wells. More than a few people who listened to that broadcast became convinced that Martians had invaded the U.S.

*State how the
public has
benefited from
their work*

In these days of movies and films that glorify blood and guts, it's good to reflect on a time when true artists didn't need special effects, sleaze or gross violence to enthrall moviegoers. Mr. Brynner and Mr. Welles reflect back to that better, more thoughtful time.

☆ *REVIEW: Look in a daily or weekly newspaper for an editorial of appreciation. Compare and contrast it to the example above.*

✔ *CHECK YOUR UNDERSTANDING of writing an editorial of appreciation by completing Worksheet #41.*

## Editorial Cartoons

The purpose of an editorial cartoon is to emphasize or clarify an issue, usually a political situation. Rarely does an editorial cartoonist recommend a solution; s/he criticizes a person or event by illustrating contradictions and absurdities. Editorial cartoons are most often critical, although they can show appreciation.

The subject must be one that can be shown in symbols or **caricatures**, exaggerated drawings of a well-known person or thing. The topic must be widely known so that readers will be able to understand what the cartoon is about without explanation. A person's features or characteristics are grossly exaggerated in editorial cartoons, either to make the person recognizable or to tell the reader something about the person. For example, people drawn with huge noses may be known for their noses -- or for sticking their noses in somebody else's business. Countries or political parties are often personified in cartoons, such as Uncle Sam signifying America.

Editorial cartoons must be simply and clearly drawn and can make only one point about something. They may have a caption below the frame, or a quote from the character may appear in a "balloon."

☆ *REVIEW: Look in a daily or weekly newspaper for an editorial cartoon which uses a caricature. Can you explain what the cartoonist is portraying?*

✔ *CHECK YOUR UNDERSTANDING of editorial cartoons by completing Worksheets #42 and #43.*

## Section 3. Sports writing.

Leads in sports stories resemble features leads. This is to avoid repetition and boredom. During any season, the same major sports are played numerous times, by prep teams, semi-professional and professional teams, college teams, and amateur teams. Using the classic news lead, each story would begin:

Arlington beat Madison, 7-10, in last night's game in Memorial Stadium.

Sports writers, therefore, most often choose quotation, question, surprise or other feature leads. Of course, the Big Six will be stated in the first two or three paragraphs, and the body of the story will follow inverted pyramid style.

Look at these examples of feature-style sports leads:

John McEnroe's stormy stay at the $1.5 million Australian Open came to a shocking stop today.

It's probably a good thing the Seattle Supersonics haven't been at home a lot so far this season. It's probably a good time for them to get out of town again.

The sight of Joe Montana hobbling to the sidelines used to trigger despair among the San Francisco 49ers and panic in their fans.

Sports writers also use a specialized vocabulary that includes synonyms for nouns and verbs that appear repeatedly -- win, lose, score, hit, run. Examples are "triumphed" for won and "ramble" for run.

Sports writers have to know the game well in order to write a good story. A single football game, for example, has hundreds of plays, involving dozens of players. After observing for three to four hours, the writer must know enough to select only the important facts and write a coherent story of a few hundred words. What were the key plays? Who played noticeably better or worse than usual? Which strategy worked, which didn't? These are the kinds of questions a sports writer must answer in his/her writing. A play-by-play narrative of each game would not only be very boring to read, it would be much too long to print in the paper.

Study the following example of a sports story:

*Feature lead*

Roosevelt High School forward Anthony Richmond stands out in a crowd. He's 6-foot-6 and has a shaved head.

With 15 seconds left in last night's Roosevelt-Blanchet Metro AAA basketball battle at sold-out Blanchet Gym, it looked as if goat horns might sprout from Richmond's smooth dome.

*Describes important plays*

Richmond missed an 18-foot prayer shot that barely hit the rim with 15 seconds to play in regulation and the score tied 68-all. Richmond's miss allowed the Braves to take a 70-68 lead with six seconds left when Blanchet's Ryan Drew swished two free throws.

*Sports jargon used in this story:*
*swished*
*jumper*
*canned*
*bomb*
*partisans*

But Richmond hit an 8-foot jumper from the baseline with 45 seconds left in overtime to break a 72-72 tie and propel the Teddies to a 76-72 overtime win over their neighborhood rivals.

Drew's free throws set up the most exciting play of last night's game.

Roosevelt's Peter Dukes threw the inbounds pass to Willie Brantley, who immediately passed the ball back to an uncovered Dukes, who dribbled to the head of the key and canned a 20-foot jumper that tied the game with one second on the clock.

Dukes's bomb resuscitated the Roosevelt partisans, who jumped to their feet and loosed an ear-splitting scream.

☆ *REVIEW: Read the leads of several stories in the sports section. Are they news or feature leads? List The Big Six.*

✔ *CHECK YOUR UNDERSTANDING of sports writing by completing Worksheets #44 and #45.*

## Section 4. Review for quiz.

1. Three kinds of feature leads are described in this chapter: (a) quotation, (b) question, (c) surprise.

2. Four kinds of feature stories are described in this chapter: (a) personality, (b) historical, (c) how-to, (d) critical reviews.

3. Two kinds of editorials are described in this chapter: (a) criticism, and (b) appreciation.

4. Feature stories use a narrative writing style, like telling a story. Editorials, features and reviews follow a specific outline.

5. Sports stories often include feature leads and a specialized vocabulary.

6. Editorial cartoons use symbols to make a point.

7. New vocabulary word in this chapter:

    caricature

# Chapter 7
# Advertising

Mass media is big business. The TV and radio programs you watch and the newspapers and magazines you read are not produced solely for your amusement. They are vehicles for advertisers who pay a lot of money for the opportunity to display messages for your consumption.

In this chapter you will learn (a) principles of advertising; (b) how advertisers appeal to consumers; (c) advertising techniques; (d) how to design advertising for each medium. Major advertising media described in this chapter are newspapers, magazines, television, radio, direct mail, and packaging and store displays.

Advertising persuades **consumers** to buy a company's **product** or **service**. A product is a tangible piece of goods, for example a candy bar, refrigerator, bar of soap, wrist watch. A service is intangible; insurance, haircuts, car lubrication are examples of services. You are a consumer, one of the prospective customers the advertisers hope to attract.

Huge sums -- in the billions -- are spent each year on advertising. Most advertising dollars are spent in these product categories: food, drug and cosmetics, automotive, tobacco, soap, beer and liquor. Advertising is the major expense in the drug and cosmetics field. Philip Morris, a tobacco products company, spends the most on advertising of any American company; they reported spending $2 billion in 1989. Others with advertising expenditures in the billions are Procter & Gamble, General Motors and Sears, Roebuck. This billion-dollar investment is risky; advertisers are gambling that they can get your attention long enough to persuade you to return some of that investment by making a purchase.

☆ *REVIEW: Can you recall a time when you bought something because of an advertisement you saw? What did you buy? What persuaded you? What do you think is most heavily advertised? Define in your own words consumer, product, service.*

❑ *TO LEARN how many advertising messages you see, complete Homework #19.*

## Section 1. Drawbacks and benefits.

Commercials and ads are popular topics of debate, and they have both benefits and drawbacks to consumers.

Ads that provide detailed information are a beneficial service, allowing consumers to "shop the ads" and compare features and prices of different brands, without leaving their living rooms. Ads which announce sales alert consumers to opportunities to save money. Advertising lets people know what is new on the market, informing them about the latest trends and improvements.

The advertising industry promotes consumer spending, which is a key part of our national economy. If consumer sales decline, manufacturing and service businesses lose money and may have to lay off employees. Some people believe the competition created by advertising forces companies to produce better products at lower prices.

Proponents of advertising believe that, without it, freedom of the press would be impossible. If advertising did not pay the bills, media would be funded by political parties or other special-interest groups, much as the early newspapers were.

On the other hand, critics of advertising claim that ads persuade people to buy items they don't really need and that they do this through exaggerated or dishonest claims. Some people are pressured by ads to buy things they can't afford. Outright lying is prohibited in advertising, but many ads make implied promises that are unrealistic.

Advertising in all its forms increases the prices of consumer goods, which is considered another drawback. These costs are passed on to the consumer, which is one reason why generic products are less expensive.

In the past, the stereotyping of sex roles, age, and ethnic groups has been a serious problem in advertising. Racial minorities are underrepresented in ads. Men and women are shown in the stereotypic roles of good ol' boys, bumbling and inept fathers, distraught housewives, or alluring sexpots. The "average" family is white, consists of mother, father, 2.6 kids and a cute dog, and lives in a nice suburban home. Older people most often are depicted as retired and inactive, selling medicine or insurance. The advertising industry has responded to this criticism in recent years by eliminating many of these stereotypes.

☆ *REVIEW: Explain at least three benefits and three drawbacks of advertising. Think of examples of each from either print or electronic media.*

## Section 2. Market research.

Because corporations have such large investments in advertising, they want to be sure to get their money's worth. No one wants to spend millions on an advertising campaign and then see it fail. The industry of *market research* has evolved mainly to take the guesswork out of advertising. Four areas are investigated: the product or service, the market for it, the type of advertising that will work best, and which media to use. Research companies gain information through in-person or telephone interviews and questionnaires.

First, an advertiser must find out about the selling points of the product. Is it strong, economical, convenient, tasty, high-tech, durable, healthful, relaxing, nutritious, beautiful? What is the best design and size for packaging? What color, shape, flavor, odor will make it most attractive to consumers? How many uses does it have and which are the best ones to sell? What do consumers expect to gain from this type of product or service? How much do they know about it already? All of this information is available through market research.

Next, advertisers must find out who is most likely to buy their product or service. Market research companies study people of different income levels, varying age and ethnic groups, living in small towns and big cities, in families or single. They find out what makes people buy something. They ask who makes buying decisions in a family. What kinds of purchases are unplanned? How often does an adult go to the store? Which purchases do the kids in a family have a say in?

Then, researchers make recommendations on the type of advertising that will work best and the media to place it in. For example, teens are big consumers of jeans, so the ads need to be upbeat and stylish. The most effective vehicles for these ads are teen magazines and the television shows most watched by youth.

Let's see how three imaginary companies use market research. Acme Toothbrush Co., Fun-Fun Family Resort, and Betterburger, Inc. want information like this: a middle-income, small-town family of four eats burgers out once a week, favors yellow toothbrushes and spends vacations visiting relatives. Small towns are a good market for Betterburger, Inc., and for Acme Toothbrush, who will be sure to picture happy people using yellow brushes. It is not a good advertising market for a vacation resort; Fun-Fun will have to look elsewhere to spend its advertising budget.

Before making a final decision on an advertising strategy, Betterburger will try it in a *test market* to see how it works. They may try out one or more ideas in a few cities across the country and see if sales increase in those areas, or use two different campaigns in different locations and compare the sales results. Another way to test is to form consumer panels which will examine different models of the same ad or package and state their preferences. Sometimes researchers station themselves in stores to watch customers' reactions to their display.

Market research has a negative image for some who believe it's not right to uncover personal information about people and then use it to sell products. Advertisers believe it is justified because they don't want to waste their advertising expenditures, and they are better able to give consumers what they want.

> ☆ REVIEW: Explain the purposes of market research and how test markets are used. Have you ever been polled about products or television shows? What kinds of limits should be placed on market research?

> ☆ REVIEW: Imagine that an alien from outer space landed on Earth, and the only source of information about our civilization came from advertising. What kind of a report would the alien make on us?

## Section 3. Advertising techniques.

In this section, you will learn four advertising techniques that are used in both print and electronic media. Most common is a straightforward ***presentation***, sometimes called the "hard sell," in which someone speaks directly to you. The presenter identifies the product and tells you how great it will be if you use it. The accompanying picture shows a person enjoying this benefit. A presenter may be a real person or cartoon character, either humorous or serious.

A variation on the presenter technique is to have someone give an ***endorsement***, usually a celebrity in sports or entertainment. The celebrity says s/he thinks this product or service is good and recommends (endorses) it.

Ads featuring experts are similar to ads using endorsements. These ads feature a brewmaster talking about beer, a doctor advising on headache relief, or a mechanic explaining about motor oil. Some use real brewmasters or mechanics, in which case names and job titles appear in the ad or commercial. Others have an actor play the role of the expert, dressed in the appropriate costume.

Another technique is called ***problem-solution***. For example, if the problem is dull, lifeless hair, the solution, of course, is to use the advertiser's shampoo. The most familiar application of the problem-solution technique is the slice-of-life drama. A woman is complaining about her problem of dull hair, and along comes a friend, conveniently carrying a bottle of shampoo, to give some helpful advice.

***Demonstration*** of the product is a part of many ads.  Two special forms of demonstrations are the torture test and the comparison test.  Advertisers have been known to go to great lengths to subject their products to various tortures to prove how well they last; this works best for a mechanical object such as a car or watch.  Comparisons set up a demonstration that proves the sponsor's product will last longer, absorb more, or taste better, than Brand X.

***Visual ads*** don't say anything specific about the product.  The look and style are intended to convey an image that brings up a pleasurable emotion -- contentment, love, excitement -- good feelings which the consumer may associate with the product or the manufacturer.  Some examples are ads showing a person sailing or skiing on a beautiful sunny day, a couple walking hand-in-hand on a beach, a group of friends playing together, or a joyous family celebration.  In television ads, they often feature MTV-style imagery with quick cuts from scene to scene and popular music.

In Chapter 11 is a discussion of deceptive advertising practices.

☆   *REVIEW: Describe in your own words five advertising techniques.  Think of an example of each from both print and electronic media.*

✔   *CHECK YOUR UNDERSTANDING of advertising techniques by completing Worksheet #46.*

## Section 4.  Product identification.

Sponsors identify their products in three ways: ***logos***, ***slogans*** or ***jingles***, and ***ID characters***.

Most businesses develop a logo for their company or product, a symbol or way of writing their name that is distinctive.  The logo is used on every bottle, tube, package, or coupon and in every print or electronic ad.  The public comes to automatically associate the logo with the product, and the more familiar it becomes the more likely people are to buy that product over others.  See if you can identify the company from these logos:  golden arches, an apple with a bite out of one corner, an alligator, a bell, an eye, a roaring lion.

Some slogans or jingles have the same effect; they are verbal logos.  "Where's the beef?", a slogan for Wendy's International Hamburgers, was repeated thousands of times in 1983-84 and became so well-known it was even used by Ronald Reagan in the presidential debates.  What company uses these slogans?  "Reach out and touch someone."  "It's the real thing."

"Oh, what a feeling." Rhyming songs about a product, called jingles, were especially popular in radio advertising in the 40s and 50s. One of the most enduring jingles is the "Oscar Meyer Weiner Song."

Many manufacturers develop an ID character which appears in all the advertising, including packaging, and may appear in person at stores or parades. The ID character may be human (Mrs. Olsen, Col. Sanders), imaginary (Tony the Tiger, Pillsbury Doughboy) or animal (Merrill-Lynch bull). Many of these characters have appeared in ad campaigns for years, and consumers immediately associate them with a specific brand name.

Building product identification or brand-name recognition is extremely important to advertisers. It results in a shopper reaching for a particular brand of shampoo or fruit juice over all the others on the shelf.

> ☆ *REVIEW: Explain the meanings of logo, slogan, jingle. Add other examples from current advertising.*

> ❏ *DEMONSTRATE HOW WELL you associate products with slogans, jingles and ID characters by completing Worksheet #47.*

## Section 5. Advertising appeals.

Since many products and services are not unique or money-saving or necessary, advertisers try to appeal to the public in other ways. They try to sell an image or indirectly make a promise that something wonderful will happen in the lives of those who buy their products.

Basic human needs are for food, shelter, and health. In addition to physical needs, people have psychological needs for love, security, acceptance and status. Advertisers play on these psychological needs and on common anxieties.

Many ads promise, through images, that by using their product you will get more love and affection. No one really believes someone will fall in love with him/her just for using a certain brand of soap in the shower. Yet, some ads imply that is just what will happen.

In the world of advertising the surest way to get friends and romance is to be physically attractive. If you look right and smell right, people will be instantly attracted to you. The more worried and anxious a person is about being attractive and having friends, the more likely s/he is to buy a lot of products that seem to promise to fulfill fantasies and relieve anxieties. Some ads imply that kids will love parents who buy them certain brands of cereal or that they will care more for a mom who washes their dirty clothes in a certain kind of detergent. All these portrayals take advantage of the universal need to have the love of family and friends.

People also need a sense of security, a feeling that they and their loved ones are safe from worry, illness or unexpected disasters. Advertising that appeals to this need implies that the product or service can assure protection. Thus, we see medicines that clear up symptoms in seconds, bankers and insurance brokers who can eliminate clients' worries about the future, and flashlight batteries that save your life.

Another psychological need shared by most humans is to be accepted. No one wants to feel out of sync with the rest of America. So, if you buy this kind of beer, you're one of the boys; if you purchase this brand of pantyhose, other women will know that you're in the know.

Teenagers are especially susceptible to this appeal. It is natural for adolescents to have an intense need for acceptance by peers and to be extremely anxious about their appearance. Advertisers take advantage of young people's anxieties in the way they advertise cosmetics, hair and body care products, and fad clothing. While one's need for clothing is fairly basic, no one has a survival need to be clothed in the newest $80 designer jeans. That is a need created by advertising.

Other ads play to men's and women's needs for status. Their implied promise is if you use the product or service you will be recognized as a well-to-do, sophisticated, important person -- a person to be envied. Luxury cars make appeals to status; so do some perfumes, liquors, and jewelry. Other ads appeal to those who gain status by having the toughest car, or tire, or chainsaw of anyone around.

Emotional advertising appeals are used when sellers cannot, or choose not to, make factual claims about their product or service. It is also more likely to be used in television advertising where 30 or 60 seconds' time is not sufficient to communicate detailed information.

☆ *REVIEW: Discuss the four psychological needs that advertisers appeal to and give some examples of each. Explain why teenagers are often exploited by this type of advertising.*

✔ *CHECK YOUR UNDERSTANDING of advertising appeals by completing Worksheet #48.*

## Section 6. Principles of advertising.

Rarely is an advertisement only used once; it is part of an ***advertising campaign***. An ad campaign is a coordinated series of ads in several media (magazines, television, newspapers, store displays) over a period of time from a month to a year.

Advertising has four basic principles which are followed in all media: (1) Get the viewer's/reader's attention; (2) give the sales message; (3) identify the product or service; (4) request action.

People want to ignore advertising. They are overwhelmed by the quantity and disinterested in much of it, so getting attention is vitally important. Estimates on the number of ads you see daily vary from 500 - 1,500; yet most persons remember fewer than ten. The average reader spends 1.5 seconds on a printed ad; TV and radio ads last 15 or 30 seconds. Print ads must catch attention with headline and picture, hoping to stop your eyes. Electronic media use louder sound levels, the audio equivalent of headlines, and, in TV, an opening camera shot that arouses interest or curiosity.

An ad is the mass media stand-in for a sales person. Its message makes a promise about what the product can do for you and explains why it is unique. It offers you a "reward" for your attention in the form of information, news, or entertainment. A sales message must be brief and believable, with one main idea. The most effective ads provide some information, in an interesting and persuasive manner.

Without brand-name identification, advertising is useless. An ad must create in your mind a link between the message and a specific product. People frequently remember a commercial but associate it with the wrong brand. In such a case, identification has failed. Repetition creates identification, by repeating the ads over and over and by repeating the name and claim several times in a single ad.

The request for action depends on the purpose of the ad. Advertising campaigns are designed to: (a) introduce a product, (b) create a preference for one brand over others, or (c) create a loyalty to one brand so customers buy it time and again. These goals are expressed in ads by commands and requests: Buy some today! Don't be caught without it! Ask your dealer for more information. Try it and see. Compare for yourself.

When you prepare advertising, use the following checklist:

1. Is is clear who the audience is?
2. Does it offer a "reward" for reading/watching?
3. Is the message limited to one main idea?
4. Does it get attention in the first second or in the headline?
5. Is the brand-name identification repeated?
6. Does it close with an action message?

☆ *REVIEW: Explain the four basic principles of advertising. How does an ad differ from an ad campaign? Describe a recent ad campaign that you recall.*

## Section 7. Advertising in each medium.

The look and style of advertising differs slightly among media, each of which has its advantages and disadvantages to an advertiser. In this section, you will practice writing an ad for each medium.

Advertising campaigns are produced by ***advertising agencies***, companies whose business is to design all aspects of ads -- making layouts, writing scripts, writing copy, inventing slogans, creating packaging and store displays, directing artists and photographers. Ad agencies also buy the space and time in the media; that is, placing an order with a magazine for a full page in specific issues or with a television network for 30 seconds on a specific program for four weeks.

An ***account executive*** is in charge of coordinating a campaign for the agency. S/he meets with the client (the advertiser) to find out about the product or service and then supervises a team of copywriters, designers, artists and photographers who translate the ideas into ads. Of these, a ***copywriter*** is the key person, the one who chooses the right words to sell the product. The written or spoken words in an ad or commercial are referred to as ***copy***.

Advertising copywriters and artists need to have some information before beginning to create a campaign. Know exactly who you are writing for; picture a person in your mind. This insures the language and image will be appropriate for your audience. Know what you have to sell, which means knowing as much as possible about the product or service. You have to be able to write a convincing sales message. If possible, tell consumers something they don't know. If what you're selling is an image or feeling, it must be believable.

Start with the headline and the picture; that's what gets attention. If those aren't any good no one will see or hear the rest. Creating advertising is a perfect opportunity for brainstorming. Meet with all members of your advertising team and list all the ideas that pop up for headlines, slogans, pictures, logos, attention-getting gimmicks.

All ads have the same elements, although the form and emphasis vary among the media. The elements are copy (including headline), picture (moving or still), and identification. No matter what the medium, certain *buzz words* are standard: new, free, introducing, secret, magic, save, mother, unique, bargain, guarantee.

Advertisers are *national* or *local*. National advertisers are companies which have products or services that are available throughout the U.S., and they try to make their brand names "household words." Local advertisers are retail stores, and they use mostly newspapers and radio, with a little bit on television and in local magazines.

## Newspapers

As you learned in Chapter 2, regular advertisers are locally owned and operated businesses such as grocery stores, department and clothing stores, movies, car dealers, and banks. Newspaper ads contain specific information; merchandise is pictured and described and prices are included.

The primary goal of local advertisers is to get a customer into the store, although the bait may be a sale or a special on a specific item. You have had the experience of going shopping for a particular item you saw advertised and coming home with something entirely unplanned. When this happens, the newspaper ad was successful.

Newspaper ads have these elements: headline, photo or illustration, copy, and store identification--name, address, phone numbers and hours.

Ads in all media reflect the business. In a newspaper, those for discount stores have big black headlines and numerous items and prices crammed in the ad -- very much like the store looks. A bank, on the other hand, presents a sedate image with a tasteful picture and small headline. An ad must call attention to itself and stand out from among news stories and other ads. This is accomplished by placing a border around it and leaving lots of white space in the ad.

On the following page are four sample layouts for newspaper ads. Notice that each has the same elements, arranged differently. White space in the ad sets apart the elements. Three of the four are symmetrical, and all of them are balanced, much like a page layout.

Secondary School Journalism - 95

## LAYOUTS FOR NEWSPAPER ADS

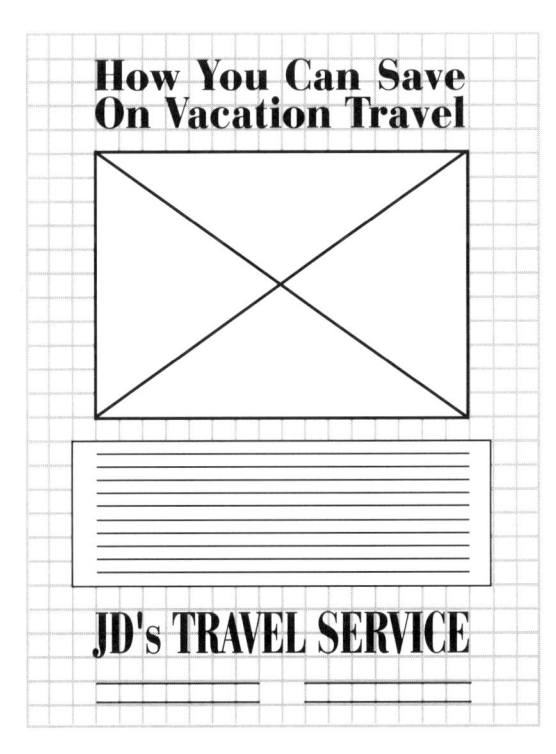

**How You Can Save On Vacation Travel**

**JD's TRAVEL SERVICE**

**INTRODUCING NEW *Diet Cola***

**Thriftlane**

New Fall Styles Are Here

*Diva's Boutique*

**BARGAINS**

*Shopper's Paradise*

Chapter 7/Advertising

Newspaper and magazine headlines make good use of the Big Six, as in "Why you should switch to . . ." or "How you can make a million . . ." or "What you should know about . . ."

> ☆ *REVIEW: Look at ads of different sizes in the newspaper. Do they look balanced? Are they symmetrical? Does each contain all the elements described here or do some omit headlines or copy blocks? Identify each element you see in the ads you study.*

> ❏ *DEMONSTRATE YOUR UNDERSTANDING of newspaper advertising by completing Worksheet #49 and Homework #20.*

## Magazines

Magazines are sold nationwide and therefore carry mostly national advertising. Magazines are a good medium for "big ticket" items like cars, computers, appliances, encyclopedia sets. Subscribers read magazines in their leisure time, so they will give ads more attention, and they generally see magazines as authoritative and informative, qualities which rub off on the ads. Magazines are kept around a long time and passed on to others, giving an advertising message a long life. Advertising in magazines can be costly; for example, a double half-page in *Time* costs $166,000. The many specialty magazines are perfect for advertisers who want to get their message out to a narrow segment of the market, persons interested in one hobby or sport.

Magazine ads rely heavily on their ability to reproduce beautiful full-color photos, something newspapers cannot do well. They frequently make emotional appeals. Eye-catching visual displays, like large photos or drawings, are their specialty, as well as broad use of color and innovative graphics.

The approach used in magazines depends on the type of product and the type of reader. Fashion magazine ads often feature only a photo and a brand name. The advertisers want to sell a "look" that comes from wearing their fashions. Magazine advertising for equipment, like cars or computers, contains a lot of detail, including diagrams and specifications. Readers who have special interests such as music, guns, knitting, or boating, want to know everything about the latest products and how they compare.

Elements of magazine ads include headline, photo, copy block, brand name or logo; store identification often is omitted. Magazines can offer advertisers special features like multi-page ads, fold-outs, and even scratch-and-sniff ads.

☆ *REVIEW: Discuss how newspaper and magazine ads differ. Analyze some magazine ads to see if they match the description above.*

✔ *CHECK YOUR UNDERSTANDING of magazine advertising by completing Homework #21.*

❏ *PRACTICE making a layout by completing Worksheet #50.*

### Television

Television is the medium everyone loves to hate, especially when it comes to commercials. The majority of television advertising is from national advertisers, who target a certain segment of the audience. Products sold on daytime soap operas appeal mostly to homemakers, the persons watching TV during the day; commercials during sports broadcasts, when the audience is mainly adult males, are for beer, cars and shaving cream; Saturday morning cartoons, with a large kid audience, are interrupted by ads for candy, toys, and breakfast cereal. Television is an excellent medium for low-cost consumable items.

A typical 30-second television commercial costs approximately $100,000 to produce. In addition, networks and stations charge high prices for air time, ranging from $1,000 per half-minute on a local station's evening news to the most expensive time, during the Super Bowl, where 30 seconds of advertising cost $1.5 million.

Some local ads appear on TV. Used car dealers are notorious everywhere for their ridiculous advertising. Remember, however, that no matter how dumb the dealers look bashing cars or sitting on a buffalo, they aren't dumb enough to waste their money. Advertising that doesn't result in more customers does not stay on the air; it is too expensive.

The elements of TV ads are the same as those in print ads, except the copy and the pictures become moving, speaking parts, with music and sound effects added. Think of a television commercial as a mini-movie. A script tells the actors or narrator what to say (the copy), and a *storyboard* describes the scenes and action, set and the props. The product will be one of the props. A storyboard is a series of drawings that represents scenes to be filmed, with the script printed below the pictures.

Most commercials are fast, loud, and flashy. They are designed to grab you before you leave the room or change the channel. It is nearly impossible to describe a typical or standard commercial because of the variety of styles. All the techniques described in Section 3 are used on television. The following brief scenarios demonstrate how each of these techniques might be used to advertise the same product: tires.

*Presentation* -- The presenter is a cartoon ID character, Tireless, who explains that Brand X tires are great because they are strong and last a long time.

*Problem-solution* -- A man sees his neighbor shaking his head and kicking his tires. In the ensuing discussion, the first man relates to his neighbor the wonders of the Brand X tires he bought. They part with a joke and a laugh.

*Endorsement* -- A well-known movie actress talks about how much she loves her Brand X tires.

*Demonstration* -- A vehicle with Brand X tires is driven non-stop across the Australian outback. At the finish, Brand X tires look as good as new. The competitor's tires, however, fell apart and the vehicle could not finish the journey.

*Visual* -- A succession of quick shots of people in vehicles with Brand X tires: on mountain roads, in freeway traffic, through placid farm country and bleak deserts. The fast pace generates a sense of excitement.

☆ *REVIEW: What TV commercials do you especially like or dislike? Which ones employ the techniques described above? Which ones don't seem to fit these categories? How do electronic ads differ from print ads?*

✔ *CHECK YOUR UNDERSTANDING of advertising techniques by completing Homework #22.*

On the following page is a storyboard for a 30-second commercial, based on the endorsement technique. Remember that most television commercials are 30 seconds, and each has to be timed to the exact second. Read the speaking parts in this script and add a few seconds for the camera shots.

## EXAMPLE OF A STORYBOARD FOR A 30-SECOND COMMERCIAL:

**VIDEO**
Long shot of a movie set. A night club scene, with the focus on a couple seated at a table.
**AUDIO**
In background.
Director: Okay, that's good. Take a break.

**VIDEO**
SF in evening gown, walks to chair and sits.

**VIDEO** Close-up.
**AUDIO**
SF: Hi, I'm Stream Fields. On the job, I'm an actress, but in all parts of my life I like to have the best products I can get. That's why I put Brand X tires on my car.

**VIDEO**
Medium close-up. SF stands.
**AUDIO**
SF: They have long life and a full warranty. I never have to worry when I'm driving in rain or snow.

**VIDEO**
SF leaving studio in street clothes. Pauses on steps, then gets in car.
**AUDIO**
SF: Whatever your job, you deserve the best, too. So, buy Brand X Tires for your car.

**VIDEO**
Close-up of tire on the car.
**AUDIO**
Orchestra music.

**VIDEO**
SF waving good-bye to guard as she drives away from studio.
**AUDIO**
Orchestra music.

**VIDEO**
SF driving along palm-lined street. Superimpose name.
**AUDIO**
Music fades.
Announcer: Have the best that money can buy. Buy Brand X tires.

❑ *PRACTICE writing a television commercial by completing Worksheet #51.*

### Radio

Most radio advertising is for a local market, and it is good for the advertiser who wants to target a specific group of people. Stations playing music popular with teens will advertise concerts, albums, clothing stores, and other places where teens are likely to spend their money. Stations whose programming is aimed at adults will have a different set of advertisers.

Radio commercials are brief -- 15 or 30 seconds. Frequently, the commercials are read by the station's disc jockeys or announcers, and they often give more specific information about sales or new products than television commercials.

The elements of radio ads are copy, in the form of a script, music or sound effects, brand name, and store ID. The scene must be set by sound effects, and the product mentioned often because a listener doesn't have the visual reinforcement of seeing the product and logo.

Here's an outline and script for a 30-second radio commercial for tires.

*CLIENT:* Rubberco
*PRODUCT:* Brand X Tires
*TITLE:* A Fine Life
*LENGTH:* 30 seconds

*ANNOUNCER:* We're on the set where "A Fine Life" is being filmed, waiting to talk with Stream Fields.

*BACKGROUND VOICE:* That's good! Take a break.

*SF:* Hi, I'm Stream Fields, and I want to talk about Brand X tires. On the job, I'm an actress, but in every part of my life I like to have the best things that I can get. That's why I put Brand X tires on my car. They have long life and a full warranty. I never have to worry when I'm driving in rain or snow.

*BACKGROUND VOICE:* OK, Stream, we're ready.

*SF:* Back to work! Remember, whatever your job, you deserve the best. So buy Brand X tires for your car.

*LOCAL ANNOUNCER:* Brand X tires are available in Kennydale at Marsdon Tire Center, 4th and Main, open daily 9-6.

☆ REVIEW: How do radio and television ads differ from each other? What radio commercials do you like or dislike? Which techniques do they use?

❑ PRACTICE writing a radio commercial by completing Worksheet #52.

## Direct Mail

*Direct mail* has become an enormous industry. It's what many people call "junk mail," brochures or letters that come addressed to Occupant. An increasing number of companies now use computer mailing lists that allow them to send "personalized" letters addressed by name to several thousand residents of a city.

Most people claim they never read junk mail, that they just throw it in the trash. However, no company is going to spend millions researching the market, writing a mailing piece, testing it, and paying for the postage unless it is selling their product or service. Direct mail advertisers hire market research companies to guide them to the right places to mail. If five percent respond, it's considered very good for direct mail.

For example, market research conducted for the resort has shown that families in the $20,000-$40,000 income bracket are the group most likely to prefer resort vacations. With that information, researchers use census information to find out which zip code areas have the most families with that income. Then Fun-Fun sends its mailing to every address in those zip codes.

Another way companies using direct mail get addresses is by buying mailing lists. Since Fun-Fun is near a ski resort, it decides to buy the subscription list of a skiing magazine. Then their copywriters prepare a letter which says that families who ski love their facility, and the company sends it to every name on the list. Names can be bought and sold dozens of times; sources are credit card companies, magazines, schools, clubs, or guest registers. This practice is not illegal, although many consider it an invasion of privacy.

Direct mail can take the form of a postcard, a letter, a brochure, or a catalog. Some mailings are fat packets containing a letter, coupon, brochure, even a sample of the product. It is a good medium, if the advertiser has a good list, because the company can send its message only to those it considers the best prospects for its business.

The first task for a direct mail advertiser is to get the recipient to open the envelope. Two approaches are used most often: (1) Make the envelope look like a business letter so the person will open it before realizing it's advertising; or (2) Print something on the outside to entice the prospective customer to look inside. Examples are "Free Gift," "Important News," "Something Special Just for You," or "You Can Win $1,000,000."

The elements and principles of direct mail are the same as other advertising: headlines, photos or illustrations, brand name and store name, and copy which includes specific descriptions and prices. Its purpose may be to get an order through the mail or to persuade consumers to go to a store.

Take note in the following example of how these principles are incorporated into one form of direct mail -- a postcard with a coupon:

```
INTRODUCING A
NEW, UNIQUE FLAVOR BAR

            FRUCH

LUCIOUS CHOCOLATE-COVERED FRUIT BITES
              PLUS
    A SECRET CAVITY-FIGHTING AGENT*
  You no longer have to worry about getting
  cavities from eating candy.  Eat all you want!

*flourotrobine
            Try some today!

Manufacturer's Coupon  Expiration Date: 12/31/92
Save $1.00 if you buy the handy six-pack of FRUCH
Not good with any other offer
```

☆ *REVIEW: Explain how advertisers get mailing lists. Study examples of direct mail that come to your home and those provided by your teacher. What form (letter, post card, brochure, catalog) is most common? What ones tempt you to read them? What happens to the direct mail that comes to your house?*

## Point-of-Purchase Displays and Packaging

*Point-of-purchase displays* are as varied as the products they feature. They display the actual product and are placed in a prominent position in a store. Store displays are used by national advertisers to introduce a new item or by local store owners to advertise a special sale.

Products also are advertised in stores through *packaging*. Does it surprise you that packages are advertisements? Millions of dollars are spent to design a package that will cause shoppers to reach for one brand of coffee, or lipstick, or motor oil, instead of the others surrounding it on the shelf. Colors, pictures, and style of type are important factors in packaging.

Store displays usually feature a poster or stand-up cutout of the ID character, logo, slogan, and maybe a headline. The display must be designed so that these elements attract attention, and the product is there as part of the display, ready to be picked up by the customer. It must attract attention but not cause a traffic hazard in the store. A classic slapstick joke involves a huge pyramided stack of cans being bumped into by a customer and rolling down the aisles.

Designing packages is an art in itself. Packages display the brand name and logo, and maybe a picture and a few words, like "new, improved." They must protect the product from spoilage, dirt, damage, and tampering, and at the same time be easy for the buyer to open. Some must be freezable or resealable; most are meant to be thrown away immediately.

Cans and bottles are forms of packaging, as well as boxes and plastic wrappers. Experts estimate that one-third of the garbage in landfills is packaging. A criticism of the packaging industry is how much waste it contributes to the environment.

> ☆ REVIEW: Analyze some packaging and decide if it includes the elements described above. What buzz words do you see? Which do you recognize as part of an advertising campaign? What elements are on the packages? How much of the packaging is thrown away immediately?

## Billboards

*Billboards* are a time-honored form of advertising, although restrictions in recent years have reduced their numbers. Billboards, signs that average about 200 feet square, once lined highways everywhere. When interstate highways were built in the 1960s, federal law prohibited billboards because they ruin the scenery and may contribute to accidents.

Billboards work best for a nationally advertised product whose name is fairly well known. Those advertising local businesses are placed on a highway leading into town for the benefit of tourists. Since copy must be limited to four or five words, it is not possible to say much about a product. The elements are picture, headline, and brand name. All elements must be big and bold; viewers must be able to take it all in at a glance.

### Alternative Media

Costs of traditional media continue to rise, and the public is becoming immune to the advertising barrage. Therefore, advertisers are turning to non-traditional media to overcome these problems. Examples are T-shirts, tote bags, electronic billboards, bus and taxi signs, placards on shopping carts, and "commercials" in movie theaters. Some companies also like to use specialty advertising like ballpoint pens or calendars.

Less traditional types of media are used successfully by stores and products who want their name to be seen a lot. Some items, bags or buttons, are given away free; others are purchased by consumers who like the product or service and want others to know it. Whatever the wearer's motive may be, the result is advertising. Are you wearing an ad right now?

☆ *REVIEW: Define direct mail, point-of-purchase, packaging, alternative media. Explain the differences.*

☆ *REVIEW: List the advantages and disadvantages to advertisers of using each medium described in Section 7. Predict the future of advertising in each medium. What new mass media might become available?*

✔ *CHECK YOUR UNDERSTANDING of advertising in various media by completing Worksheet #53.*

## Section 8. Review for quiz.

1. Benefits of advertising:

   a. gives consumers information for comparison shopping and helps consumers keep up-to-date on new products and trends;
   b. helps the economy by promoting consumer spending;
   c. contributes to freedom of the press by keeping media free from political control.

2. Drawbacks of advertising:

    a. persuades people to buy things they don't need and can't afford;
    b. is sometimes misleading or deceptive;
    c. increases the price of goods and services;
    d. perpetuates harmful stereotypes.

3. Advertising appeals to people's needs for:

    a. love and affection;
    b. security;
    c. acceptance;
    d. status.

4. Market research is used to decide:

    a. what kind of advertising campaign will work best;
    b. what media to use;
    c. what group of people will be the target population.

5. Advertising media are newspapers, magazines, television, radio, direct mail, billboards, and non-traditional media. Each has its own style and advantages and disadvantages for an advertiser.

6. Four advertising techniques are:

    a. presentation;
    b. problem/solution;
    c. demonstration;
    d. endorsement.

7. advertisements are structured to:

    a. get attention;
    b. deliver a sales message;
    c. identify the product or service;
    d. request action.

8. Three techniques for brand-name identification are:

    a. logos;
    b. slogans or jingles;
    c. ID characters.

9. Ads contain the same basic elements: copy, headline, picture, product identification, store name and address. The way they are combined depends on the medium.

10. New vocabulary in this chapter:

    account executive
    advertising agency
    advertising campaign
    billboard
    buzz words
    consumer
    copy
    copywriter
    direct mail
    local advertiser

    logo
    market research
    national advertiser
    packaging
    point-of-purchase display
    product
    service
    storyboard
    test market

# Chapter 8

# Magazines

Americans in all walks of life enjoy reading magazines. In addition to serving numerous special interests, magazines serve different age groups -- children, teens, and adults from early 20s to senior citizens. In one research study, teens said magazines were their favorite reading material. Magazines also are called *periodicals* because they are published periodically on a regular basis -- weekly, biweekly, monthly, or quarterly. In this chapter, the focus will be on *consumer magazines,* those for sale to the general public. "Magazine" comes from the French word, *magasin,* which means storehouse. As you learned in Chapter 7, readers see magazines as excellent sources of information about trends, new products, new ideas, and special hobbies or interests. Often, people turn to magazines for in-depth information about something they read about in a newspaper or saw on television.

In this chapter you will learn (a) twelve categories of periodicals; (b) structure of magazines; (c) how to edit and publish a magazine; (d) problems in the industry; (e) advertising; (f) history and future.

## Section 1. Categories of magazines.

Estimates of the number of magazines fall between 9,000 and 12,000, depending on the definition being used. A simple way to study such a huge industry is to divide it into categories and discuss the best-known examples in each division. The categories in this section are news/opinion, business, women, men, children/teens, sports/leisure, general interest, science/technology, home/shelter, city/regional, farming, religion, and minority.

### News/Opinion

The grandparent of news magazines, *Time,* was started by Henry Luce and a partner in 1923, at which time a year's subscription cost $5. *Newsweek* is its closest competitor. News magazines report national and international current events, as well as news about lifestyles, the arts, sports, science and business. Their coverage of events is more detailed than newspapers because usually they have more time to gather information. Each has thousands of writers and researchers who submit information on a topic, after which it is reduced to a story of a few hundred words.

National news magazines have printing plants in several cities across the U.S. and in foreign countries. (The pages are relayed to these locations by telecommunications.) They also publish regional and specialized variations of each issue to attract advertisers who want to reach a specific market such as West Coast residents or top business executives.

Weekly news magazines are at a disadvantage covering a "late-breaking" story because their deadlines are several days before press time, instead of hours like a newspaper. What happens if something occurs to change the cover story just before deadline? On stories that could have more than one outcome, like an election or a trial, two different covers and stories are prepared. Sometimes, it's too late to make significant changes.

The third major news magazine, *U.S. News & World Report*, has a different style and purpose than the two leaders. It concentrates on national and international news and has fewer departments.

Opinion magazines and magazines of ideas are like collections of editorials or essays. They analyze and interpret news, frequently offering criticism and solutions. Many are strongly identified with a political viewpoint; *National Review* is conservative, *The Nation* is liberal. *Columbia Journalism Review* monitors and reports on the actions of the mass media. Other magazines of ideas, like *Harper's* and *The Atlantic*, include short stories and poetry as well as essays.

## Business

Business is a high-interest topic. Newspapers are expanding and improving their business sections, and business magazines are gaining popularity. *Business Week* is a weekly news magazine about various aspects of business, like marketing, finance, management, production, and technology. Other business magazines, *Fortune, Money, Forbes, Changing Times,* and *Inc.* are written for different markets: business owners, investors, corporate executives, or people seeking guidance in personal finances.

## Women

Women's magazines have gone through enormous changes in the past 20-30 years. The feminist movement and the dramatic increase in women working outside the home have resulted in a shift in the older magazines and a large crop of new ones. The traditional leaders, sometimes called "the seven sisters," are *Ladies' Home Journal, McCall's, Good Housekeeping, Redbook, Cosmopolitan, Woman's Day,* and *Family Circle*. They were severely attacked in the 70s for stereotyping women and not treating them seriously. Since then, changes in editorial policy have resulted in articles and advertisers more in tune with modern women's lifestyles: divorce, financial planning, careers, child care.

The amazing success story of *Ms.* (founded in 1972), with its new approach to women readers, fostered a series of women's magazines with a different look. Instead of emphasizing cooking, crafts, and kids, they consider all contemporary issues from an independent woman's viewpoint. Many have an editorial focus on women with jobs, such as *Working Woman, Working Mother,* and *Savvy.*

A sub-category of women's magazines are the "glamour rags" like *Harper's Bazaar* and *Vogue,* which restrict their articles to high fashion, makeup, and lifestyles of the "beautiful people."

Other magazines which have mostly women as readers are those about romance or soap operas and movies. The stories in the romance and confession magazines usually are written by professional writers, some of whom write dozens of "true confessions."

## Men

It's hard to say which have been more energetically attacked -- traditional women's magazines for stereotyping women as housewives or traditional men's magazines for stereotyping women as sex objects. The current leaders, *Playboy, Penthouse,* and *Hustler,* continue to be the targets of protest for what many consider to be their pornographic content.

Two other popular men's magazines, *Esquire* and *Gentlemen's Quarterly,* do not rely on female nudity but have an editorial content that includes stories about fashions and contemporary issues from a male point of view.

## Children/Teens

Periodicals for young people are written for a specific age group and feature high-interest topics written with appropriate vocabulary. Included in this category are *Highlights, Sesame Street, Ranger Rick's Nature Magazine, Boy's Life, Seventeen,* and *Teen.*

If there is any one topic that nearly all teens have an interest in, it is music. While young people may disagree about what kind of music is best, they all like to read about their favorites. Magazines which fill this need include *Tiger Beat, Bam,* and *Creem. Rolling Stone* does the same for an older audience.

## Sports/Leisure

This is a huge and rapidly expanding category, because it includes all the hobby and special interest magazines. However, a few general sports magazines stand out as leaders. *Sports Illustrated* is a weekly news magazine about sports, published by Time Inc. In the sub-category of hunting and fishing, *Field & Stream, Sports Afield,* and *Outdoor Life* have long been popular.

Leisure-time magazines include a large number devoted to travel, as well as specific leisure-time activities. You probably cannot name a sport, recreation, or hobby for which there is not a magazine, as a visit to a large supermarket or bookstore will demonstrate. Advertisers have discovered these little magazines are very effective in selling products and services related to the readers' interests.

## General Interest

General interest magazines try to offer something for everyone. *Reader's Digest* is the undisputed leader in this category as well as one of the all-time best-selling magazines. Its original purpose was to condense, or digest, 31 articles each month from different magazines so readers could get the benefits of numerous publications. Today, most of its articles are prepared by writers hired by *Reader's Digest.* It is published in 16 languages in 163 countries.

The other top-selling magazine, alternating in first place over the years with *Reader's Digest,* is *TV Guide.* It is the only magazine in the world to sell one billion copies per year. It publishes 100 regional editions, an amazing feat for a weekly magazine, aided by its pioneer use of computers. In addition to program listings, it features articles on all aspects of the television industry.

Rounding out the big three is *National Geographic,* which was first published in 1888 by the National Geographic Society and still is sold as a "benefit" of membership in the society. It is probably the most-saved magazine in the world. Most families have a hoard of *Geographics* in the back of a closet somewhere.

The newcomer in the general interest category is *People,* published by Time Inc. Although criticized for containing only "soft" news and personality journalism, it has been very successful.

## Science/Technology

Science and technology is one of the fastest growing magazine categories. New starts in recent years include *Science, Discover* and *Omni.* The rate of technological expansion is so fast, it is a rare person who can keep thoroughly up to date. These magazines attempt to fill that need. They join *Science Digest* and *Scientific American,* which is the oldest in the field, founded in 1845.

Computer magazines reflect the up-and-down personal computer industry, as many are published by computer companies for their users. The *Popular* series *(Mechanics, Science, Electronics)* also maintain a large readership.

### Home/Shelter

Home and shelter magazines offer tips on how to improve and beautify homes, inside and out. The best-known is *Better Homes and Gardens;* others include *Metropolitan Home, House Beautiful, Apartment Life* and *House and Garden.*

### Farming

In addition to many specialized and state farming magazines, three general farming magazines are widely circulated: *Successful Farming, Progressive Farmer,* and *Farm Journal.* The latter prints 300 variations, matched by computer to subscribers' special needs.

### City/Regional

Except for *The New Yorker,* city and regional magazines are relative newcomers. *The New Yorker* is one of the great old magazines which has long enjoyed a nationwide audience for its articles, fiction and nonfiction.

The best-known regional magazines are *Sunset* (West), *Yankee* (Northeast), and *Southern Living* (Southeast). Most major metropolitan areas and many states now have their own magazines. They try to balance articles about the glories of their areas with more thoughtful articles about problems such as conservation, pollution, and unemployment.

### Religion

Religious magazines may be independent *(Christian Century* and *Guideposts)* or church-sponsored *(Catholic Digest* or the Methodists' *Upper Room).* Their market is readers who not only want devotional reading but a religious viewpoint on society and world events.

### Minority

Minority publications are like general interest magazines, except their audience is a specific ethnic group. The biggest is *Ebony,* started in 1945 because black people were largely ignored by the major periodicals. Publisher John Johnson also started *Jet* and *Ebony Jr.* and was the first to use black models in advertising. *Nuestro* is a magazine for Hispanics. Although the "color bar" has been dropped in most print media, minority magazines continue to attract an audience with their editorial focus on the concerns of a particular ethnic group.

☆ *REVIEW: Describe the 12 categories of magazines. Look at examples of publications in each category. Try to classify all the magazines in your classroom or library into one of these categories. Do you find some that don't fit? Which of these categories interests you?*

### The Top Magazines

Which are the most successful magazines? It depends on how success is measured. The magazines which have the largest paid circulation are (in order): *Modern Maturity, NRTA/AARP Bulletin, Reader's Digest, National Geographic, Better Homes & Gardens, Family Circle, Good Housekeeping, McCalls, Ladies Home Journal* and *Woman's Day.* It seems most of the popular magazines are general interest and traditional women's magazines, with the two top ones designed for senior citizens.

### Other Types of Magazines

Besides consumer magazines, thousands of others are published. Professional and technical magazines, often called **journals**, are published for persons in every possible occupation. Just a few of the approximately 3,000 in this category are *Clinical Nuclear Medicine, Teaching and Computers, Electronic Component News, Hardware Age, Food Engineering International, Poultry Tribune,* and the *Pet Food Industry Journal.*

Another several thousand magazines are distributed at no charge by companies. Sometimes called "house" magazines, these publications go to their employees, customers, stockholders, sales people, or technicians and service people. Large corporations publish several magazines -- one for each of these groups. Anyone who has flown on a major airline is familiar with one example: the in-flight magazine.

☆ *REVIEW: What do the lists of top ten magazines say about the magazine-reading public? What kind of people are they? What do they like? Do you have a personal top ten of magazine favorites?*

## Section 2. Magazine structure.

There are several ways to read a magazine. You may pick it up and skim through the pages. If a headline or picture catches your eye, you will stop and read all or part of the article. If you are familiar with the magazine, you probably have favorite departments that you turn to first. If you're the systematic type, you will turn to the table of contents, read down the list, then turn to the article that looks most interesting. Magazine researchers have discovered this interesting fact: 25 percent of readers start at the back.

All magazines have some elements in common. They have (1) cover with a nameplate, (2) table of contents, (3) masthead, (4) departments, and (5) a variety of articles, often called features.

The magazine publishing business is highly competitive. As you learned in Section 1, each category has several similar publications trying to attract the same people. Therefore, a cover is the most important element in selling a magazine, because it is the cover that first attracts a shopper's attention. This is the same principle as attracting buyers through packaging. All popular magazines feature a striking color photo on the cover. All have a distinctive **nameplate**, in which the name always appears in the same size and style of type. Also on the cover is the date and price. The date is the day it goes OFF sale. Many magazines feature teasers, or **blurbs**, on the cover which contain a few words about each of the major articles.

The **table of contents** lists all features and departments and the page each starts on. Sometimes the table of contents is livened up by more blurbs and small photos. You also will see something like "Vol. 8, No. 4." In this example, the volume number is the years of publication (eight years); the other number is the number of issues so far in the current calendar year (April or the fourth in the year if it is a quarterly). The **masthead**, a listing of the publisher and editors, is printed within the first few pages. Also included "up front" are postal and copyright information.

Most magazines have regular departments which appear in each issue. A well-known example is *The Reader's Digest's* "Laughter Is the Best Medicine." Nearly all magazines have a "Letters" department.

Nonfiction magazine articles are like feature stories in newspapers, and they can be labeled in the same way: how-to, historical, information, humor, personality, human interest, or news-related.

Many magazines buy articles and photos from **freelance** writers and photographers, who sell their work to various publications. Rates paid to freelancers vary from a few cents per word to $1 or more per word. The name of a freelance writer appears as a byline. If no byline is on the story, assume the article was written by one of the staff, which is a group of writers employed by the magazine.

Titles and photographs are the key to getting readers' attention. Magazine titles are not like newspaper headlines. They are labels; they don't necessarily have a subject and predicate nor do they summarize the lead. They are written to attract attention and to stimulate interest, so they are descriptive or suspenseful. Often subtitles are added to draw the reader into the article. Look at the following examples:

*Title:* Education: Where will we be in 20 years?
*Subtitle:* An in-depth look at America's schools

*Title:* How to Get Better Grades
*Subtitle:* Five tips to raise your GPA

*Title:* Skier's Paradise
*Subtitle:* Try Oregon in the Spring

Nearly all articles in consumer magazines are illustrated by photographs, and a lead photograph is selected to attract attention and express the main idea of the article. Some magazines publish photo essays, a collection of photos on a single theme, with little or no text. In addition, illustrations or graphs may be included.

☆ *REVIEW: Describe the five elements common to all magazines. Define blurb and freelance. How are magazine headlines, photos and articles like or unlike those in newspapers?*

❑ *LEARN ABOUT magazine structure by completing Worksheet #55.*

## Section 3. Editing magazines.

Editors at magazines work several months in advance; i.e., planning for a December issue may start in June. Monthlies establish a year-long calendar and plan each issue around a theme. For example, seasonal themes focus on various holidays, vacations, or back-to-school. Even news magazines plan coverage far ahead for known events, such as elections, the Olympics, the Super Bowl, or Nobel prizes.

The number of pages is determined by the amount of advertising sold for each issue. Each publisher has a ratio of editorial to advertising content. A ratio of 60/40 means if 60 pages of ads have been sold, the editors have 40 editorial pages to fill. If only 30 pages of ads were sold, the editorial content drops to 18 pages. The preferred, and most expensive, places for ads are the back cover and the two inside covers.

Once the editors know the number of pages and have decided on a theme, the stories, photos and illustrations are assigned. Editors then make a miniature dummy of the whole magazine, with a rough layout of each page. As in newspapers, ads are placed first.

A typical staff includes a publisher, who is responsible for seeing that the entire business makes money; an executive editor or editor-in-chief, who oversees the content; other editors for photos, features and departments; an advertising manager, who supervises artists, copywriters, and sales people; and an art director, who does layout and supervises artists in the editorial department.

Magazines offer an opportunity for tremendously creative layout. Art directors can use ***typography,*** the style, size and arrangement of type, to design a special look. Magazine layouts are not bound by the restrictions on use of space that newspapers have. They can leave large areas of white space, alter column widths, and use pictures of various sizes and shapes. Color is another element that can be applied effectively--in drawings, borders, titles and subtitles.

Art directors often work with ***double-page spreads,*** two pages facing each other. Because of the size of magazines, a reader's eye takes in two pages at once. Two tricks to keep spreads balanced and coordinated are: (1) work from the inside out, placing elements in the center area first and leaving most of the white space on the outer edges, and (2) align elements on vertical or horizontal lines. Photos are usually most effective if they are grouped together rather than scattered throughout the story. A layout must have a dominant element that attracts the eye and cues the reader where to start. Study the following example:

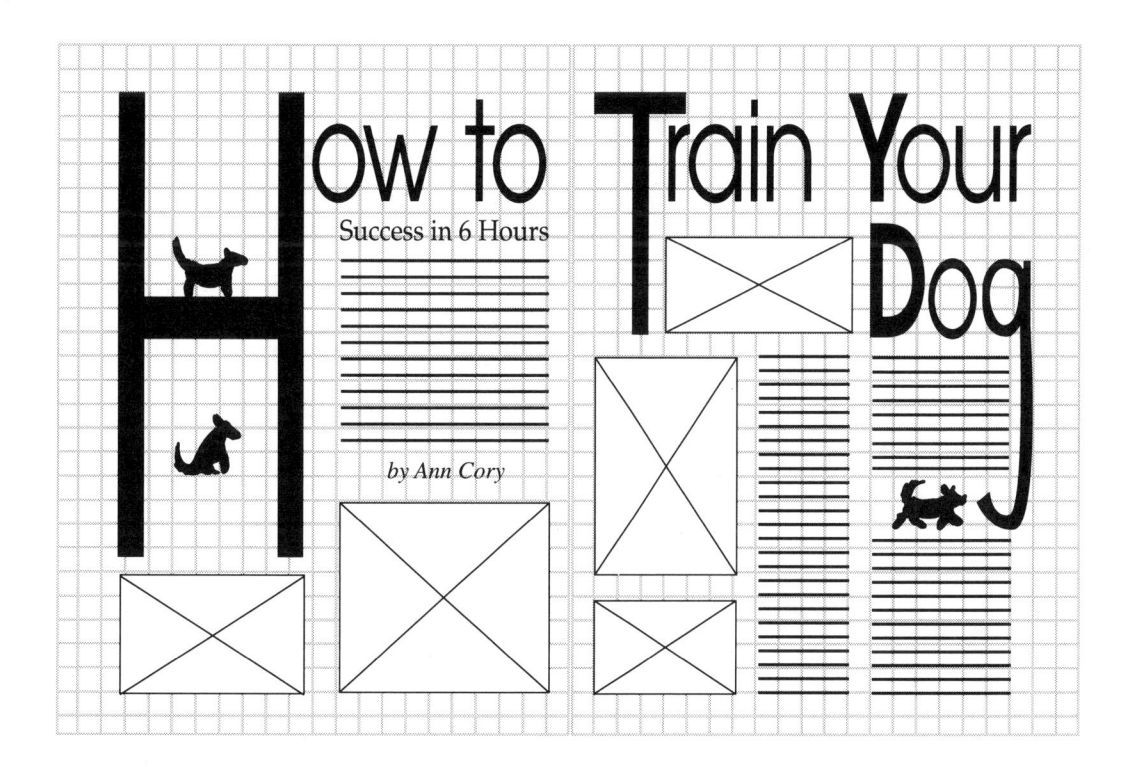

Note the alignment of various elements (dotted lines), dominant element (the big H), varied column widths, grouping of photos, and the use of a large expanse of white space around the outer edges.

> ☆ *REVIEW: Explain the roles of magazine editors, art director, and advertising manager. What are two points to remember in magazine layout? Find double-page spreads in several magazines. Critique the use of white space, color, typography and column width. How well does the layout attract attention and direct a reader's eye?*

## Section 4. Advertising and research.

In Chapter 7 you practiced preparing magazine ads. Because magazines compete heavily with each other, they must advertise themselves. A common practice is to offer large discounts for introductory subscriptions and use schools or other organizations to promote them. Some of you probably have sold magazine subscriptions for a school fundraiser.

Advertisers consider two factors, rates and circulation, before choosing which magazine to use.

Circulation figures are the key to advertising rates. Magazines guarantee a certain minimum circulation. The rates for advertising are based on a formula for computing the ***cost per thousand readers (CPM)***. CPM is the rate for one page divided by the circulation multiplied by 1,000.

$$CPM = \frac{rate}{circulation} \times 1,000$$

So, if an advertiser pays $500 for one page in a magazine that has 100,000 readers, the cost is $5 per thousand readers:

$$\frac{\$500}{100,000} \times 1,000 = \$5$$

This is more useful than considering the cost of the one page, because the same price ad in a publication with only 50,000 readers costs $10 per 1,000 readers.

One more factor must be considered -- ***demographics***. Who are these readers? They fall into the categories you learned about in Section 1. Magazines hire researchers to learn all about readers--their income, marital status, housing, cars, boats, hobbies, occupation. If you want to advertise outboard motors, for example, you might consider buying a page in *Time* for $97,000. That's a lot, but their circulation is 12 million, and several million of those readers own motor boats. The CPM is $8. Or you might look at a magazine like *Lakeland Boating,* circulation 46,000, advertising rates: $1,000 per page. The CPM is $21, higher than the big magazine, but you can be guaranteed that almost every reader will be interested in outboard motors.

☆ *REVIEW: Explain CPM and demographics.*

✔ *CHECK YOUR UNDERSTANDING of the relationship between advertisers and publications by completing Worksheet #56.*

## Section 5. Production.

The production process for magazines is very much like that of newspapers. Copy editors and proofreaders perform the same functions. Unlike newspapers, many magazines do not do their own typesetting, paste up, or printing.

The use of computers has been as revolutionary in magazine publishing as elsewhere. A few publications perform all editorial and production processes on computers, with the end product being completed pages in ***signature*** sets ready for the platemaker. Publishers can transmit text and photos across the country via satellite to distant printing facilities.

Pages are printed in sets called signatures; for most magazines, a signature is 16 pages. Pages must be added or subtracted from a publication in even numbers, in this case multiples of four. To demonstrate this, use an 8-1/2 x 11 piece of paper. Fold it in half once, short end to short end. Now you have four pages (count both sides). Fold again, eight pages. Once more, 16 pages. If you number the pages in order, 1 - 16, then unfold the paper, you can see how the signature goes through a large press, printing eight pages per impression (some print both sides at once).

A magazine can be bound together two ways: ***insert*** or ***stack***. See the following illustration. Depending on the type of binding, a 16-page signature may be the first 16 pages of a magazine (stack) or the first eight and last eight (insert).

INSERT

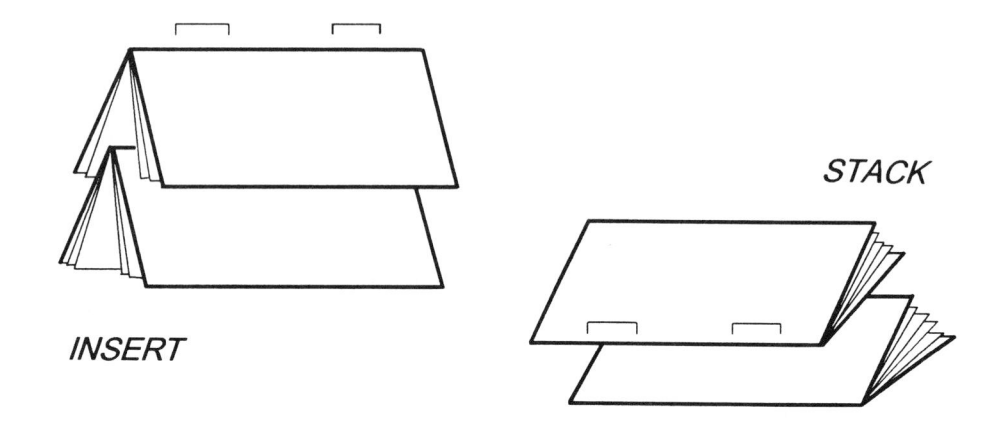

STACK

The cover is printed separately. After printing, a signature is folded, bound, then trimmed on three sides. An editor must know what pages will be in each signature when planning where to place color and in preparing signatures to send to the printer.

As you can imagine, the distribution process of magazines is complex. Subscriptions must be mailed on schedule, ideally to arrive at homes before the issue appears in stores. Mailing lists must be kept up-to-date as thousands of subscribers start, renew or drop.

Distribution companies handle the placement of each issue in stores (newsstand sales). The merchant receives 20 percent of the profit on each magazine sold, plus an additional 10-15 percent for those occupying the premium spaces near the checkout stands.

☆ *REVIEW: Define signature, insert, and stack. Compare and contrast newspapers and magazines in terms of writing, layout, production, and readers.*

✔ *CHECK YOUR UNDERSTANDING of magazine vocabulary by completing Worksheet #57.*

## Section 6. Review for quiz.

1. Magazines are divided into 12 categories: news/opinion, business, women, men, children/teens, sports/leisure, general interest, science/technology, home/shelter, city/regional, farming, religion, and minority.

2. All magazines have five elements in common: (a) cover, with nameplate; (b) table of contents, (c) masthead, (d) departments, and (e) features or articles.

3. Rules for magazine layout: (a) work on double-page spreads; (b) work from the inside to the outside; (c) group photos together; (d) align elements on vertical or horizontal lines.

4. New vocabulary in this chapter:

| | |
|---|---|
| blurb | masthead |
| consumer magazine | nameplate |
| demographics | periodical |
| double-page spread | signature |
| freelance | stack |
| insert | table of contents |
| journal | typography |

# Chapter 9

# Radio

Radio is the medium that is most constantly available to consumers because people can do other things while listening to the radio. No other medium allows you to split your attention in this way. With portable radios, people can listen while driving, jogging, bicycling, even showering. More than 80 percent of teens and adults listen to the radio sometime each week. The average home has 5.5 radios.

In this chapter you will learn about (a) types of radio programming; (b) radio advertising; (c) writing radio news; and (d) radio production.

## Section 1. Types of radio programming.

Most radio stations have an all-music *format.* This means their broadcast time is filled with music, with brief breaks for news, announcements and, of course, commercials. Other formats are all-news, ethnic, and religious programming.

### Music Format

The stations teenagers listen to feature a Top-40 or contemporary hit format of popular singers and groups. The announcers are called *disc jockeys* because when music formats first became popular the music came only on records (discs), and DJs alternated two turntables in order to play songs one after another. Through Top-40 stations, teens are introduced to new groups and new albums, as well as hearing their favorites over and over (and over and over).

Other music formats are aimed primarily at older audiences. They include country-western, classical, jazz, MOR (middle of the road) or light rock, easy listening and adult hits. Newspapers list local stations and their formats.

Disc jockeys are very important to all-music stations because they attract and hold listeners. If several stations in an area have the same format, the listeners will choose the one which has the most entertaining disc jockeys. Many develop comedy routines and special on-air "personalities."

Some stations purchase pre-taped music programs in their format instead of having their disc jockeys select each album. Because stations across the country use nearly identical formats, the same "canned programs" can be sold to numerous stations.

### All-News Format

All-news stations broadcast news bulletins and news features. Radio's speed and flexibility are shown to best advantage in its use of telephone interviews. Interviews are done anywhere, and they can be broadcast without the need for a film crew or the graphics necessary for television.

Radio announcers are skilled questioners, and interviews may be broadcast *live* or taped. A live broadcast is one in which the audience is hearing it at the same time it is being recorded. Live broadcasts often are taped also and repeated later. All-news stations schedule telephone interviews with people all over the world. Other interview subjects are visitors to the area who come to the studio to be interviewed.

### Religious Format

Like religious magazines, Christian radio stations are for those who prefer a religious viewpoint on issues. They offer music, news, and features with a Christian perspective, as well as worship services.

### Ethnic Format

Ethnic formats are aimed at black, Native American or Hispanic audiences. Ethnic stations attract listeners of all kinds who like the music. These stations may broadcast in their native language and emphasize news and features of particular interest to its listeners.

### Public Broadcasting

Public broadcasting stations are non-commercial, which means they do not sell advertising to support themselves. Their funds come from donations and government or corporate grants. Programming is more educational than commercial stations and aimed at an adult audience. Many are operated by universities.

### Other Programming

Telephone talk shows are popular with some listeners. Listeners call in to ask questions or share their opinions, and their conversation with the host/ess is broadcast. A caller's voice is delayed a few seconds to screen out obscene or violent language.

Sports broadcasts on radio generally are limited to the three main professional sports of football, basketball, and baseball, with occasional broadcasts of college games. Special events like the Indianapolis 500 are broadcast live each year. It's not unusual to see someone at a sports event listening to the play-by-play commentary on a portable radio. Radio sports announcers use colorful language to help the listener picture the plays they are describing.

> ☆ REVIEW: Describe the four most common formats. Which ones do you enjoy?

> ❑ LEARN more about different formats by completing Homework #23.

## Section 2. Advertising.

In Chapter 7, you studied radio advertising and practiced writing a 30-second radio commercial. In this section, you will learn how stations sell commercials.

Radio and television sell time the way print media sell inches of space. A contract for radio time will state, for example, that a commercial will be broadcast five times per day at a specific time for one month. The advertiser pays a fee for each broadcast, from several hundred to several thousand dollars for 30 seconds. Commercials are prepared by advertising agencies, which send the tapes to the station. In some cases, the announcer reads a script provided by the advertiser or agency.

The cost for 15 or 30 seconds of advertising depends on two things: the time of day it is scheduled and the station's ratings. Advertisers pay more for *prime time,* the hours when the largest number of people are listening. Prime time covers commuting hours, before and after the work day, or for young people, before and after school. A commercial will be heard by more people at 8 a.m. than at 4 a.m., so it costs the advertiser more.

Ratings measure the number of households which are tuned into a station at a specific time. Two ratings services, Arbitron and Pulse, issue reports three times per year announcing each station's rating. They gather information through interviews with a random sample of people in each listening area, or by asking a representative sample of homes to keep listening logs (called diaries).

Stations use ratings like print media use circulation figures. Stations with the greatest number of listeners can charge the most for their advertising time. Competition in the "ratings game" is very strong. Stations change disc jockeys or entire formats if they believe it will improve their ratings.

☆ *REVIEW: Explain prime time and ratings. Do you listen most often during prime time?*

❏ *PRACTICE writing a radio ad by completing Worksheet #58.*

## Section 3. Writing broadcast news.

Writing for radio and television is different than writing for a newspaper or magazine. A person does not naturally speak in the same way s/he writes. Your brain does not process messages you hear in the same way as those you read. You cannot remember and understand a complex sentence that would be perfectly clear in writing.

In broadcast writing, use short sentences and simple language. Humans have to breathe, which means verbal sentences are shorter than written ones. You have a larger reading than speaking vocabulary; therefore, use short simple words to communicate verbally.

Speak in the present tense, instead of the future. Whenever possible, say "you are listening" instead of "you will be listening."

Here is an example of a DJ introducing a record:

> *ANNCR:* Stay tuned to hear the latest hit from the top group in the country. You're listening to KXXX -- the rockin' station!

A typical radio newscast is five minutes long. In that five minutes, announcers make opening and closing remarks (about 10 seconds each), give a weather report (30 seconds), maybe a Wall Street or livestock market report (another 30 seconds), and pause for commercials (60-90 seconds). That leaves about three minutes for news. If an announcer covers six stories, each will have 30 seconds.

In the opening and closing comments, the announcer identifies him/herself and the station and gives the time. The closing will include a mention of the next newscast and upcoming programming. Stations are required by law to identify themselves once each hour.

Nearly all the words you hear spoken on radio and television are being read from a script. They are spoken in a casual conversational manner, but very little is truly **ad lib,** that is, spoken without any plan beforehand. Newscasts are carefully scripted from the opening teasers ("Norway invades Sweden. Back in a minute with details.") to the closing ("That's the news at 5:00. Tune in at 5:55 for the latest update.") It is important to stay with the script because of the careful timing needed to include everything in the time allocated. On music shows, an announcer may ad lib. However, commercials and news must come on at the scheduled times, so DJs must plan to have the music end at the right second.

A news item to be read on the air is written in short sentences that sound like natural speaking when read aloud. In the limited time available, the main facts, the Big Six, are mentioned, but very few details.

The body of a news item is brief and to the point. It is about five typed lines, mentioning only the most important details necessary to round out the lead.

Compare a newspaper story to a broadcast story by studying the following example. The radio story uses a surprise lead.

*NEWSPAPER STORY*

Two teenagers were rescued yesterday after a night on a narrow ledge of Mt. Townsend. Neither John Worthy or Lynda Smithfield, both 16, were seriously injured.
Another hiker heard their cries for help and alerted authorities. A rescue party, unable to work in the dark, went up at dawn.
Temperature dropped to the mid-30s during the night. Both were dressed in shorts and tee shirts.
The accident occurred when Worthy slipped and Smithfield attempted to help him. They were not able to climb up again unaided.

*RADIO STORY*

Two local teenagers spent Saturday night outdoors in near-freezing temperatures. John Worthy and Lynda Smithfield, both 16, were stuck overnight on Mt. Townsend. They were brought down yesterday. Neither was seriously injured.

❑ *PRACTICE: Read the above story aloud, enunciating every word clearly. The average rate of speaking is 120 words per minute.*

✔ *CHECK YOUR UNDERSTANDING of radio news by completing Homework #24.*

Leads are short and catchy; they need to attract a listener's attention before s/he changes stations. Use a straight news lead or a type of feature lead. Study the following examples of leads:

*News lead* -- Six men and six women will decide the fate of accused murderer Robert Charles Miller.

*Question lead* -- What's the hottest ticket in town this weekend?

*Surprise lead* -- You may find a little something extra in your paycheck next month.

❑ *PRACTICE writing broadcast leads by completing Worksheet #59.*

A lead story is the first one, and it will be the most important and interesting story, one that will attract listeners who most likely then will stay tuned for the rest of the broadcast.

Radio stations have a style book. The purpose is to make the script as easy as possible to read. Occasionally, a hurried announcer may not even see a script before s/he goes on the air.

Three basic rules will improve your scripts and make them simple for announcers to read.

1. Triple-space the copy to make it easy to read without skipping lines.

2. Do not write any abbreviations. We are trained to pause and let our voices drop when we see a period, so an abbreviation may confuse an announcer. A mistake could occur in the following example:

   ANNCR: A big accident on Main St. tied up traffic for two hours this morning.

3. Write phonetically any words, especially names, that may be unfamiliar. For example: Geraldo (Heh-rahl-doh) Rivera (Reh-ver-ah).

Radio stations use the same sources for news as newspapers: wire services, staff reporters, syndicated reporters and press releases.

Wire services have a separate line for radio and television stations. The stories are transmitted in broadcast style. Many editors and announcers rewrite the stories before the newscast and try to include a local angle. On stations with a small staff, an announcer may "rip and read," that is, pull a story off the terminal and read it on the air without having seen it before. If you hear announcers stumbling over words, this is probably what happened.

Broadcast media can react faster than newspapers to a news event. Frequently an announcement will be on the air within minutes after something happens. On important stories, stations interrupt regular programming to report the latest developments. Many times, the first newspaper reports are not available for several hours or until the next day.

Any non-profit organization can send a ***public service announcement (PSA)*** to a radio station. Stations devote a certain amount of time each month to PSAs, without charging the sponsoring organization for the air time. The station chooses which ones to put on the air. Those that are well-written and clearly in the public interest will be used at times when the station needs fillers. Examples of PSAs are naming agencies to call for help with problems, or announcing campaigns against drinking and driving. Stations also air other public service programs, often on religious or educational topics. Because these programs attract few listeners, they most often are broadcast early in the morning or late at night, usually on Saturday and Sunday.

☆ *REVIEW: Explain three kinds of leads used in broadcast news. Compare and contrast print and broadcast news. Define PSA. Can you remember hearing any PSAs recently?*

✔ *CHECK YOUR UNDERSTANDING of writing broadcast news by completing Worksheet #60.*

## Section 4. Production/Technology.

Stations are network affiliates or independents. A ***network*** is a group of stations across the country linked by telephone, satellite, and microwave relays.

The four commercial networks are American Broadcasting Company (ABC), Columbia Broadcasting System (CBS), National Broadcasting Company (NBC), or Mutual Broadcasting System (MBS). National Public Radio (NPR) is the public broadcasting network. Only one station in each broadcast area can be a network affiliate, so any other stations are independents. Network affiliates have the advantages of using shows produced by the networks and live reports from network correspondents. They get national advertisers sold by the network sales staff.

Anyone with the desire and the bankroll can start a newspaper or magazine. However, electronic media are different. Each station must be licensed by the ***Federal Communications Commission (FCC).*** The airwaves cannot be owned by individuals, and a limited number of frequencies are available. FCC licensing limits the number of stations transmitting so they won't interfere with each other.

Radio waves are transmitted in cycles and measured by the number of cycles per second. The cycles can be changed, or modulated, in two ways.

One is *amplitude modulation (AM)*, which adjusts the size of the cycle; the other is *frequency modulation (FM)*, which adjusts how often the cycle repeats. AM was invented first. It travels farther than FM, but FM produces a wider range of tones.

The first letter in a station's call letters indicates its location. W is east of the Mississippi River and K is west, although one or two early "K" stations can be found in the east. The other letters can be anything the owner wants as long as no other station is using them.

The FCC prohibits over-commercialization. The National Association of Broadcasters has adopted a code which limits commercials to nine minutes and 30 seconds per 60-minute period in prime time. Outside of prime time, the limit is 16 minutes in any 60-minute period. The number of program interruptions also is limited.

Occasionally, your listening pleasure is interrupted by a test of the *Emergency Broadcast System.* All stations are required to maintain emergency broadcast equipment. In an emergency, all regular programming is halted and designated stations broadcast messages. All other stations must go off the air.

☆ REVIEW: Using your own words, explain these terms: affiliate, independent, network, FCC, AM, FM, Emergency Broadcast System.

The staff of a radio station includes a general manager, who is like a managing editor of a newspaper; program director, who decides what the program content and schedule will be; news editor, who decides what news stories to use each hour; reporters, disc jockeys, announcers, engineers and other technical staff.

Each hour's newscast is broadcast live, and each one must have a new script, even though some items will be repeated. It may include an *actuality,* a voice report from the scene of a news event. Actualities may be live and transmitted on the telephone, or a reporter may make a tape and bring it to the studio for editing. A long interview may be cut so that only a few second are played as part of the newscast.

The engineer operates the controls of the tape machines and various microphones so the actualities, announcements, and commercials are played at the right time during the newscast. The engineer has a copy of the script, which includes *cues* for when to play a tape. The cues are the first and last words of an actuality, as in this example.

REPORTER: ... We asked Mr. Kingsley what he saw.

IN CUE: A big wall of mud ...

OUT CUE: ... lucky to be alive.

TIME: :30

With time checks and cues in the script, announcers and engineers can monitor themselves to be sure they are coordinated and on schedule. The time check in the example means that item ends 30 seconds after the beginning of the show. It tells the announcer if s/he has to speed up or slow down.

☆ *REVIEW: Give an example of how actuality and cue are used in a script. Explain the roles of editor, announcer, engineer and reporter. Listen to some radio newscasts and identify the actualities.*

## Section 5. Review for quiz.

1. A station's format is defined by what kinds of programs it broadcasts. Music is the most popular format. Others are all-news, ethnic, and religious.

2. Rates for radio advertising are determined by a station's ratings and the time slot for the commercials.

3. Guidelines for writing radio scripts:

    a. Write the way you talk. Use short words and short sentences.

    b. Every word to be spoken must be in the script and timed to the second.

    c. Write in the present tense as much as possible.

    d. Except for a really important story, limit news items to 30 seconds.

4. News items often use feature leads, especially surprise.

5. Stations are licensed and regulated by the FCC.

6. Stations broadcast on AM or FM cycles.

7. New vocabulary:

| | |
|---|---|
| AM | FCC |
| actuality | FM |
| ad lib | format |
| cue | live |
| disc jockey | network |
| Emergency Broadcast System | PSA |
| rating | prime time |

# Chapter 10

# Television

Few inventions since the telephone have had as significant an impact on modern society as television. In the space of a half-century, television has changed the way people receive news and information, altered the use of leisure time and made the idea of a "world community" a reality. In 1950, nine percent of U.S. households had a television set; today, 98 percent do.

Everything you learned about market research and demographics applies to television. It has been studied in great detail. More homes have a television than have a refrigerator or indoor toilet. Sunday evening is the time when the most people watch. Teenagers watch the least of any age group; women over 50 watch the most. Adults with the least education watch more than those who have been to college.

The "tube" has been blamed for increased violent crime, rising illiteracy, the breakup of the American family, corruption in college athletics and the election of unqualified candidates to high office. It is said to be the most financially successful industry in history; it has not lost money since 1950. The impact of television continues to be one of the most controversial issues of our time.

Each of you grew up in the television era. If you were like many children, you were placed in front of a TV screen before you could walk. You have your favorite shows and favorite stars.

In this chapter you will learn about (a) the controversies surrounding television viewing; (b) types of programming; (c) kinds of television; (d) advertising; (e) writing and producing television shows; (f) technology.

❑   *LEARN more about your viewing habits by completing Homework #25.*

## Section 1. Controversy and praise.

Critics of television are more vocal than supporters. Those who like it the way it is are sitting in front of the screen quietly watching. Following is a discussion of some of the major areas of controversy plus some words of praise. This information will help you to evaluate the programs you and your family watch.

The debate continues over whether heavy television viewing increases the likelihood of a person's committing a violent crime. The argument is that children who watch a lot of TV see thousands of violent acts (assaults, murders, car accidents, robberies), and that they will copy that behavior. (One study reported that the average high school graduate has seen 18,000 murders on television.) Many people fear that, in later life, these children will tend to resort to violence to solve problems. Many studies have shown that watching television makes children more aggressive, although critics also lay blame on violence in movies and videos. It seems reasonable that a person who watches seven or more hours of TV per day (a heavy viewer) will be influenced by what s/he sees. After all, advertisers believe they can influence our behavior with 30-second messages. How strong the media's influence is depends on other factors in a child's life; such as family, church, school.

Another frequent criticism of television is that it doesn't portray the world in a realistic manner. Certain types of behavior and lifestyles are emphasized, and these rarely match the lifestyle of the average American family. In the worst cases, these distortions create harmful stereotypes. Let's look at three examples of unrealistic situations.

Often programs feature families with a housekeeper or other servant. In truth, only a tiny percentage of wealthy families in the U.S. employ live-in household help.

For dramatic effect, certain crimes and illnesses are shown frequently. Rape occurs in television programs in much greater frequency than in the real world. Life-threatening illnesses and hospitalization happen with regularity in television-land, far more than in a normal family. Television characters have a high incidence of mental illness, which is always portrayed as involving violence.

On the other hand, many popular programs are about families who seem to have no serious problems at all. The parents are wonderfully understanding. Brothers and sisters, in spite of a few arguments, are loving and supportive. No one ever becomes unemployed or chronically ill. Their houses are always clean. No problem is too complicated to be resolved in a half-hour. These families are as unrealistic as the family with a new disease every week.

Only a small percentage of men and women are employed in the legal, medical, or other "white collar" professions. The majority of citizens have careers as teachers, sales people, factory workers, or similar jobs. However, these less glamorous careers rarely show up on the little screen.

People who rely on television for most of their information about the world will have a very distorted view. For example, studies show that heavy television viewers believe the world is more dangerous than it really is. They are much more fearful of being a crime victim than people who don't watch so much. They also describe their lives as lonely and boring.

Television news gets its share of scorn, too. It is called shallow, more entertainment than news. Stories are selected less for the news value than for the film quality. All issues, even those of great complexity, are reduced to a report of one or two minutes. News announcers are chosen for their appearance rather than for their abilities as journalists. In spite of this, one study showed that 60 percent of adults get ALL their news from television.

It is obvious that television and radio have changed family life. Once when families gathered together, they played games or had conversations. Now families gather to watch TV, which doesn't allow for much interaction. New inventions came into being with this medium, such as TV dinners and TV trays.

The decline in learning ability often is blamed on television. In the past, children and adults filled their leisure time with reading, for entertainment and for information. The quick pace and flashy style of television production makes other types of instruction pale in comparison. No wonder a classroom teacher is dull to a child who was raised on Sesame Street and spends leisure time watching music videos. Studies show that children who are heavy viewers show less imagination and creativity than other children.

Political analysts generally agree that the media image of a candidate is more important than his/her abilities or opinions. Candidates hire media consultants and market research firms, and they are packaged for sale to consumers (voters) in much the same way as a new model of car. This was first noted in the 1952 presidential campaign when it was said that Stevenson made speeches; Eisenhower made commercials. Eisenhower won.

Finally, the lack of positive role models for children is considered a drawback of television. Some of the biggest stars are male "detectives." They frequently use violence to solve problems and get away with breaking laws. TV characters often are shown smoking and drinking alcohol, providing a poor example for young viewers.

Well, this is a heavy indictment. With all the bad news about television, does it do anything right? In surveys, people say they watch TV for relaxation, escape, entertainment, learning, and keeping up to date. Despite the problems, it is a fine source of cheap, accessible entertainment, especially for those homebound or unable to afford to go out.

Citizens throughout the world have learned about their global neighbors through eyewitness accounts of other cultures. We have been able to see important events from across the oceans -- battles, ceremonies, tragedies, sports contests. Television allows armchair travelers to visit the most remote sections of the planet. Cultural events such as plays or ballets that once would have been seen only by those who could afford to travel now can be enjoyed by a wide audience.

Documentaries and interpretive news programs provide information to persons who otherwise might not take the time to read about an issue. Escape into a fantasy world is a time-honored form of relaxation and stress reduction.

☆ REVIEW: Explain the benefits and drawbacks of television. Which of these do you think is a serious problem? What do you use television for?

✔ CHECK some of these assertions about the negative aspects of television by completing Homework #26.

❑ LEARN more about television's influence by completing Homework #27.

## Section 2. Types of programming.

Television programs can be divided into nine categories: sports, drama, comedy, soap opera, news, game/quiz, children's, talk and public service shows.

### Sports

Football dominates sports programming from August to January. Once there was Sunday Afternoon Football, then came Monday Night Football; now we have Thursday Night Football, Saturday Afternoon Football, and Sunday Morning Football. And that's just the professional teams. Television revenues have become critically important to many college football programs, and some cities have local broadcasts of high school games. During spring and summer, numerous telecasts of basketball and baseball games fill the void. Every weekend, additional coverage is given to less popular sports. An avid sports fan has no trouble spending 20 hours or more per week watching televised games.

### Drama

Dramatic series have a regular cast and a theme -- private investigator (private eye), police, medical, legal, science fiction, or espionage. Themes are like fads; they are popular for a few years, then something else becomes popular. Once, western dramas were on every channel ("Bonanza" was one of the most popular), then "Star Trek" started a space theme. Detective shows are perennial favorites. They vary from realistic police drama to the pure fantasy of the shoot-'em-up private eyes. Another fad is a father-daughter, husband-wife, or operator-sidekick detective team.

Network programmers try a few new ideas each season, but many shows are copies of other popular programs. Therefore, the dramas tend to be very similar.

### Comedy

*Sitcom* is TV-speak for situation comedy -- a weekly humorous show with the same cast of characters shown in the same situation, usually a family or work setting. Like the dramas, sitcoms follow fads. One season they are built around cute adopted kids; another season around people with supernatural powers. In many cases, pre-recorded laugh tracks are coordinated with the script to make it appear the actors are performing in front of an audience.

### Soap Operas

Soaps are the staple fare of daytime television and some have been on the air for decades. They tell a continuing story and maintain a constant cast of characters. For years, soaps were on daily in the morning or afternoon. This means actors have little rehearsal time between shows. Acting in soaps is very demanding because of the need to learn a new script each day.

Soap opera fans are among the most faithful in the world. Newspapers print weekly summaries in case viewers miss something during the week; magazines are devoted to the actors. Many fans talk about the characters as though they are people they know.

Because of the great popularity of these shows in daytime, soaps moved into prime time (evening hours) with "Dallas," which was a huge hit in the U.S. and abroad. A version of soaps, the mini-series, also became popular. Mini-series are stories divided into three or four parts, often based on historical novels.

### Game/Quiz

Game shows are the other mainstay of daytime television. Most are based on a quiz format in which contestants must answer some questions in order to win. However, the longest-running game, "Let's Make a Deal," is based on a form of gambling wherein participants guess the price of prizes or take a chance on getting more valuable rewards.

Contestants are selected from applications submitted in advance. They are chosen on the basis of enthusiasm and appearance. Game shows are taped in front of a live audience, which directors consider important to generate an air of excitement. Audiences are "warmed up" before the taping by a staff member who comes out to tell jokes and rehearse the audience in responding to cue cards, which tell them when to applaud.

## Children's

Network programming aimed at children is limited to Saturday morning cartoons and a few specials. Quality children's programs are shown in the morning and afternoon on public television, before and after school. Shows like "Sesame Street" and "Mr. Rogers" teach specific skills to children in an entertaining manner.

The violent nature of many cartoon shows has come in for special criticism. Many parents also object to the commercials which take advantage of young children's lack of knowledge about advertising techniques. Some shows seem to be little more than vehicles for selling toys based on theme characters.

## News

Television news is an important part of any station's or network's success. Radio listeners become loyal to one station, but television viewers build loyalty to specific programs. News is the exception, and viewers acquire the habit of watching news on the same station. News *anchors* are the most important part of a news show; an anchor is the main announcer. Over the years, some anchors have become stars. It was said that Walter Cronkite, anchor of CBS Evening News for many years, could have been elected president. Polls showed he was the most trusted man in America.

In addition to anchors, network news has correspondents who become well known, especially those covering the White House and Capitol Hill (the U.S. Senate and House of Representatives). Correspondents, or reporters, broadcast from "on location." Since TV news must have a picture, they often are filmed standing at the site of a news event.

Standard additions to newscasts are the sports and weather. Sports reporters relate the scores and report on important contests, accompanied by film clips of key plays or finishes.

Weather reporters frequently develop an on-air personality that includes a humorous style; they illustrate their reports with graphics to demonstrate changes in the weather.

Networks also broadcast *news magazines* and news specials. "60 Minutes," one of the longest-running shows on TV, is the model for news magazine shows. Each week, its investigative reporters cover three or four stories, usually an expose of some misdeed. Other features are interviews with famous people.

A news special is an hour or half-hour show devoted to an in-depth report on one subject, terrorism or AIDS, for example. News specials provide the background information and expert opinions that are impossible to include on the nightly news.

Another form of news special is a *documentary*. Documentaries relate facts about a subject in an entertaining way; subjects most often are historical, biographical or scientific. Most are shown on public television.

### Talk Shows

Talk shows on television are not call-in shows like the radio programs. They are based on a series of short interviews with celebrities or experts in some field, psychology for example. Questions from the audience are part of some talk shows but not all. Each network has a morning talk show, a daytime talk show and a late-night talk show, each with a different style and format. NBC, for example, has "Today" in the morning, "Donahue" in the afternoon, and "The Tonight Show" and "Late Night with David Letterman" at night, each of which has successfully beaten back its competitors on other networks.

### Public Service

Television, like radio, airs public service programs and announcements and, like radio, tends to concentrate these on Sunday morning, when they have the fewest viewers. PSAs on television often are from the big disease organizations (American Heart Association) or large charities (United Way). Drug-prevention PSAs are aired frequently.

☆ *REVIEW: Describe the nine categories of television programs. Give an example of one program in each category. Think about the new shows you have watched this year. What is the current trend in drama? In comedy?*

✔ *CHECK YOUR UNDERSTANDING of television programs by completing Worksheet #61.*

## Section 3. Kinds of television.

The divisions in television are similar to those in radio. Three big networks, National Broadcasting Company (NBC), American Broadcasting Company (ABC), and Columbia Broadcasting System (CBS) have dominated the airways for years. Recently, they have been challenged by the Fox Network. Each network has an affiliate in each **market**, the geographical area the signal can reach. Several independent stations also exist in each major market. Independents do not have the resources to produce their own shows. Their programming tends to be old movies, reruns of network series, and less-popular sports. All expenses of affiliates and independents are paid by the sale of air time for commercials.

Public Broadcasting System (PBS) is the non-commercial network and like NPR is supported by public funds and grants. It is often called educational television because the programming leans heavily to documentaries and news specials.

Since 1970, **cable networks** have made heavy inroads into the audience that used to belong to the networks. Cable television is also called pay television. Each household pays a monthly fee to receive programs, and viewers are spared commercials. Many cable channels specialize in one format: music videos, movies, sports, arts, religion or news.

The FCC requires each cable system to reserve one channel for **public access.** Anyone who wishes to prepare a program can have his/her show aired on the public access channel and those without television production experience can receive instruction.

☆ *REVIEW: Explain market, cable, public access. Discuss the differences among commercial television, public television and cable television. Check your local listings to identify commercial networks and cable networks.*

## Section 4. Advertising.

In Chapter 7 you learned about television advertising and practiced writing a commercial. As in other media, the price networks can charge for advertising time is based on the number of viewers they can "deliver" to their clients. This is the basis of **ratings**. Ratings of television programs are similar to ratings of radio programs.

Programs with the highest rating (the most viewers) can charge the highest fee for 15 or 30 seconds. Ratings are measured four times per year by the A. C. Nielsen Company. A random sample of households across the country is chosen to participate in the Nielsen survey. A monitor attached to the television records what channel it is on and who is watching. Each member of a Nielsen family has a code number that s/he punches into the monitor every 15 minutes while watching. One rating point in the Nielsen survey represents 859,000 homes. A rating of 30 or above is considered a hit; below 20, a failure.

Television prime time is any 3.5-hour block between 6 p.m. and midnight, designated by each individual station. Advertising costs the most in these hours, but it is limited to nine minutes and 30 seconds in each 60-minute period. Outside prime time, 16 minutes of commercials can be aired in one hour.

Pilots, often in the form of a two-hour made-for-TV movie, are made for most new series. If the ratings for the pilot are good, the network will make from four to eight episodes. The ratings for these are evaluated, and programmers make a decision whether to continue the show or replace it. This is why some shows go off the air in a month or two -- the ratings were too low. Programs are planned to attract high-income persons, aged 18 to 35, because those are the people most advertisers want to reach.

The schedule is adjusted to help the ratings of some shows. A show that is scheduled at the same time as a highly rated show, "60 Minutes" for example, doesn't have much of a chance. This is why you often have to choose between two good shows. Each network is scheduling its best programs to compete for your attention.

☆ *REVIEW: Explain why ratings are important. How do ratings affect what you see? Check the newspaper to see which of the current programs have the highest ratings.*

❑ *PRACTICE preparing a television ad by completing Worksheet #62.*

## Section 5. Writing and producing for television.

### Newscasts

Guidelines for writing television news are the same as for radio news. Leads are short and simple; don't try to get the Big Six in the first sentence. The items are longer because the newscasts are 30 minutes instead of five minutes. A 30-minute newscast contains about 14 to 15 minutes of news, six to seven minutes of commercials, two minutes of opening and closing remarks and teasers before the commercials, two to three minutes of sports news and two to three minutes of weather. Many newscasts use feature stories to lighten up the program, and some have regular features like a consumer hotline.

Both radio and television news staff use the same criteria as newspaper editors: timeliness, nearness, importance, drama, people's names, famous people, and unusual items. In addition, television news looks for a story that is **visual**, one for which good film footage is available. TV news that is nothing but "talking heads," with no action sequences or on-location scenes, quickly becomes boring.

One story could have these pieces: a **live remote,** the reporter on camera relating the facts of the story; interviews with the people involved; footage of the site or event; file footage (perhaps still photos transferred to tape); and graphics.  All this for a three-minute story; obviously, each bit is only a few seconds.  Reporters usually come up with about 20 minutes of footage; the editor selects bits and pieces to get two to three minutes to use on the air.

Let's follow a news story from the time the news editor assigns the reporter to cover it until the announcer reads it on the evening news.

At about 10 a.m., the news director, producer, and editor meet to go over the budget.  They decide on the lineup of stories (in what order they will be reported) and how much time to give to each.  The editor has assigned a reporter to cover a story about a fire that destroyed a middle school.  The news team--reporter, camera operator, electrician and a sound technician-- are on the scene now as firefighters mop up.  They will shoot about 20 minutes of videotape, including interviews with the paper carrier who first noticed the flames, the principal of the school, and the captain in charge of the firefighting crew.  The reporter will write a short introduction, and s/he will be filmed reading this with the smoking building in the background.  The team must be back at the studio at least one hour before broadcast time in order to allow the editors to prepare the story.

Editors of broadcast news perform a different function than editors on newspapers.  They arrange the elements of the story and cut them to fit the few minutes allocated on the newscast.  In this example, the editor works with several pieces:  the voice of the reporter explaining what happened (telling the Big Six), plus the film of the reporter standing alone and additional film of the three interviews.  The edited version looks like this:  Opening shots are views of the wreckage with a *voice over,* the reporter's voice reading his/her script.  Then it cuts to the reporter standing in the playground as the lead ends, a shot known as a "talking head."  The next scene is a few seconds from the interview with the paper carrier.  The story closes with quotes from the interview with the fire department captain.  The 20 minutes of film was edited to a story lasting three minutes.

As they write the entire newscast, the editors work backwards from the end.  They know how much time is allocated for the weather, for sports, and for commercials.  The remaining time is divided among the news stories.

❑   *LEARN more about newscasts by completing Worksheet #63 and Homework #28.*

A television announcer must look at the camera.  Therefore, the script is written on a *teleprompter.*  News announcers and talk show hosts use teleprompters so they don't have to memorize everything they say.  It is a screen on which the printed script is scrolled up at a speed easy to read.  The teleprompter is placed next to the camera, so it appears the speaker is looking into the lens.  Some announcers like to have written scripts in front of them as well.

## Scriptwriting

Regular series -- dramas, sitcoms, soaps -- employ a staff of writers to prepare scripts for each program. Scripts for television include the dialog for each character, camera directions, and stage directions. Most scenes are shot in the studio, and the same set is used in each show -- the apartment, the office, the hospital. Other scenes are filmed *on location,* which is anywhere outside the studio.

Scriptwriting is a special form of writing. The story must be clear from the action and the dialog, and the dialog must sound natural.

## Section 6. Technology and production.

Two quite different technological advancements have changed television since it became commercially available in the 1950s. They are *satellite communication* and *minicams.*

In the 1960s satellites were launched into synchronous orbit with the earth, meaning they rotate at the same speed as the earth, thereby staying at a fixed spot above the ground. Communications companies--radio, telephone, television--are able to use these communications satellites as transmitters. Television companies no longer have to transmit signals from tower to tower across the land; a satellite is cheaper, and it broadcasts to a huge area.

A television satellite receives high-frequency microwave transmissions from ground stations and broadcasts the signals across the northern hemisphere. Local stations pick up the signals on their channel and broadcast them through a relay tower or antenna to individual homes, where they are received by the antenna attached to your television set. Satellites also are used to send a live transmission across the country or around the world. Newscasts frequently make use of this to bring you live reports from overseas. Other special programs, the Academy Awards for example, use satellites to broadcast and communicate from two widely separated locations. Radio stations also transmit via satellite.

Cable companies receive a license or franchise from local government to install cables; they use public utility poles or go under public streets. Cable programs also are transmitted by satellite.

People who live in rural areas, outside the range of standard television transmissions and beyond the areas covered by cable companies, have the option of installing a private microwave dish. Dishes receive signals directly from satellites. Television companies now are scrambling their signals, and dish owners must pay for unscrambling devices.

Minicams, lightweight portable videotape cameras, have improved the quality and speed of on-the-scene broadcasting. News teams can move quickly to the scene of an accident, for example, make a tape at the scene, then edit on the spot in their van. Camera operators are not restricted by the weight of their equipment; they can follow troops in a battle zone, for example. Minicams have improved sports coverage also.

> ☆ REVIEW: Explain the relationship of satellites, minicams, and microwave dishes to television programming.

> ✔ CHECK YOUR UNDERSTANDING of television vocabulary by completing Worksheet #64.

## Section 7. Review for quiz.

1. Television is controversial. The major issues are its depiction of violence, its lack of realism, its superficial news reporting, the changes it has brought about in family life, its effects on learning, and its influence on the political process.

2. People like to use television for escape and relaxation, information and entertainment.

3. Nine categories of programs are sports, drama, comedy, soap opera, game/quiz, news, children's, talk and public service shows.

4. Ratings determine which shows stay on the air and what rates will be charged to advertisers.

5. Kinds of television networks are commercial, public and cable.

6. Television ratings are measured by the A. C. Nielsen Company. The ratings determine the cost of advertising.

7. Television news must be visual -- something with a good picture. Most news items are two or three minutes long.

8. Two important technological advancements were communications satellites and minicams.

9. Vocabulary words in this chapter:

anchor
cable
communications satellite
documentary
live remote
market
minicam
news magazine

on location
public access
ratings
sitcom
teleprompter
visual
voice over

# Chapter 11
# Media and Society

You already have learned that the mass media wield a tremendous force in society. That force touches nearly every part of our lives. Because of that strong influence, equally strong conflicts develop over how to use or control the power of the mass media -- power that can be positive or negative. In this chapter, you will learn about controversies in the media. They are: (a) conflict between our constitutional right to freedom of speech and the government's need to insure national security and safeguard public morality; (b) conflict between an individual's right to privacy and the public's right to know; (c) conflict between free enterprise and consumer rights; (d) conflict between propaganda and information.

**Section 1. Freedom of speech vs. government control.**

*Congress shall make no law respecting an establishment of religion, or prohibiting the free exercise thereof; or abridging the freedom of speech, or of the press; or the right of the people peaceably to assemble, and to petition the Government for a redress of grievances.*

" . . . or abridging the freedom of speech, or of the press . . . "

From these ten words in the First Amendment to the U. S. Constitution has come a huge body of law related to what can and cannot be published or broadcast.

In Colonial times, the royal governors prohibited any form of public criticism of their actions. The government had the power to close down newspapers which printed critical remarks and to punish people who spoke out in opposition to royal decree. The writers of the Constitution knew that to maintain a democracy, citizens must feel free and safe to express their views. They also wanted to be sure the press had full knowledge about government actions so citizens could make informed choices. This is how we insure what is called the public's *right to know* -- an open exchange of ideas and a lack of secrecy in government affairs.

is called the public's *right to know* -- an open exchange of ideas and a lack of secrecy in government affairs.

> ☆ REVIEW: Study the First Amendment until you can say it or write it without looking. What does it mean to you? Can you explain its relationship to your life?

## Censorship

*Censorship* means to prohibit the printing or broadcasting of information, in whole or in part. In America the government censors material that it believes will be harmful to the national security or public morality. Examples of the kinds of material that are censored are military secrets and sexually explicit books or films. Censorship is done in two ways: by banning access to information, usually for reasons of national security, and by passing legislation which restricts access to items considered morally objectionable.

Government documents can be *classified*, kept secret from the public and from reporters. Classified information usually is about military and diplomatic matters, such as the location of nuclear submarines or plans for secret missions in foreign countries. Reporters, of course, try to gain access to classified documents to be sure the government is not trying to cover up mistakes or illegal actions by stamping "Secret" on the reports.

However, our government does not censor through *prior restraint*, which means an official reviews a story first and has the power to order the media not to use it. Exceptions to this are reports from war zones. In some parts of the world nothing can be published until the government censor has seen it in advance. Stories the censor does not approve must be omitted, sometimes resulting in newspapers being published with blank spaces where the stories were. Another means of censorship in other countries is government ownership of the communications media, including radio and television stations. In these places, broadcasts contain only the news the government wants the public to hear.

> ☆ REVIEW: Look at today's newspaper. What stories might not appear if we had a system of government censorship? Do you see any stories that you believe have been censored? What do you think should be the limits of censorship?

## Obscenity

Most of the time you hear of censorship in relationship to *pornography*. Pornography is material which is *obscene*, usually because it is sexually explicit. The dictionary defines obscene as deeply offensive to morality or decency, repulsive, or especially designed to incite to lust or depravity. The problem, one the courts have struggled with for years, is to decide exactly how to use this definition. A book that is deeply offensive to one person is acceptable to another; a movie that seems repulsive to the residents of one community does not arouse the same degree of disgust in another part of the country.

Courts are asked time and again to ban the sale or distribution of a book, magazine, film or tape because it is obscene. A legal definition arose from the 1973 case of *Miller v. California.* From that Supreme Court decision came three tests for obscenity: (1) whether the average person in a community would find that the work, taken as a whole, appeals to an unhealthy interest in sex; (2) whether the work portrays, in an offensive manner, sexual conduct specifically prohibited by state law; (3) whether the work, taken as a whole, lacks serious literary, artistic, political, or scientific value.

In other words, a book or film cannot be judged obscene based on one person's complaint; it must offend the standards of the average person in the community. It also cannot be judged on the basis of one part; the work must be considered as a whole, since descriptions of sexuality could be appropriate in some artistic works.

An artist or writer whose work is banned can claim the right to free speech. Generally, the courts have favored the constitutional right to individual expression, even if that expression is considered pornographic by some people. Legislators have allowed these works to be sold, but limit who can see them.

Most people agree that some restrictions on the distribution of obscene material is desirable. For example, children under 18 are not allowed to see X-rated movies. Many cities have set aside specific downtown zones for "adult book stores." Yet children have unrestricted access to movies and music videos on cable television and to tapes and records, some of which have X-rated themes.

People who want more censorship believe the widespread availability of pornography is responsible for an increase in sexual violence and a decline in moral standards. Those who want less censorship say that once we allow one group to impose its standards on society, it will be hard to draw the line. Next, they say, will be a call for censorship of disagreeable political viewpoints.

The most outspoken defender of free speech, the American Civil Liberties Union (ACLU), is a frequent target of criticism for their insistence on protecting the rights of everyone to free speech. They have defended writers and speakers from the American Communist Party, The Order (a Nazi-style organization), and other extremist groups which preach revolution against our present form of government. However, we continue to have legal protection for everyone. If we silence viewpoints such as these which most of us find objectionable, it would be possible to use the same laws to silence rightful protest.

A recent wave of challenges to books used in schools has caused the issue of censorship to be raised in that arena. Parents have asked that various books be removed from school libraries and from reading lists, most often due to the presence of profanity, racial stereotypes, or sexually explicit scenes. Some of the well-known books that have come under attack are *Huckleberry Finn* by Mark Twain, *Of Mice and Men* by John Steinbeck, *Catcher in the Rye* by J. D. Salinger, and *Romeo and Juliet* by William Shakespeare. Since these books are considered by many people to be literary classics, the outlines of the conflict are clear.

Few people can argue that the best censor is personal initiative. No one is forced to buy pornographic magazines or enter an X-rated movie theater. Every television set and stereo has an "Off" button. The controversy begins when people, on both sides, try to impose their personal standards on others.

☆ *REVIEW: Explain censorship, classified, prior restraint, obscenity, pornography. What limits do you think should be set on pornography? Explain the importance of a free press.*

❑ *EXPRESS YOUR OPINION on First Amendment issues by completing Worksheet #65.*

## Section 2. Right to privacy vs. right to know.

Each of us has a legal right to privacy, to go about our business without having an account of it published or broadcast. However, we forfeit our right to privacy by being involved, even accidentally, in a newsworthy event. If you are in a car wreck or speak at a public hearing or are named in a lawsuit, you have no legal right to prohibit the media from using your name and picture. Anything that is on public record (arrests, real estate sales, tax assessments) is public information and can be used by the news media. A picture taken in a public place, such as a park, can be used without your permission.

Abuses occur when reporters go beyond a legitimate right to know. In their zeal to cover the news, for example, reporters appear to be insensitive as they intrude on families in the midst of tragedy. Television reporters especially have been criticized for asking, and filming, responses to such inane questions as "How do you feel about your house being flattened by a runaway bulldozer?"

In special circumstances, you are protected from the exercise of the public's right to know. It is illegal to use names of minors (people 18 or younger) who have committed crimes, and many court proceedings involving juveniles take place in the judge's chambers, away from the eyes and ears of journalists. Most news media do not use the names of victims of sex offenses.

The Sixth Amendment protects our right to a fair trial by an impartial jury. To insure this right, judges can restrict the media during trials. They may close the courtroom or not allow cameras. This protects the right of the defendant to a fair trial by an impartial jury, which outweighs the public's right to know everything about it. Once a jury is impaneled for a trial that has received a lot of publicity, a judge usually forbids jurors to read or listen to any reports of the proceedings. Extensive news media coverage can prejudice people against the accused so it becomes impossible to find jurors who haven't already decided s/he is guilty.

In a landmark case in 1954, the Supreme Court reversed the conviction of accused murderer Sam Sheppard because of the influence of the press coverage on the trial. The pre-trial publicity caused what one lawyer called "mass hysteria generated by an over-zealous press." Newspapers printed interviews with witnesses and with jurors; the press related information from police and lawyers regarding evidence. All this made a fair trial by an impartial jury impossible. New rules for covering trials were adopted after this decision.

If you become famous -- or try to become famous -- the rules change. People who place themselves voluntarily in the limelight (politicians, athletes, entertainers) forfeit the right to privacy in their personal affairs. Anyone who publishes a book or acts in a play must expect his/her performances to be criticized by reviewers, who may be very insulting. Critics are paid to give their opinions.

Famous or unknown, you are protected from having untrue stories told about you. It is illegal to print or broadcast something known to be untrue about a person if it exposes that person to hatred, makes him/her seem ridiculous or damages his/her reputation or earning power. To do so is called ***libel.*** This is why editors want reporters to check and double-check all information; they don't want to be sued. Editors have a good defense against a charge of libel if they can prove one of two things: (1) what was published is true and can be proved, no matter how incriminating or embarrassing it is; (2) it was published in good faith without "malice," or intent to harm, even if it later is shown to be incorrect. All the above applies equally to all news media.

As a reporter, you can use several techniques to avoid libel charges. Use the words "alleged" and "accused" when referring to suspects of a crime. Since a person is presumed innocent until proven guilty, no one can be called a murderer or a thief before being convicted in a court. For example, "Jones is accused of masterminding the robbery" or "The alleged murder was committed in December." Be sure every quote has an ***attribution,*** which means to state who is being quoted. If a source needs to be protected, use a phrase like "a highly placed official" or "an administrator close to the president." This tells the public you have promised to keep the name a secret but that it is a genuine quote. If you are doubtful about the information, find a second source to confirm the story.

Of course, you can write an eyewitness account if you were on the scene. However, be careful to describe only what you saw and not draw conclusions. Say "The suspect gestured wildly and shouted incoherently" not "The suspect acted insane."

If an error has been made, a newspaper will print a ***retraction,*** a statement correcting the misinformation and making a public apology.

☆ *REVIEW: Explain right to know, privacy, and libel. Look in the newspaper for an example of retraction and attribution. What actions can a reporter take to avoid libel? Do you agree that truth or acting without malice are adequate defenses against libel charges?*

❑ *DEMONSTRATE your understanding of libel by completing Worksheet #66.*

## Section 3. Individual rights vs. free enterprise.

Democracy and free enterprise are inseparably joined in America. Conflict arises when a company's right to pursue a profit clashes with individuals' rights to receive honest and complete information. This problem affects each of us directly in the area of consumers' rights to fair advertising practices. A less direct effect is the restriction on information through control of the media by a few corporations.

### Deceptive Advertising

Advertisers are prohibited by law from making untrue or unprovable claims. A manufacturer cannot say, "If you eat this cereal, you will grow two inches taller" or "If you use this toothpaste, you will have three new friends." Some ads, however, are deceptive in the way the product is pictured or in the way the copy is worded.

One misleading trick is to put a ***qualifier*** in fine print. A qualifier is a statement that makes it clear exactly what you will get for your money, even if a picture or headline make it seem you get more. For example, a toy ad or package may show an extensive set, and the qualifier will say "All parts (or all accessories) sold separately."

Similar qualifiers are used in food advertising. A package may contain two frozen drumsticks. The picture on the front shows a full plate covered with two drumsticks, mashed potatoes, and peas. The qualifier, in fine print, says: "Serving suggestion. Contains two drumsticks." However, a consumer could easily believe s/he was buying a complete dinner.

Other ads in which a consumer should check for qualifiers are those which promise to give something away for free. The fine print usually reveals a requirement to buy something in order to get additional products free.

Deceptive advertisers frequently use ***dangling comparisons,*** such as "our detergent makes clothes whiter" or "these jeans last 50% longer." Whiter than what? Those washed with baking soda? Last longer than what? Cotton shorts? The implication is that the detergent is better than other detergents and the jeans last longer than other jeans, but the ad doesn't say that. An advertiser could only make a claim like that if it could be proved in scientific tests.

Another practice is the use of ***weasel words.*** Examples of weasel words are "*fights* cavities" or "*attacks* dirt." The ad does not promise to eliminate cavities or dirt, just to fight and attack. It gives the impression the products are effective, as in fact they may be, but the language is misleading.

***False endorsements*** are misleading. While it makes sense for athletes to endorse athletic clothing and equipment, they can also be seen endorsing insurance plans, home furnishings, airlines, and other things they probably know no more about than anyone else.

Intense competition in the marketplace, a hallmark of our consumer society, leads to these deceptive practices. Many products are nearly identical; only the effectiveness of their advertising can result in sales better than others like them.

☆ *REVIEW: Explain these deceptive advertising practices: qualifiers, dangling comparisons, weasel words, false endorsements. Give some examples of each. Should advertisers be permitted to do this? Why or why not?*

✔ *CHECK YOUR UNDERSTANDING of deceptive advertising practices by completing Homework #29.*

## Media Control

Cynics like to say that freedom of the press is reserved for those who own one. Like a lot of jokes, this one has some truth to it. Our right to know can be limited in two ways. First, the owners of a newspaper or radio station can slant the news their way. Second, large advertisers sometimes threaten to cancel their ads unless the media accept their demands.

News can be slanted in several ways. Some you learned about in Chapter 3: tell only one side of the story, use portions of quotes that change the meaning of a statement, include editorial opinions in news stories.

A less obvious means of slanting is to over-report or under-report. If a station owner is in favor of an issue on the ballot, for example, it will get lots of coverage--a story every night on the news. However, if s/he is opposed, it will get only one short story. Placement in the newscast or newspaper and length of a story also can be a means of slanting. A front-page story gets more readers than one on page 20; the item at the top of the news gets more attention than one 15 minutes later.

This kind of slanting makes it harder for us to get complete information and is harmful if even one magazine or television station does it. It is a far more serious problem if many magazines, newspapers, radio and television stations are doing it.

As in other industries, economic conditions favor large companies, so media ***conglomerates*** have been formed. These huge corporations own several magazines, newspapers, book publishing houses, television and radio stations. For example, the Hearst Corporation owns 13 newspapers, 20 magazines, four television stations, and seven radio stations. (1980 figures)

Competition used to be fierce between two newspapers in the same city. Reporters raced to be the first to get a good story--to get a ***scoop*** or to ***scoop*** the competition. Each was quick to point out the other's mistakes. With each newspaper striving to be the best, readers benefited from careful and thorough coverage. Now, many independent newspapers have gone out of business, sold out to newspaper chains, or merged under one owner. Seventy-five years ago, nearly 700 cities had competing newspapers; now fewer than 50 have. Magazines are the best place to read diverse opinions. Yet, they fail at an alarming rate. Most blame their problems on rising expenses. The cost of labor, paper, and especially postage has become so high they cannot make a profit.

Some people fear that if this trend continues, the flow of information through the media will be controlled by a few powerful conglomerates, who would be able, if they wished, to slant the news to their own uses.

Another battle for control of the media takes place between advertising and editorial departments. Advertisers are the main source of income, and they can apply tremendous pressure. If a company is spending thousands of dollars, it isn't going to be too happy about a story that will hurt its business or its reputation. For example, large advertisers have been known to cancel their ads in newspapers which refuse to slant news their way. In some cases, sponsors have threatened to pull out if a network won't change a documentary about problems in their industries, such as strikes against the company or environmental problems it is involved in.

Critics say many consumer magazines are biased in favor of advertisers. For example, writers mention only their advertisers' brands in stories about new products or trends. They, too, may change or drop stories that reflect badly on an advertiser's company or industry. In some magazines it is difficult at first glance to tell the difference between ads and articles. Federal law requires that ads that look like a publication's editorial content must be labeled "Advertisement."

Responsible editors, writers, and broadcasters will resist these pressures. If they don't, the public will lose faith in their truth and accuracy.

> ☆ REVIEW: Define scoop. How do advertisers and conglomerates influence the media? Who controls the media? Who protects the public interest?

This chapter has described conflicts between kinds of rights and the laws that have been passed to insure those rights. Another conflict occurs within a person who has to do what s/he thinks is right. This is a conflict between law and *ethics*. Ethical behavior is what is honorable and upright, but it is individual. It is what your conscience tells you to do, whether or not it is legal. If you work in the media, you have to decide not only what is legal and constitutional, but what is ethical as you make decisions about what to print or broadcast.

## Section 4. Propaganda.

To use *propaganda* means to spread ideas or information deliberately to further your cause or damage an opposing cause. Propaganda has become a dirty word, always something that another country or another political party does. In fact, much of the information we get from the media is propaganda. Advertising is propaganda; political speeches are propaganda. The U.S. spreads propaganda about our country and ideas to other parts of the world, and so do the U.S.S.R. and Japan and Israel, and everyone else who wants to gain allies or attract tourists. As with deceptive advertising, if the purpose of a message is persuasion, you are rarely getting both sides of the story. You are getting propaganda.

By this time you are well-equipped to detect propaganda. You can recognize deceptive advertising and slanted news, which are two propaganda techniques. You have learned that what is called news on television is what has good film with it. You know that some publications mix advertising and editorial content. You know that newspapers can slant stories to support one political party.

Another propaganda technique is to try to appeal to your emotions rather using logic.

"Waving the flag" is a tried-and-true propaganda technique. This means to associate a particular position with patriotism by using the flag as a symbol or suggesting that anyone who disagrees is disloyal to our country. Because we all want to be seen as patriotic, we may allow the propaganda to hide the real issue. These are also called "motherhood and apple pie" issues; they are presented as ideas no one would dare speak against.

Using "loaded" words is another means of propaganda. "Yes, I was there," *admitted* the boy. He may simply be saying where he was. However, the word "admitted" usually means confessing wrongdoing -- it is a word loaded with negative meaning.

Labels also are loaded words. You are labeling if you call someone radical, right-wing, egghead, hawk, dove, or women's libber. This kind of propaganda tries to get you to accept a negative stereotype instead of examining the facts.

> ☆ REVIEW: Define propaganda and ethics. Give examples of slanted news, waving the flag, loaded words, labels.

## Section 5. Review for quiz.

1. The concept of a free press comes from the First Amendment to the Constitution.

2. Censorship is done in two ways:
   a. by classifying documents to keep them secret;
   b. by passing laws restricting distribution of material.

3. Material is obscene according to law if it meets three tests. However, the definition is still controversial.

4. The public has a right to know about current events, but individuals have a right to privacy.

5. Advertising can be deceptive by using qualifiers, dangling comparisons, weasel words, or false endorsements.

6. The free exchange of information can be restricted by owners of communications media and by large advertisers.

7. Propaganda attempts to persuade by appealing to your emotions rather than your reason.

8. New words in this chapter:

| | |
|---|---|
| attribution | pornography |
| censorship | prior restraint |
| classified | propaganda |
| conglomerate | qualifier |
| dangling comparison | retraction |
| ethics | right to know |
| false endorsement | scoop |
| libel | weasel words |
| obscene | |

# Chapter 12

# History & Future of the Mass Media

Your life is different from that of your parents and grandparents largely because of changes in the mass media. Your grandparents never dreamed of television when they were your age; your parents never dreamed of personal computers. Yet, you take these for granted. The importance placed on the press from the beginning of this country's history has insured a central role for the mass media. Thomas Jefferson said:

> *The basis of our government being the opinion of the people, the very first object should be to keep that right; and were it left to me to decide whether we should have a government without newspapers, or newspapers without government, I should not hesitate a moment to prefer the latter.*

It's hard to say if he would have felt the same about television.

In this chapter you will learn about the history of the major mass media -- newspapers, magazines, radio, and television. You will study some predictions for the future direction of each medium and how a new medium, computers, opens another avenue of communications.

## Section 1. Newspapers.

Newspapers have always existed in some form in America, but those printed in Colonial times would not be recognized as newspapers today. Until the mid-1800s, newspapers were propaganda sheets, published by men who wished to promote themselves and their political views or to attack those of their opponents. This propaganda was often vicious and resulted in lawsuits, fistfights, horse-whippings, and an occasional duel with pistols. Our early presidents, Washington, Jefferson, and Adams, were all reviled by the press, but nonetheless defended publishers' rights to print their views. The propaganda press continued through the Civil War, and Lincoln was attacked and insulted by many newspapers.

During this period, a famous newspaper editor, James Gordon Bennett, started the *New York Herald,* the forerunner of modern newspapers. Bennett's primary goal was to make a lot of money by selling more newspapers than his competitors. He promoted his paper by aggressively covering the news, instead of printing whatever attracted the fancy of his writers. He sent reporters to the scene of news events, anywhere in the world, and he was the first to have reporters cover beats.

The Civil War was an impetus to this type of reporting. It was close; reporters sat on the edge of battlefields and wrote firsthand accounts of the battle in progress, accounts which were eagerly read by the folks back home. Northern newspapers profited from the war by improving their reporting techniques and establishing a loyal readership; most Southern newspapers were destroyed.

Modern news-writing style became standard practice at this time. Telegraph communications, established in 1844, were a great improvement in getting more up-to-date news. Previously, news sent by mail or carried on horseback didn't get into the paper for days or weeks after the event. However, the telegraph was still unreliable, and reporters wrote all the main facts in the first few paragraphs so if part of their transmission was lost or delayed, the most important information would reach their editors. Today we call this the inverted pyramid style of writing.

In the latter part of the nineteenth century, the competition for readers got out of hand, and resulted in an era called *yellow journalism*. In their unending drive for readers, newspapers printed the most sensational and scandalous stories they could find. They hired "stunt reporters," who created news by daring deeds, like Nellie Bly going around the world in 80 days -- sending back a daily dispatch, of course. This was the purpose in sending Stanley to find Livingston in Africa. The most disgusting episode was the fight between Joseph Pulitzer, *New York World,* and William Randolph Hearst, *New York Journal.* Their inflamed, distorted stories from Cuba are said to have been mostly responsible for pressure on President McKinley to declare war on Spain, resulting in the Spanish-American War.

Newspapers changed in look around this time, too. They started using varied page layout, adding photographs and larger headlines. Earlier ones had page-long columns of type with small headlines at the top of each column.

After the Civil War, the seeds of responsible journalism were planted, and during the next few decades, newspapers began to see their role more as informing the public rather than persuading it to their beliefs. A number of newspapers gained readers by fighting corruption in government and promoting the public good in issues such as child labor. Investigative journalism exposed scandals in city and state governments, and newspapers called for reforms, setting the tone for today's editorial policies.

The excesses of yellow journalism turned most newspapers into more moderate businesses. Around the turn of the century, advertising revenues, for the first time, began to exceed income from circulation. This meant that newspapers had to present an image that would attract and keep their advertisers' support.

The role and appearance of newspapers has not changed much in this century, although the total number has dropped. Radio and television eliminated newspapers' monopoly on reporting news. Many combined with other newspapers, which is why today they have names like Post-Dispatch or Herald-Tribune. The fierce competition between newspapers is gone; few cities have more than one. Big chains own hundreds of newspapers, as well as radio and television stations, across the country.

The look of newspapers is changing once again, with many of them adopting magazine-style graphics and broad use of color. Foremost in the new look was *USA Today,* the first national daily newspaper. Rapid technological advances in typesetting and printing have resulted in radical behind-the-scenes changes.

Newspapers continue to face strong challenges from television news, which can bring information to your home in minutes. Owners of personal computers already have the option of subscribing to stock market news, and it won't be long before other feature services will be available by subscription. Although some speculate that entire newspapers will be transmitted electronically to home computers, others believe the cost is prohibitive and not efficient, since few readers read every page.

In summary, newspapers have undergone many changes in the past 200 years:

1. Their purpose has changed from propaganda to public service;

2. Their writing has changed from opinionated narrative to objective reporting;

3. Their appearance has changed from dull columns of type to lively layout;

4. The competition has changed from newspaper vs. newspaper to newspaper vs. electronic media;

5. Their technology has changed from hand-set type and hand-fed presses to totally automated, high-speed processes.

☆ *REVIEW: Describe the changes in American newspapers since 1776.*

## Section 2. Magazines.

The first two magazines in the U. S. started the same year--1741-- in Philadelphia. Ben Franklin published one of them and gave it the catchy title, *The General Magazine and Historical Chronicle, For All the British Plantations in America.* It didn't last too long.

The "golden age" of magazines came after the Civil War. This is the time when advertising became accepted. Publications had more income; therefore, they could afford to print more copies. The magazines of this time were influential magazines of ideas. They changed public policy through their opinion articles about unjust conditions. Some magazines still popular today that started in the late 1800s include *Ladies' Home Journal, National Geographic, McCall's, Good Housekeeping, Scientific American, Harper's, Atlantic Monthly* (now called *The Atlantic* ), *House Beautiful, Nation,* and *Cosmopolitan* (which was originally a journal of opinion).

The great historic general interest magazines were *Look, Life* and *Saturday Evening Post.* Each of these died and was revived in the 1970s; *Look* unfortunately died again and the other two have never attained their former glory. These magazines, in the decades from 1930-1970, did for people what television does today. They were the best source of news and entertainment, in color. *Life* photographers, especially, were outstanding, and their work has been collected in a book called *The Best of Life. Saturday Evening Post* did not publish great photos like the other two, but offered readers touching and entertaining stories about everyday happenings.

The modern era has seen the rise of thousands of small specialty magazines. The trend to special interest and local/regional magazines will continue as advertisers retreat from national markets.

Like newspapers, magazine publishers are looking to the future and deciding how their industry will fully enter the computer age. They may be better candidates than newspapers for electronic transmission, since readers tend to read most or all of a magazine. In the future, computerized magazines will have sound, which will be activated by a scanner.

Another possibility for home computer users is entry into an indexing and retrieval system, for searching through print documents like newspapers, government reports, or legal and technical journals. Readers, comfortably seated in their home information centers, could request all material related to a specific topic of interest. The computer would do the job you do now by checking *The Reader's Guide to Periodical Literature,* but the index would contain many more documents.

Magazines will continue to face competition from television, particularly as cable networks specialize more--something they already do with all-news, all-sports, and all-arts channels.

☆ *REVIEW: Explain how magazines have changed in the past century. How might they be different in the future?*

## Section 3. Radio.

The golden days of radio were the 1930s and 1940s. Families gathered for an evening around a big wooden console radio in the living room the same way families watch television now. Performances were done live, often with the actors in costume. Elaborate systems were developed to produce sound effects like doorbells, hoofbeats, or footsteps coming up the stairs. Radio shows were forerunners of early television, which copied the comedy, detective, western, and drama shows which were so popular on radio. Soap operas started as daytime radio dramas which were sponsored by soap companies.

In the early days, sponsors (advertisers) bought a whole hour, and the show was named for the sponsor, like the "Colgate Comedy Hour." It wasn't until the 1950s that programs started using multiple sponsors. This change occurred because production costs were rising and because networks wanted more control over program content.

Although it was not intentional, one of the greatest hoaxes ever performed was a radio broadcast called "War of the Worlds," which was broadcast in 1938. In was written, directed, and acted in by Orson Welles. It sounded so realistic that many listeners were convinced they were listening to an actual report of an invasion from Mars, instead of a play. People panicked and were injured as they fled the "invasion"; cars of those trying to escape crowded the highways.

Radio lost popularity as television took over home entertainment in the 1950s. The old formats would not work any longer because television could do them so much better. The three major radio networks easily moved into television.

Then music formats became popular and radio audiences started to increase in size and attract advertising again. Another setback occurred with the *payola* scandals in the 1960s. Radio personnel on several popular stations were discovered to have taken payments from recording companies to play their records. This meant, of course, that those records became big sellers, while others were not given the opportunity to be heard.

Today radio is increasing in popularity again. Nearly 1,500 new stations have started up in the past 10 years. An increasing number are network affiliates, which can take advantage of the worldwide news coverage of network correspondents. Radio continues to increase its advertising sales.

☆ *REVIEW: Describe the importance of radio in the 1930s and 1940s. Contrast that to its role today.*

## Section 4. Television.

Televisions started appearing in a large number of homes in the 1950s. Early television shows often were a continuation of radio shows, although not all were able to make the transition. Comedy and drama shows were filmed live in front of a studio audience. Each show was like performing in a play; the actors had no chance to go back and do it again if they made a mistake. Of course, some great bloopers came out of those days.

Following the pattern of radio, sponsors produced the shows. Instead of a series of 15- and 30-second commercials for different products, the commercials were all for the same product, and the show was named for the sponsor; i.e., "The Hallmark Hall of Fame." This changed for two reasons: the costs of production were becoming too high for one company, and the networks wanted to have more control over program content.

The television industry is continually changing. Trends in programming have come and gone over the past thirty years. Color television has replaced black-and-white. Sets have very large screens or very tiny ones, like wrist TV. Many homes now have as many television sets as radios, including under-the-cupboard for the kitchen. Cable channels and direct-to-home satellite transmission reduce the power of the networks because viewers have many more options. New technology will expand the number of available channels into the hundreds.

In the future, television and computers will be linked as part of an overall home entertainment/information center.

☆ *REVIEW: What changes have occurred in television in the last generation? What changes can you expect in the future?*

## Section 5. Advertising.

Advertising has changed and developed over the years as the mass media have progressed and expanded. It continues to faithfully reflect the society and times. When newspapers were dull and gray, the advertising was very similar in appearance and writing style. Studying the advertising of any era is as good a clue as anything to that period's customs, morals, styles, and values. It mirrors the people it hopes to persuade.

The advertising industry has been the source of many advances in media. In the early days of radio, when the sponsors were responsible for the whole hour or half-hour, they produced classic radio dramas and comedy programs that are still remembered fondly. Advanced filmmaking and animation techniques were developed for television commercials. The fight for consumers' attention causes advertising creators to seek something that will amaze and startle consumers. Techniques of persuasion and market research developed for advertising have been adopted by candidates for public office and other groups or organizations who wish to improve their public image.

Our economic base is shifting toward businesses that provide services rather than products such as recreation, education, vacations, sports, hobbies, health, travel. Presently, most advertising sells products, but it will gradually shift to reflect the realities of the marketplace and sell more services.

Advertisers will continue to refine methods of identifying a specific target market, so their messages reach only those who are the very best prospects for a sale. National advertising, a shotgun approach in all media, will decline. On the other hand, consumers will continue to be creative in their efforts to evade, avoid and otherwise ignore the avalanche of advertising.

☆ *REVIEW: What changes have you seen in advertising in your lifetime? What do you predict for the future?*

## Section 6. The next era -- computers.

Information is expanding in our world at an exponential rate. More information is available than a single person can ever hope to learn about. It is disseminated through the various media you have studied. If you never slept and only read newspapers and magazines or watched television and tuned to the radio, you still could never keep up.

Computers as a medium of communication allow a consumer to sort through this avalanche of messages quickly and efficiently. In the future, the home computer may be the major medium for news and advertising, in somewhat the same way that television (especially when coupled with a video cassette recorder) has joined books and movie theaters as a major medium of entertainment.

It is possible now to tie your personal computer to several databanks by using a *modem,* which is a telephone hookup. For a fee, you can then access an encyclopedia, airline schedules, or the daily stock market report. Japan already has thousands of telephone information services. This capability will be expanded as cable companies install *optical fiber* cables. A single strand will be able to carry 1/2-billion bytes (bits of information) per second. This means you can have *interactive television;* the cable will carry two-way signals. You will be able to talk to your TV instead of having it only talk to you. For example, you will shop through television. Direct mail will be replaced by electronic catalogs; shoppers will view selections on their television screen and place orders. If you subscribe to a videotex service (an electronic magazine), you will check the index or watch the pages scroll past, then choose the page you want to read.

Already computer bulletin boards serve a few users. Using a computer bulletin board, you can put in a message that is read and answered by other computer users. In the future, they could replace classified advertising.

Personal computers, even the inexpensive ones, remain a luxury item. Remember, however, that forty years ago only a few wealthy homes had a television. Three generations ago, a telephone was a rare item; now it's the most commonplace piece of equipment we own. Similar changes will occur in the next few decades in the computer industry.

All this means that the consumer will exercise more control over the mass media. You will have the ability to make many choices instead of being the passive recipient of whatever the media puts out.

> ☆ *REVIEW: Explain how computers are a medium of communication. How do you imagine you will use computers in the future?*

## Section 7. Review for quiz.

1. Newspapers have changed in five significant ways in their history.

2. Magazines have been very influential in American life: the journals of opinion in the late 1800s; general interest magazines from 1930 - 1970.

3. Radio once had the role of a major entertainment medium, until it was replaced by television in the 1950s. It has regained popularity using all-music formats.

4. Future developments in television include interactive programming, more specialized cable companies, and the decline of the networks as hundreds of channels become available to every television owner.

5. Advertising is a mirror of each decade.

6. As computers become standard equipment in every home, they will become the basis of a complete home entertainment/information center.

7. New vocabulary in this chapter:

>interactive television
>modem
>optical fiber
>payola
>yellow journalism

# Chapter 13
# Careers in Journalism

In the next few years, you will be learning more and more about careers. Before high school graduation, you will probably have some idea of what career you want and how to prepare for it. In this chapter, you will learn about the skills and personality traits that fit with a successful career in the mass media.

### Section 1. Types of jobs.

Throughout this book, the jobs of different kinds of workers -- reporters, artists, copywriters, camera operators -- have been described. The same types of jobs can be found in more than one medium, as you can see from the following list:

WRITERS
* newspaper stories
* wire service stories
* advertising copy
* newspaper features and editorials
* magazine articles
* radio and TV news
* story scripts (teleplays)

EDITORS
* newspaper and magazine--copy
* newspaper and magazine--layout
* television and radio news

ARTISTS
* advertising layout and design
* newspaper and magazine layout and design
* illustrators
* cartoonists
* comic strip artists

PHOTOGRAPHERS
* newspapers
* advertising
* magazines
* wire services

SALESPEOPLE
* newspaper and magazine advertising
* newspaper and magazine circulation
* advertising account executives
* radio and TV advertising
* radio and TV promotion
* recordings

PERFORMERS
(includes actors, singers, dancers, musicians)
* radio and TV advertising
* radio and TV programs
* video and audio recordings
* radio and TV announcers, including disc jockeys

TECHNICAL JOBS
* press operators
* plate makers
* sound technicians
* camera operators
* typesetters

OTHERS
* directors
* proofreaders
* researchers
* circulation managers

Persons with the same skills may choose one media over another, depending on what purpose they wish to serve: information, persuasion, or entertainment. For example, if you are a good writer, you could become a newspaper reporter or an advertising copywriter or a script writer for television shows. If you become interested in a career in the mass media, you will have to decide in which area to specialize.

## Section 2. Is journalism the career for you?

To pursue a career in journalism, you must like to communicate -- in writing, by speaking, through drawing or photography, with acting. You will be part of a business that believes it can change people's lives through communication.

Choosing a career is based on several things: your interests, your skills and abilities, your personality, your lifestyle, and your education or training.

## Skills and Abilities

Here are some of the skills and abilities associated with journalism:

1. Language -- writing, speaking, editing

2. Research -- reporting, interviewing, observing, listening, reading

3. Intuition -- knowing why people act as they do, guessing what will happen next

4. Creativity -- thinking of something in a new way, visualizing what something might look like

5. Graphic arts -- putting original designs on paper

6. Logic and analysis -- knowing how to arrange information in sequence; completing tasks efficiently

7. Assertiveness -- refusing to take no for an answer

## Interests

The interests you have today will change in the next few years. However, successful journalists have some interests in common. Consider these questions: Do you like to read? Do you like to learn new information? Do you feel the need to communicate what you learn? Are you curious? Are your hobbies related to journalism in some way? Do you have an interest like sports or fashion that people want to know about?

## Personality

Your personality characteristics determine what kind of job will make you happy. Work environments vary with different jobs. Some workers sit at a desk or drawing-board all day. Others are physically active--making deliveries or operating machinery. Journalists frequently are "do-gooders," people who want to cause changes that will solve problems.

The media field is very people-oriented. Journalists like to talk to people and to prepare material for others' entertainment or information. They interact with clients and members of a news or advertising team each day. As a journalist, you will have to take criticism: a time will come when an editor won't like your story, a client won't like your ad layout, or a television viewer won't like your looks.

The mass media involves daily deadlines, which are a source of stress for many people. In journalism, it is not possible to put a job aside and say,

"I'll finish this tomorrow." Many times a reporter or photographer must stay with a story until its finished, which may mean working long hours, day and night. Journalists do not automatically work an eight-hour day.

Journalists must be assertive, even aggressive, to succeed. Reporters and photographers compete with each other to get a scoop. Ad agencies are pitted against each other to get big advertising accounts. Freelance writers and photographers must be persistent to get an editor's attention and get a sale.

As you consider a career choice, take into account whether you have the type of personality that can accept criticism, likes deadlines and working with others.

## Lifestyle

To a large extent, your lifestyle is determined by the salary level you choose. A person who wants a lifestyle filled with luxuries will aim for a high-paying job and complete the education and training necessary to get it.

Another factor in determining your lifestyle is where you live, in a large city or a small town. Journalists who get to the top of their field live and work in large cities, such as New York, Washington, D.C., Los Angeles. Magazines are published in large population centers. The competition for jobs in these markets is extremely tough. However, jobs in the mass media are available in all parts of the country. Even very small towns have a weekly newspaper; many small cities have radio stations.

Most media jobs are in the middle-income range ($20,000 - $50,000 per year). A few television anchors have multi-million-dollar contracts, but, as in other professions, this is the exception rather than the rule.

Following is a list of average salaries for a sampling of media jobs. If you want a job such as those listed below, plan to complete a college degree. Many journalists start as interns while they are still in college.

| Job | Salary |
| --- | --- |
| Newspaper reporter | $31,000 |
| Newspaper copy editor | $36,000 |
| Newspaper display ad salesperson | $34,000 |
| Newspaper photographer | $19,000 |
| Staff writer, large consumer magazine | $34,000 |
| Production manager, large consumer magazine | $36,000 |
| Television anchor | $56,000 |
| Television technician | $22,000 |
| Junior copywriter, advertising agency | $20,000 |
| Radio news reporter | $26,000 |

❑ *ASSESS YOUR INTEREST AND APTITUDE for a media job, by completing Worksheet #67.*

## Section 3. Review for quiz.

1. Types of jobs fall into these categories: writers, editors, artists, photographers, salespeople, performers, technicians.

2. Seven skills and abilities are associated with journalism.

3. Journalists like to work with people, can work under pressure, and can take criticism.

4. Choosing a career is based on skills and abilities, interests, personality, and the lifestyle you prefer.

*NOTES*

**SECONDARY SCHOOL JOURNALISM**

# School Publications Handbook

# Handbook Chapter 1
# School Newspapers

You may think no similarities exist between a big daily newspaper and a middle school newspaper. Although the end product looks very different, the component parts and the step-by-step processes are alike in many ways. In this chapter you will learn to apply each step to a school newspaper. All you learned in earlier chapters about newspapers will help you now.

### Steps to Newspaper Production

1. Editor or teacher makes story assignments.
2. Reporters get information and write stories.
3. Page editors prepare rough layouts.
4. Reporters submit stories before deadline.
5. Editors mark copy, write headlines, and return any copy which needs to be rewritten.
6. Layout editors prepare layouts (by hand or on the computer).
7. Word processor types stories in justified columns.
8. Proofreader marks typed copy; typesetter makes corrections.
9. Paste-up artist letters headlines, pastes up each page, or layout editors make final adjustments on the word processor.
10. Pages are printed, collated (placed in order), and stapled or folded.
11. Newspapers are distributed.

## Section 1. Structure.

### Staff Organization

The tasks to be completed are different depending on how your newspaper is printed. Usually, it will be in one of three ways:

1. Student staff writes and marks copy, writes headlines and marks headline size, prepares layouts. Outside printer sets all type, screens photos, and prepares for offset printing. Students may or may not do proofreading.

2. Students do all of above except actually printing the pages. Camera-ready paste-ups are sent to the printer, ready to be photographed and made into plates. Your school may or may not have the equipment to screen photos.

3. Students do everything at school, including printing, and process photos by whatever method is available.

The role of adult staff and volunteers will be different in each school.

Following is an outline of tasks to be performed by each staff member:

Managing editor or editor-in-chief:
-- Makes assignments for news, editorials, features
-- Assists page and copy editors
-- Settles disagreements
-- Holds all staff members accountable for the performance of their duties

Copy editor:
-- Marks copy
-- Checks word count and writes page number in upper right corner
-- Writes headline on separate half-sheet, places slug in upper left corner, writes headline's size and page number in upper right

Page editor:
-- Makes rough layout for each page
-- Prepares final layout or dummy for each page
-- Negotiates with managing editor if too much or too little is indicated for any one page

Typesetter:
-- Types all copy for printer, or
-- Types everything in correct column width
-- Types corrections

Proofreader:
-- Reads everything that has been typed and marks corrections

Paste-up artist:
-- Makes headlines with press type or stencils
-- Pastes in corrections to typed copy
-- Pastes up each page according to layout

Printer:
-- Operates duplicating equipment
-- Assembles pages in order; staples or folds if necessary

Circulation manager:
-- Organizes and supervises distribution of each issue
-- Counts money collected and follows procedures for turning it in

Business manager:
- -- Keeps records of income and expenses
- -- Sends bills and tear sheets to advertisers

Advertising manager:
- -- Prepares ad layouts
- -- Calls on prospective advertisers
- -- Makes assignments to sales representatives
- -- Prepares advertising contracts

Advertising sales representatives:
- -- Calls on regular advertisers
- -- Relays new ads to advertising manager

Exchange editor:
- -- Reviews exchange papers for story ideas, exchange columns
- -- Sends a copy of each issue to schools and individuals on the exchange list
- -- Files copies of each issue

Stringer:
- -- Writes school news stories to send to local daily and weekly newspapers

In reality, most secondary school newspapers are small enough that the staff can work together informally. The same person may be copy editor and page editor; the jobs of business and circulation manager can be combined; the managing editor may be the stringer. Jobs may be rotated from issue to issue. Whatever system of staff organization your teacher assigns, all the tasks must be completed for each issue.

☆ *REVIEW: Explain the responsibilities of each staff member.*

## Section 2. Writing news stories.

Criteria for school news are the same as those described in Chapter 3. Let's review them again and see how they can guide you to write news stories appropriate to your student publication.

***Nearness*** -- Any recent event that involves students or staff at your school may be news; the same event at another middle school is not. Examples are additions to the staff, changes in class offerings or curriculum, assemblies, dances, and other extracurricular activities.

*EXAMPLE:*

### LEADERSHIP STUDENTS SURPRISE TEACHERS
### By Valerie Jones

Student leadership class members served homemade baked goodies at the Nov. 25 faculty meeting to show their appreciation of the teachers.

Students greeted the faculty at the door and escorted them to their seats. They then gave them a thank you note and served them homemade ice cream, pies, cookies, brownies, and cheesecake.

"I really enjoyed it. I thought the food was delicious and the students were very nice," said Noelle Delore, librarian.

Barbara Miller, leadership adviser, contributed by organizing and baking for this activity. The next teacher appreciation project will be on Dec. 17 when a potluck luncheon will be served both lunch periods in Room 104.

*Webster Warrior*
Daniel Webster Middle School
Stockton, California

*Importance* -- The more people in your school affected, the bigger news it is. An all-school Halloween party is more important than a party in one class. Changes in school policy or special events that involve everyone in the school have the greatest importance.

*EXAMPLE:*

### ELIGIBILITY CONTROVERSIES ARISE AFTER YEAR OF PLANNING
### By Joyel Rollow

In response to increased concern about academic achievement and participation in school activities, the Western Heights school board adopted a new eligibility policy for the next school year.

This rule requires that all students make a 2.0 grade average and pass five of six classes. Grade checks will be made every four and one-half weeks. Any student who does not meet the requirements will not be allowed to participate in extracurricular activities for the next four and one-half week period. That includes sports, band, choir, journalism, and club parties and field trips.

After the first grade check the band discovered that some of its members would be ineligible for the next period, as were several athletes and others. Some band parents and the program directors became concerned about what effect this would have on the planned band performance at the Gator Bowl in Florida over the Christmas holidays.

Following a special school board meeting held Oct. 9, the decision was made to leave the eligibility policy intact.

> *Jet Express*
> Western Heights Jr. High
> Oklahoma City, Oklahoma

***Drama/conflict*** -- Dramatic incidents occur in students' lives all the time. In the closed environment of a school, however, you must be sensitive to the effect on students and their families of revealing personal information. Reports of accidents, burglaries, assaults by outsiders are appropriate. Controversy within the school district or the parent organization may also provide news.

*EXAMPLE:*

FIRE HITS CENTRAL
By Gabriela Dellatorre

A fire started in the stairway of the girls' restroom on October 21. The building was evacuated in less than five minutes.

No injuries were reported, and the damage was minimal. Due to quick detection and responsible following of procedure, a terrible tragedy was avoided.

Custodians Bob Jackson and Jack DeMoss and Charley Cordill, security guard, discovered the fire and together put out the flames.

The fire was started allegedly by a girl who was skipping her first hour class.

"We think someone must have been hiding out in there," Mr. Johnson stated, "but we don't want to say anything until the investigation is complete."

He added that students and teachers should be commended for acting intelligently and for knowing and following proper procedure.

> *The Centralian*
> Central Middle School
> Mission, Kansas

***Names*** -- A school is the best possible place to get stories with lots of names; clubs, musical ensembles, sports teams, honor roll, class officers, and student government are good examples. Anytime one of these groups does something, you have an opportunity to print the names of its members.

*EXAMPLE:*

### McGRATH SETS 3 SCHOOL SWIM MEET RECORDS
By Jeff Jackson

Five new school records were set in the swim meet June 5. These records were:

100 Medley Relay: Amy Thessan, 58.84;
Girls 100 Individual Medley: Heidi Atkins, 1:l4.29;
Boys 100 Individual Medley: Eric McGrath, 1:09.64;
Boys 50 Back: Eric McGrath, 2:31.97;
Boys 100 Freestyle: Eric McGrath, 1:03.11.
Other results were as follows. . . .

(Names of 35 students and their times follow.)

*The Trojan Horse*
South Shore Middle School
Seattle, Washington

**Famous people** -- This is the toughest one for a school newspaper, since famous people are covered in detail by general circulation media. However, your school may have a famous alumnus, or have been visited by a famous person.

*EXAMPLE:*

### DAN CLARK APPEARS ON ASSEMBLY PROGRAM

Thanks to the Assembly Committee and Student Council, LJH had its share of entertainment. Dan Clark, former professional athlete, visited on April 24.

One of the topics discussed during the assembly was suicide. According to Clark, suicide is not a way to cope with your problems. He also gave students helpful hints on how to build up your self-confidence. Some hints he gave were to be yourself and don't get caught by peer pressure.

Dan discussed stories of his sports friends, such as O.J. Simpson, and how he achieved his dream to someday be a football player.

*The Black and Gold*
Lebanon Junior High
Lebanon, Missouri

**Amusing, unusual** -- In a school, this also must be handled with sensitivity so you don't ridicule anyone. However, many opportunities for amusing stories will present themselves: mixed-up locks, a bird in the building, humorous projects and speeches.

*EXAMPLE:*

## LIVELEYBROOKS TAKES TO SKIS
### By Molly Sims

Science teacher Lisa Liveleybrooks and three neighbors set out for the Fifth Street Market on skis! They all live in Southwest Eugene, and the trek to the market was eight miles. They went on this expedition when the city shut down with a record six inches of snowfall. The group skied for five hours altogether.

"We went to the market for fun. Besides, in Eugene you don't have much chance to ski," smiled Mrs. Liveleybrooks.

As the 25 degree temperature began to shoot up and the snow began to melt, the adventuresome group had a problem.

"We really had to hurry on the way back so we wouldn't be stuck halfway home with no snow," laughs Mrs. Liveleybrook.

*The Scribe*
Madison Middle School
Eugene, Oregon


As you go through your daily routine, keep these criteria in mind and be alert to news tips. Tips come from what people say, bulletins, or other publications. For example, the daily newspaper may have a story about changes in school district policy that will affect schools. This is a tip to ask the principal what changes you can expect at your school as a result. Give news tips to your teacher or editor-in-chief.

✔ *CHECK YOUR UNDERSTANDING of applying news criteria as a school reporter by completing Worksheet #68.*

✔ *CHECK YOUR UNDERSTANDING of recognizing news tips by completing Worksheet #69.*

Before you write news stories for your school newspaper, review the lessons on writing a lead and using an inverted pyramid style. Use the list of reminders in Chapter 3.

Because student newspapers publish on monthly or semi-monthly schedules, it is nearly impossible to use spot news. Ninety-nine percent of the stories you write will be advance or follow-up. Be aware of the publication date when you write a story.

At some point, you will be assigned beats. In a school, beats usually include the offices of the principal and other administrators, counseling staff, nurse, librarian, heads of departments (music, science, P.E.), PTSA, coaches, club advisers, lunchroom manager, and head custodian. Additional sources of stories are exchange papers from other schools, the daily newspaper, press releases, and other students.

## Slug

To make typing and editing easier, learn to identify your news stories with a *slug*, like professional reporters do. A slug is placed in the upper left hand corner of the paper and consists of three lines. The first line is your last name. The second line is a one- or two-word label that will distinguish this story from others. After your story is done, count the words and put the total on the third line. The slug for a story about your swim team winning a meet could be "SWIM WIN."

JONES
SWIM WIN
260 words

Whether you type or write by hand, always double space your stories. That means to leave one blank line between each written line.

At the end of the story, place a symbol to let the editor and typist know it's the end. Traditionally, ### or -30- is used as the closing symbol.

If the typed or handwritten copy has more than one page, place the word "more" at the bottom of page one. At the top of page two, as a third line of the slug, write "2-2-2"; do the same for all subsequent pages.

☆ *REVIEW: Explain the correct way to prepare your news copy and headlines. Practice writing a slug and using symbols for more than one page and the end of a story.*

❑ *PRACTICE: Write news stories based on facts of current events in your school. In these and all future practice assignments, use a slug and double-space the copy.*

## Getting Information

Much of the information for news stories will come from interviews, mostly interviews with faculty and students in your school. Follow all the steps described in Chapter 5 for a good interview story.

It is possible to get an interview with a famous person or an invitation to a press conference. Write to make the request as far in advance as you possibly can. Write to stars in care of their television network, recording company, or movie studio. Expect your reply to be from a press agent; you may receive a press kit with information about the person whether or not you get an appointment.

You will have opportunities to do speech stories on assembly speakers or other special guests at your school. In some cases, it may be appropriate to combine information from a speech and an interview with the speaker.

Occasionally, your teacher will receive a press release. It can be used two ways: as background information for an interview if it is about something that can be developed into a good story, or it can be rewritten to fit your newspaper's style and used as an advance or follow-up story. Remember that many people who issue press releases are looking for free advertising. Rewrite the story to be objective by removing any slanted words or phrases.

## Section 3. Writing Features.

Because of the infrequent publication schedules, school newspapers are ideal places for feature stories. Here are some suggestions for writing the kinds of features you practiced in Chapter 6.

### Polls

Poll stories are popular features. Be sure to adhere strictly to the guidelines to insure your credibility.

*EXAMPLE:*

ADULTS HAVE MIXED VIEWS ABOUT TEENS AT LOCAL MALL
By Trisha Rubino & Charity Pontow

Hanging out in shopping malls is becoming a popular national pastime for teens. In a recent "Peanuts" comic strip, Charles Schulz referred to young mall-goers as "mallies."

"I like going up to the mall on Friday and Saturday nights because everyone goes there. I can hang out with my friends," said Jenny Williams, eighth grader.

Interviews with adult mall shoppers yielded opinions about mallies ranging from dress to drugs. The majority of the 20 adults interviewed said that the way teens dress is all right. A few adults felt the way teens dress is offensive.

Several adult shoppers interviewed said they avoid Bannister Mall on Friday and Saturday nights. One of the reasons they gave is that the mall is too crowded on those nights. Alecia Hatfield, eighth grader, said her mother doesn't allow her to go to the mall on those nights because the high school kids take over and it's too rough.

Although many of the 30 students surveyed think that the mall is the "in" place to be, some students feel uncomfortable there.

"Almost every time I go to the mall, druggies offer me a cigarette or something else. When I say no, they stand there and call me names," said Pam Darter, eighth grader.

*The Pathfinder*
Ervin Junior High School
Hickman Mills, Missouri

Here are some possible topics for a poll feature: "What is your favorite . . . ice cream flavor, place to hang out, excuse for being late?; Yes-no poll on a political issue, such as "Should the U.S. have a national health plan?;" Opinion poll on a school issue, such as discipline policy, bus rules, homework requirements.

❑ *PRACTICE: Pick a topic from this list and prepare an opinion poll for your school newspaper or use a topic of your own.*

## How-To Feature

Write about something you know how to do, and use one of the three types of leads you practiced earlier.

*EXAMPLE:*

NEW BEDROOM DESIGNS CAN BE INEXPENSIVE
By Kristine Erickson & Heather Pauling

You can change or redo your room inexpensively in many ways.

If you want to change the color or make designs on something like a cloth lamp shade, here is a fun and simple idea. Fill a spritzer bottle with Rit Dye. Place tape over places that you do not want to be sprayed. Then spray in even, light strokes. Pillows and bedspreads can be done by filling a bowl with dye and using a sponge on cloth. If you want designs, use masking tape. Rit Dye can be purchased at drug and craft stores.

Another fun idea is to paint simple designs (like squares or triangles). You can do this by taping trim tape around your shape and then painting the inside. Let this dry for at least four hours, or even overnight. Trim tape can be purchased at hardware stores.

If your room is a bit "unorganized," you can invest in a few helpers. At Target are many helpers like plastic cubes, mini-bins, and shelves. You can store these things in your closet, under your bed, in drawers or stacked up on the floor in your room.

When you want to change your room, think about these ideas and have fun.

*The Centurion*
Central Middle School
Eden Prairie, Minnesota

Here are some possible topics for a how-to feature: How to repair and maintain your bicycle, skateboard, cassette player; how to be a successful paper carrier, babysitter, grocery clerk; how to train your dog, cat, parakeet; how to feel more confident, make new friends, say no to drugs.

❑ *PRACTICE: Pick a topic from this list and write a how-to feature for your school newspaper or write about a topic of your own choosing.*

## Historical

Base your historical feature on library research, referring to the resources listed in Chapter 5. Use one of the three types of leads described in Chapter 6.

*EXAMPLE:*

HOLIDAY ORIGINS UNCOVERED
By Patti Edwards

Ding-dong. The sound of the doorbell interrupts the latest Rodney Dangerfield commercial.

"Trick-or-treat" yells a strange assortment of ghosts, baby witches and monsters. The only explanation for this is, of course, Halloween.

While trick-or-treating is one aspect of Halloween, people celebrate it many different ways. Many students will be attending tonight's Student Council-sponsored costume dance in the cafeteria.

Different Halloween customs arose from different groups of Celts all over the world. In Scotland, people paraded through fields and lit bonfires to drive away evil spirits.

The one legend giving us the majority of our customs came from Ireland. Their Halloween festivities included people begging for food in a parade that honored Muck Olla, a god. The leader of the parade wore a white robe and a mask made from the head of an animal.

Begging for food evolved into our present-day children ringing the doorbell and saying "trick-or-treat." The white robe became plastic and cloth outfits depicting different characters, not all scary. The animal head became makeup and plastic masks.

*The Cougar Print*
Chaffin Junior High
Fort Smith, Arkansas

Here are some suggestions for topics: history and significance of one of the national holidays; anniversary of a historical event; birthdates of famous Americans; curriculum, clubs, rules of schools 25 or 50 years ago; what existed at the site of your school 100 or 200 years ago?

❑ *PRACTICE: Pick a topic from this list and write a historical feature for your school newspaper or write on a topic of your own.*

## Personality

Follow up on your news tips for personality features. Use your best interviewing skills to get the information.

*EXAMPLE:*

MRS. SCHUESSLER FAMILIAR FACE IN CAFETERIA
By Michelle Gentry

For 25 years, Mrs. Josie Schuessler has been serving lunches to students in the Cape Girardeau schools. For 13 of those years, Mrs. Schuessler has been cooking for students at Schultz, where she serves as manager of the cafeteria staff.

Favorite lunches down through the years, according to her, have remained the same. "Chili, hamburgers, hotdogs, and pizza have been the favorites," she said. "Spinach has been the all-time least favorite."

Mrs. Schuessler's interest in cooking began when she was only 12 years old. Since she grew up on a farm on Bloomfield Road, she had to help her mother prepare food for their family. Nine people were in her family then, including her six brothers and sisters.

"Today, I have just me and my husband, Victor, at home. I have three children, but they have families of their own now. We have eight grandchildren."

"I fix supper for some of them every Friday evening before they go bowling," she said. German potato salad, lasagna and coffeecake are some of her favorites.

Outside of school, Mrs. Schuessler enjoys many interests. She likes to go fishing with her husband. One of her hobbies is quilting.

"The best thing about Schultz," Mrs. Schuessler explained, "is that I love to work with young people. It's something to be proud of when you feed them a good lunch. Sometimes at home maybe, they won't get the right food or enough."

*The Paw*
Louis J. Schultz Middle School
Cape Girardeau, Missouri

Some of the following people may be good subjects: teachers, students or parents who have interesting hobbies, volunteer jobs or backgrounds; business people in the community; members of local bands; adults in the community known to students, such as librarians, police officers, recreation leaders; outstanding students from secondary schools, high schools or local colleges and universities.

❑ *PRACTICE: Write a personality feature for your school newspaper.*

## Reviews

School plays and concerts are topics for (tactful) reviews. You may also review movies, TV shows and restaurants that appeal to teenagers. Reviews of movies and concerts must be timely, however. If your publication date is two or three weeks after an event has closed, it may be just as well to omit a review.

*EXAMPLE:*

BILL COSBY PROVES TO BE CAPABLE TV COMEDIAN
By Nathan Wiedenman

As the high school boy complains to his father, "If I go out with Christine in this shirt, she'll never want to be seen with me again!" the boy's father consoles him while the father is trying to stop laughing at the outlandish garment.

This is but one of the numerous (and familiar) family crises dealt with on the new NBC living-room sitcom, "The Bill Cosby Show."

The stars of this show are the father, Cliff Huxtable (Bill Cosby); the mother, Clair Huxtable (Phylicia Ayers-Allen); and the children: Denise, (Lisa

Bonet), Theodore (Malcolm-Jamal Warner), Vanessa (Tempest Bledsoe), and Rudy (Keshia Knight Pulliam).

On the show, Cliff is a pediatrician who has his practice on the first floor of their New York City brownstone, while the family living quarters are on the second and third floors.

While this show may sound like another poor attempt at the overused living-room sitcom format, "The Bill Cosby Show" revolutionizes this type of plot, creatively blending the humor of Bill Cosby's established comic career with realistic situations.

With appealing realistic scenes of problems that could be from many American families, and with great humor from Bill Cosby, "The Bill Cosby Show" has been a hit with television viewers, ranked number three overall among television shows last week.

*The Eagle Eye*
South Junior High School
Anaheim, California

❏ *PRACTICE: Write a critical review of a movie, television show, play, concert, or restaurant. Write at least five paragraphs, following the outline in Chapter 6.*

## Editorials

It is tempting to start writing editorials of criticism about everything at school you don't like. That is why it is especially important to follow the outline in Chapter 6. If you are going to blast your school's rules or policies, be sure to get all the facts, state the problem clearly, and propose an alternative solution and course of action. It's not enough just to say you don't like something.

*EXAMPLE - Editorial of Criticism:*

LACK OF TRANSPORTATION LEAVES SOME IN THE COLD

Because the forces of nature are uncontrollable, animals, plants, and humans have learned to adjust to them. With the change of seasons comes a change in lifestyles. Birds fly south, and bears hibernate. But why do the junior high students still walk to the high school?

Being neighbors with the high school has some advantages. They share their auditorium, gymnasium, higher level math classes (beyond algebra), as well as their band, choir, and foreign language departments with us. However, students enrolled in these classes are required to walk to the high school unless it rains or snows. Then a bus is provided. But what about wind, frost, and 30 degrees Celsius?

It is understandable that the classes cannot be brought to the junior high because the number of students (about 10 in each) in foreign language and geometry do not meet the required minimum size. But would it be unreasonable to ask for a bus on days when the temperature and wind chill are below average?

Since the school cannot bring these classes closer to home and students cannot provide transportation for themselves, they have had to compromise to be in these classes. It seems only fair that the school should compromise also to meet the needs of these students.

*Jet Express*
Western Heights Junior High
Oklahoma City, Oklahoma

*EXAMPLE - Editorial of Appreciation:*

### CENTER GOOD IDEA

We would like to congratulate the recently formed committee that is studying the possibility of allowing area teenagers to use the Civic Center for various activities.

This is a good idea because teenagers would have a place to gather for a variety of activities such as dances and movies. The place would not become "old" because of the diversity of activities that would be possible. Also, this would give students a chance to meet students from other schools while keeping them off the streets and out of trouble.

Any money generated could be used to purchase equipment such as jukeboxes and video games for the teenagers' use at the Civic Center.

We support this group and their idea, and we encourage the use of the Civic Center for this purpose.

*The Cougar Print*
Chaffin Junior High
Fort Smith, Arkansas


Editorial topics must have two of the same news values as stories: nearness and importance. Following are some topics which might make interesting editorials of criticism and appreciation.

*Criticism:* closed campus, discipline policies, vandalism, truancy.

*Appreciation:* unsung heroes (secretaries, custodians, bus drivers), volunteers and other community supporters, parents, retiring staff members.

❏ *PRACTICE: Write editorials of criticism and appreciation for your school newspaper. Follow the guidelines in Chapter 6.*

## Sports

Inter- and intra-mural sports are fun to cover for a school publication and offer wonderful opportunities to use lots of names. Arrange to get names and statistics from a coach or teacher before or after the event. As you watch, take notes on key plays or outstanding performances to use in your lead.

*EXAMPLE:*

### JACKETS LOSE OPENER TO OZARK

Eighth-grade boys opened their season with a loss to Ozark, 28 to 46.

"I expected the guys to play nervously and they did. Ozark was a fundamentally sound team for eighth graders," said Mr. Dave Plassmeyer, eighth-grade basketball coach.

The leading rebounder was Harold Capps with nine rebounds.

The next game for the Jackets brought Lebanon another loss when the Waynesville Tigers came to town. The Tigers defeated the Jackets 26 to 64.

"In this game, they found out that basketball is really a passing game by making either bad or good passes. The pressure forced us into some bad passes which consequently gave Waynesville some easy lay-ups," said Coach Plassmeyer.

Richard Groce scored 10 points for the night to lead Lebanon.

The Jacket B team defeated the Tigers, 28 to 18.

William Foster was the leader with 12 points, followed by Adam Richert with six.

*The Black and Gold*
Lebanon Junior High
Lebanon, Missouri

❏ *PRACTICE: Attend a sports event and write a news story about it.*

## Section 4. Editing Your School Newspaper.

An editor's job is extremely important and needs to be taken seriously. Everyone working on the newspaper must accept the importance of meeting deadlines and turning in acceptable copy. If an editor asks a reporter to do a rewrite, it should be understood that s/he is doing what is necessary to produce a good paper.

### Style Book

Each newspaper has its own style book for writers and editors to follow. Your teacher may follow the suggestions in Chapter 4 and add rules as necessary or buy a copy of a style book written for another newspaper. The important point is to pick one style and be consistent.

### Headlines

Writing headlines is part of a copy editor's job. A headline should be written on a separate half-sheet of paper and slugged exactly like the story it goes with. Write in the upper right corner the headline size (as it appears in your headline schedule) and page number it goes on.

If your paper is sent out to a typesetter, then you write the headlines according to the printer's instructions and deliver with the copy. Copy that goes to a printer for typesetting must first be typed.

### Estimating Length

After editing a writer's copy, a copy editor counts the words in the story and writes that number in the upper right corner of the first page. A simple way to find the approximate number of words is to count the words in three or four lines and find the average number of words per line. Then count the total number of lines and multiply the two figures.

A layout editor can then convert this figure into the number of inches long the story will be when printed. This, of course, will vary depending on the size of type and the column width. If, for example, you print 45 words per column inch, then the story of 300 words will print out to be about 6-3/4 inches. To be safe, allow seven inches on the layout.

❑ *PRACTICE: Using this method, compute the approximate number of words on this page. At 45 words per column inch, how long a column would it be?*

## Layout

Layout sheets are the exact size of the newspaper page and are pre-printed with columns and inches marked. They are used for rough layouts, final layouts and dummies. A *dummy* is made for a printer to follow. The layout editor cuts up the proofs and pastes up each page exactly as it is to look when printed, marking in headlines and leaving the precise space for ads and cuts. The dummies are sent to the printer if s/he is to do the final paste-up.

Rough layouts are drawn on layout sheets when stories are assigned. At that time, editors know what stories will run and the approximate length. They also know what ads, if any, will be placed on each page. Rough layouts will show where holes may appear or which pages are too crowded. They will be revised when stories are turned in, and a final layout is prepared after deadline for the paste-up artist to follow.

Each page has a *folio line* at the top. A folio line contains the page number, publication name, and date. The page number goes to the outside on the left for even-numbered pages, the right for odd-numbered pages:

*(left)*      2 - The Messenger, Dec. 5, 1986
*(right)*     The Messenger, Dec. 5, 1986 - 3

No folio lines appear on page one.

Your paper may be too small to have sections, but it can have pages devoted to news, editorials, features, and sports. Here is a suggestion for page content of a four-page newspaper:

Page 1 -     Three or four major news stories
                 Flag

Page 2 -     Editorials, editorial cartoons, letters to the editor
                 Masthead
                 Major feature

Page 3 -     Sports
                 Fun features (puzzles, comics, advice column)
                 Other types of features
                 (Ads)

Page 4 -     News from around the school (collected from beats)
                 (Ads)

On the next page are sample layouts for a four-page publication. The same basic layout can be followed for every issue; these are easily modified according to the number and length of stories. It is helpful to have standing headings for each page. Examples are *EDITORIALS, SPORTS, AROUND THE SCHOOL* and *CALENDAR*.

# SCHOOL NEWSPAPER LAYOUTS

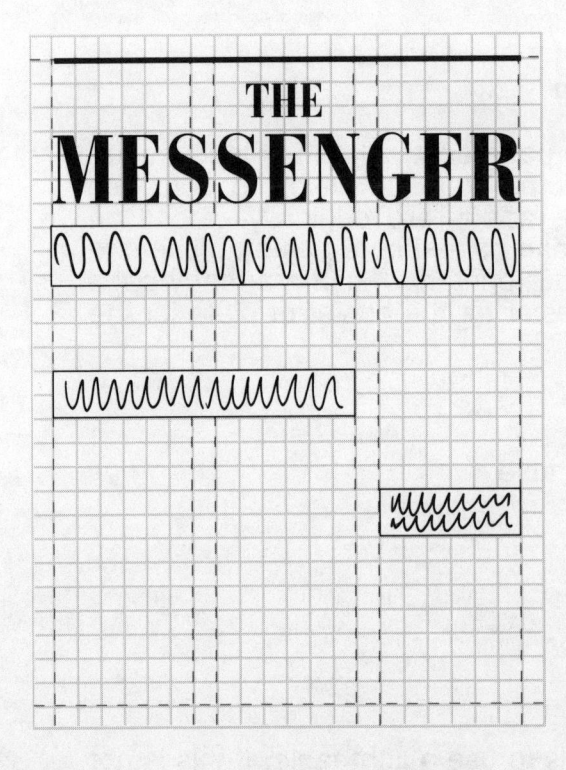

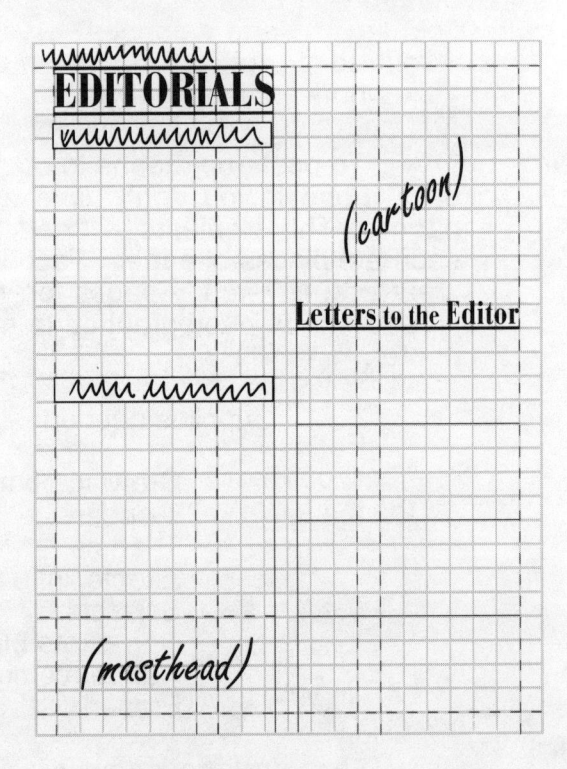

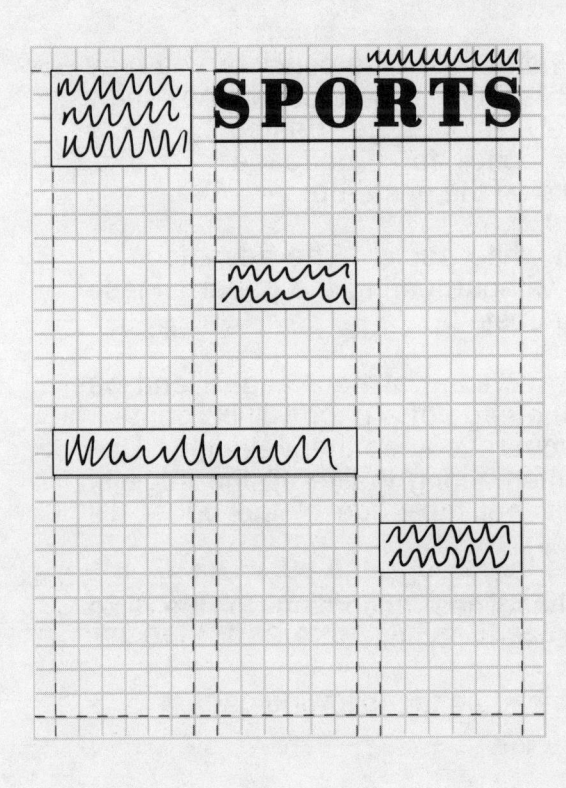

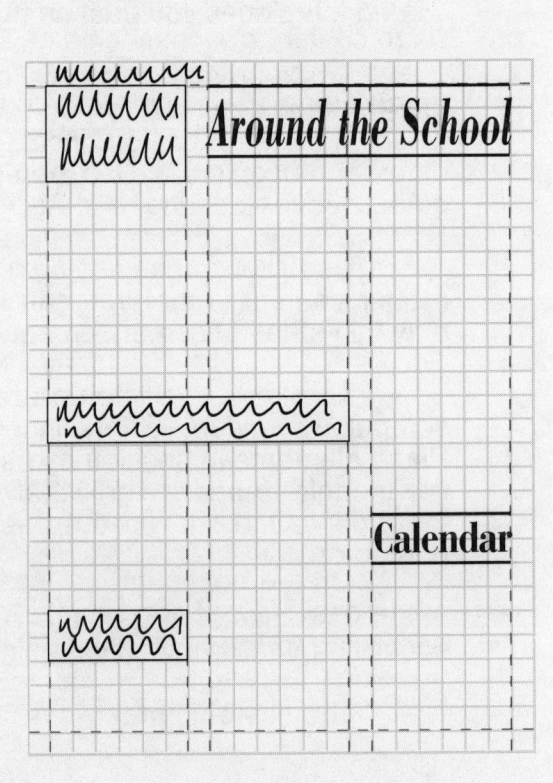

❑ *PRACTICE doing a school newspaper layout by completing Worksheet #70.*

### Paste-Up

To paste up means to prepare each page as it will be printed. Paste-up is done if you don't have a computer program on which to complete pages. The elements -- headlines, copy, ads -- are originally placed on separate pieces of paper. Each is cut out and pasted on a paste-up sheet to create camera-ready pages for you and your printer. A camera-ready page is ready to be photographed to make a master for the copier or plate for the printer.

Supplies needed:

Drawing board or light table
T-square
Triangle
Exacto knife
Scissors
Non-photo blue pencil
Rubber cement
Eraser

The best arrangement for paste-up is to use a light table. If this is not available, a drawing board will do. A T-square and triangle are essential to line up the pieces you past on the sheet.

Paste-up sheets can be drawn with non-photo blue pencil or you may use those pre-printed in non-reproducing-blue ink. This blue will not show when photographed for offset; unfortunately, it does get printed by some older photocopiers. Use non-photo blue pencil for proofreader's marks, guidelines for lettering, and ANY other marks on the paste-up.

Use rubber cement or hot wax, not white paste. The advantage of rubber cement is that you can lift a piece without tearing the paper. Place only thin strips of cement on each piece you paste up.

The keys to paste-up are to keep everything at right angles and be scrupulously clean. Grimy fingerprints on the edge of a page will be printed. Place elements in position by using the T-square to keep them straight. Use the triangle to adjust vertical alignment, remembering to line up the edge of the type to the line on the paste-up sheet, not the edge of the paper it's printed on.

The paste-up artist prepares all headlines according to the size specified by the copy editor, using stencils or press type.

The paste-up process is further described on the following page.

# THE PASTE-UP PROCESS

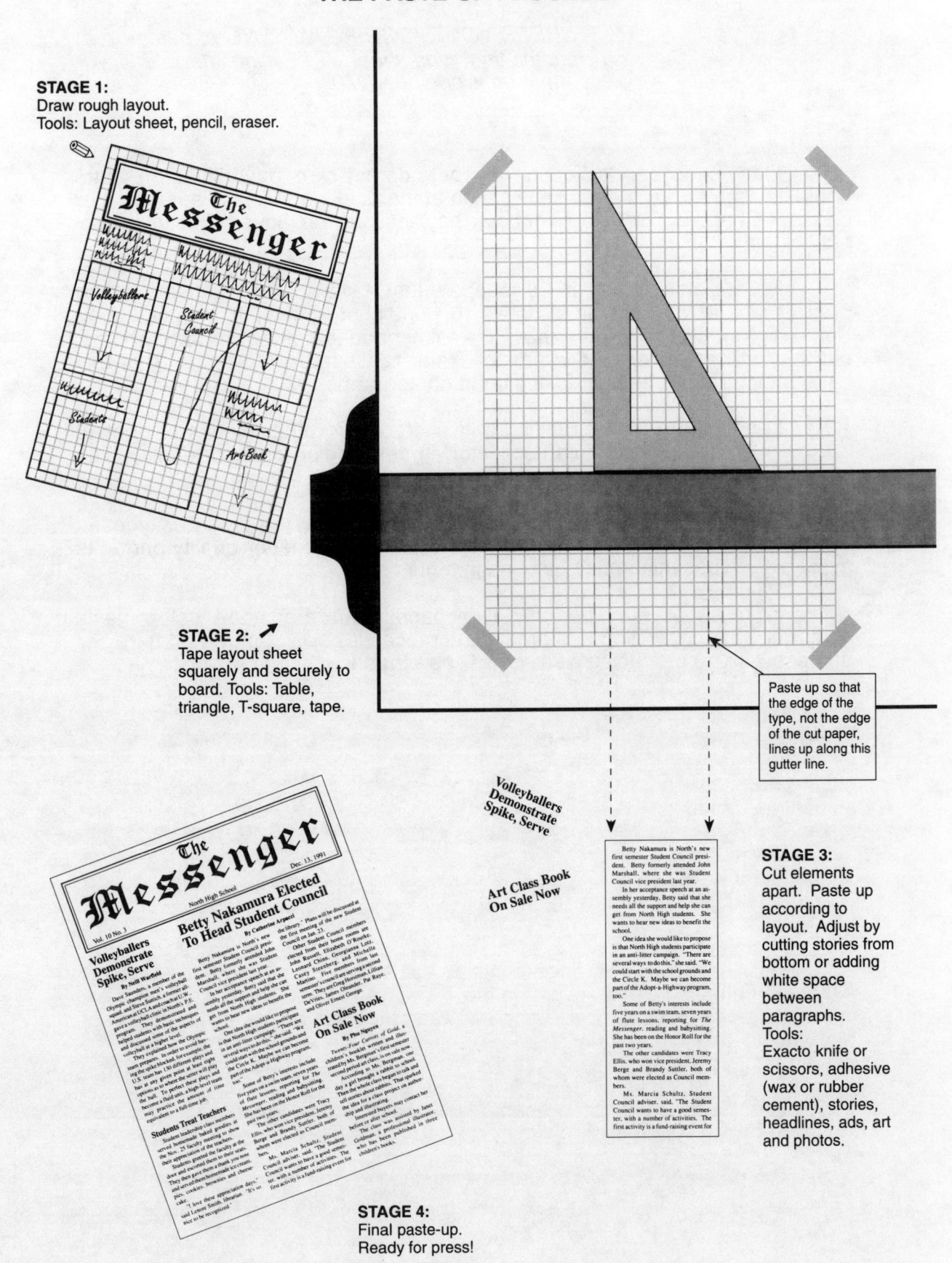

**STAGE 1:**
Draw rough layout.
Tools: Layout sheet, pencil, eraser.

**STAGE 2:**
Tape layout sheet squarely and securely to board. Tools: Table, triangle, T-square, tape.

Paste up so that the edge of the type, not the edge of the cut paper, lines up along this gutter line.

**STAGE 3:**
Cut elements apart. Paste up according to layout. Adjust by cutting stories from bottom or adding white space between paragraphs.
Tools: Exacto knife or scissors, adhesive (wax or rubber cement), stories, headlines, ads, art and photos.

**STAGE 4:**
Final paste-up. Ready for press!

✔ *CHECK YOUR UNDERSTANDING of paste-up by completing Worksheet #71, using the layout you made on Worksheet #70.*

Many secondary school newspapers do not carry advertising. If yours does, you may have a classified section at the back and display ads on other pages. Chapter 4 of this handbook has lessons on advertising in school publications.

Photos only appear in newspapers that have access to offset printing presses, so it may not be possible to print photos in your school paper. Some high-quality copy machines do a fairly good job of reproducing photos, but they still are inferior to a press. Refer to Chapter 2, Section 3, of this handbook for guidelines on taking good photographs.

In addition to offset printing and photocopier, other means of printing are by mimeograph and fluid duplicator, in descending order of quality. The latter two are in all schools.

Depending on the budget, your newspaper may be typed or typeset. Typing can be done in school on a word processor if a letter-quality printer is available. Typesetting must be done in a print shop.

Your paper may be only four pages, but the step-by-step news gathering, writing, editing and production processes you learn about here will be necessary to producing a top-quality newspaper.

# Handbook Chapter 2
# Yearbooks

A highlight of every school year is distribution of the yearbook or annual. It is a memory book to be treasured for years, and it certainly provides humorous reading for future generations. How many of you have chortled over your parents' yearbooks, exclaiming over the clothes, hair styles, and corny slang?

In this chapter you will learn about these aspects of yearbook production: (a) planning; (b) photography; (c) writing; and (d) editing.

## Section 1. Planning.

At planning sessions at the beginning of the year, you and your fellow staff members will decide what to include in the yearbook, page by page. The number of pages will be decided far in advance, based on your budget. The more pages, the more expensive the book will be. Most yearbooks for small high schools and secondary schools are between 40-60 pages, and the cost is less than $15 per copy.

The theme is a single idea expressed throughout the book. It sets the tone and unifies the yearbook because it is repeated in each section. A theme may be humorous or serious; frequently it is expressed in a phrase or quotation. Examples are "Keys to Learning," "Challenge of the Future," "All the World's a Stage."

A yearbook is divided into sections. Part of planning is to decide how many pages will be in each section. These are the most common: title page; faculty; classes by grade; activities (clubs, music and drama groups); sports; advertising; and school life (a section of candid photos with or without captions). Some add a dedication page, a table of contents, or an introductory section which sets the *theme*.

Choose a theme that relates to students' lives or to events in the world or community. Try to have a logo--a drawing, phrase or photo--that symbolizes the theme and can be used throughout the book.

If a picture or story or *caption* does not contribute to fulfilling your goals, it does not belong. A caption is the same as a cutline--it describes or explains a photo.

> ☆ REVIEW: Define caption and theme. Brainstorm lists of possible themes for the upcoming yearbook.

The title page carries the name of the school, the year, and the name of the yearbook *(The Totem, The Wrangler, The Islander)*. Some yearbooks use as a title the graduation year (Class of 88).

The faculty section includes pictures of all faculty and non-teaching staff, identified by name and position. Teachers also may be identified by grade level or the subject they teach.

In the class sections, the graduating class usually is pictured first. Their pictures are printed larger and may be in color if the budget allows. Then the next grade lower is pictured, with the lowest grade in the school placed last. The individual portraits are taken by professional photographers -- the ones that do "school pictures." It is important that the staff make extra effort to get every student's picture. Few things are more disappointing than to be omitted from the yearbook.

Clubs, sports, and other organized groups like band and orchestra are featured in separate sections. Group pictures of each organization are used with a caption naming each member. Students appearing in each photo must be identified accurately. Some yearbooks devote a separate page to each group, with group photo, candid shots, and officers pictured. Others, with fewer pages available, limit pictures in this section to group photos.

School Life is a popular section and is a good place to include photos of students who are not part of an organized group. One of your goals should be that each student is pictured twice: the portrait, and another photo in a different section. Avoid the temptation to fill the School Life section exclusively with your friends or with silly pictures of people caught off-guard. Make it a cross-section of your school routines, from students studying in the library to clowning in the hallway.

Look outside the school for significant events that happened during the school year, particularly if those events had some impact on students' lives. If your city hosted a world's fair or was hit by a tornado, that is important enough to be included in your memory book.

As you plan pages and sections, the managing editor will record the contents of each page on a *ladder diagram*. This shows accurately if your pages will come out even and will be important in planning layouts. Following is an example of part of a ladder diagram. *Signatures* (groups of 16 pages printed in a sheet, eight to a side) and *multiples* (groups of eight pages or one side of a signature) are marked on the ladder diagram. This is the same type of layout you studied in Chapter 8.

| | | | | |
|---|---|---|---|---|
| | | | 1 | title page |
| dedication | 2 | | 3 | dedication |
| table of contents | 4 | | 5 | division page |
| 9th grade | 6 | SIGNATURE | 7 | 9th grade |
| 9th grade | 8 | | 9 | 9th grade |
| 9th grade | 10 | | 11 | 9th grade |
| 9th grade | 12 | | 13 | division page |
| 8th grade | 14 | | 15 | 8th page |
| 8th grade | 16 | | 17 | 8th grade |
| 8th grade | 18 | | 19 | division page |
| 7th grade | 20 | | 21 | 7th grade |

Plans will be based on the deadlines you have to meet. Yearbooks are sent to the publisher in signatures or multiples, each with a different deadline. The first section to go in the mail, sometime in November or December, must be planned first.

☆ *REVIEW: List the sections in a yearbook and discuss ideas for the contents of each section. Define ladder diagram, signature and multiples.*

✔ *CHECK YOUR UNDERSTANDING of planning a yearbook by completing Worksheet #72.*

## Section 2. Writing for the yearbook.

Much of the writing you do for the yearbook will be composing picture captions. The caption writer's primary task is to be sure every person is correctly identified and every name is spelled right. Either the photographer or writer records the names when the picture is taken. After a print is made, ask the group adviser to verify the names of all students. In the caption, help the reader locate those pictured by naming them in order by row.

*EXAMPLE:* Swing choir members are (front row) . . .

Don't state the obvious in picture captions ("Students eat lunch in the lunchroom") and don't try too hard for cute slogans ("Ain't we cute?"). Avoid such trite statements as "Studying hard!" or "Sure looks good!" Limit the caption information to The Big Six. If further details about an event are necessary, write a feature story to go with the picture.

*EXAMPLES:*

Student council officers chaired their first meeting Sept. 22. They are Randy Oster, president; June Ritenhouse, vice president; Michael Trent, secretary-treasurer.

The winning basket against Trojan Junior High was made by Wendy Sloan in this game on Jan. 10.

☆ *REVIEW: Explain the two suggestions mentioned above for writing captions.*

**Feature stories** review the year in general or describe specific events. Be sure someone from the staff attends each major event and writes a story immediately afterward. Use the information on feature writing you learned in Chapter 6. An account of the year may be a personal narrative, or may be based on interviews and polls of students and staff. Study the following examples, the first a year-end review story and the second describing one event.

## MARCHING TO THE RIGHT BEAT

"I hated early band practices because they were a hassle and I had to get up early every morning," said freshman Shawna Rackley.

"Early practice was a pain, but it was one that we had to bear because it was the only way to improve the band," said freshman Mai Nguyen.

This is the way most of the freshmen in the high school band felt about getting to school an hour early every day to practice music and marching routines.

But all of the practice and hard work paid off. The band won first place in regionals which were held here at Western Heights on October 31.

On November 7, the band went to a state contest held in Lawton, Oklahoma. They took first place in class 4A.

"I was really proud because of all the effort we put into our show," said freshman Melody Martin.

Then on November 9, the band won second place in an open class competition held in Carthage, Missouri.

The eighth-grade band also did well this year. At a parade held in Weatherford, Oklahoma, the eighth graders took first place.

"I thought we were good, but I was astonished when we won," said eighth grader Dustin Mustain.

According to Mrs. Martha Walker, the junior high band director, the seventh-grade band is a good band with a lot of potential.

"It's an easy class but you have to work hard at it. It's like having homework every night," said seventh grader Tammy Baldridge.

Other concerts and contests that were attended by the junior high bands were the Winter Concert on December 12, the contest concert on February 6, the Elk City Band Contest on February 19, the District Solo Contest held here at Western Heights on March 8, and the Spring Concert on May 15.

By Jennifer Traviolia

### ONCE IN A LIFETIME -- DREAMS REALLY DO COME TRUE

Do you have spirit? If so then maybe you took part in some of the activities during Spirit Week.

The first day of Spirit Week was Bum Day. The second was Nerd Day. The students got to wear their "Jams" on the third day.

"I liked wearing my 'Jams' and I thought Spirit Week was really fun," said freshman Mark Young.

On the fourth day everyone wore red, white and blue, the school colors. Finally, on Friday the students got to dress-up as their favorite star.

The purpose of the various days was to get the student body into the spirit of homecoming.

Apparently there was not a lot because only a few students took part on most of the dress up days. Jams Day and Nerd Day were the most successful.

By Jennifer Traviolia and Jana Wilson

(Both feature stories from *Jet Log '86,* Western Heights Junior High, Oklahoma City, Oklahoma)

✔ *CHECK YOUR UNDERSTANDING of writing yearbook features by completing Worksheets #73 and #74.*

## Section 3. Photography.

Without good photos, and lots of them, your yearbook will be a flop. Here are some hints for taking good pictures:

1. Get action shots, not posed pictures. Shoot students as they go through the daily schedule: working in science lab, drawing in art class, giving a report, waiting in the cafeteria line, groaning through aerobics.

2. Make a goal of getting a candid shot of everyone in school. It's not fair -- and not good journalism -- to take pictures only of your friends.

3. Don't try to be funny by picturing anyone in an embarrassing or misleading photo. Schools, students, and teachers have been sued for this.

4. Compose each shot so it has a focal point and is balanced.

5. A closeup of one student or two to represent an activity usually is more effective than a shot of a group. This is especially important with large groups such as band or a football team.

6. Shoot at least two pictures of everything -- one horizontal and one vertical. When you're taking the pictures, you don't know how they will be used in a layout. Having a choice of both horizontal and vertical composition helps the editor design pages.

It is the editor's job to plan photos in advance. Be sure to schedule a photographer to attend all major events, such as sports contests, social occasions, assemblies and other special presentations.

If your budget permits color photos in one section, plan those first. The publisher must have them earlier than others to process them.

☆ *REVIEW: Restate the hints for taking good photos. Look at the photos in your own or another school's yearbook. Discuss whether they follow the suggestions made in the previous section. Pretend you are a photographer. Explain how you will get good photos.*

## Section 4. Editing.

Each yearbook editor is in charge of one section. Editors have the job of writing headlines, editing copy, preparing layouts and meeting deadlines. What you learned in studying newspaper and magazine editing will help you edit the yearbook.

### Style Book

Follow your newspaper style book for usage, abbreviations, numbers and names. Use these guidelines for captions:

1. Write in the present tense.

2. Start with the front row in identifying people in a group photo. Since readers naturally look from left to right, you don't need to write that in the caption.

3. Use capital letters or boldface type to highlight each row and make it easier for the reader.

   *EXAMPLE:*

   FRONT ROW: Jane Allen, Owen Lester, Naomi Sutton, Shonelle Howland; SECOND ROW: Roy Matthiesen, James Reardon, Trang Nhu, Marcus Holden; BACK ROW: Maria Sanchez, Suzanne Olivier, Mary Pat O'Hara, Mario Santos.

4. Look at the punctuation in the example above. Use commas between each name. Omit the "and" before the last name in each series. Follow "first row" with a colon. End the list of each row except the last with a semicolon.

5. Use the first and last name of each person.

6. When identifying people by title, use commas and semicolons as in the following example:

   *EXAMPLE:*

   Computer club officers are Roy Chinn, president; Luella Grossman, vice president; Francis Noland, secretary; Bang Nguyen, treasurer.

☆ *REVIEW: Look through your yearbooks again to see if they follow this style for captions. If not, can you state what their style rules are?*

✔ *CHECK YOUR UNDERSTANDING of writing yearbook captions by completing Worksheet #75.*

## Headlines

Yearbook headlines are like magazine headlines. Usually limited to one line, they label the page and attract attention. Don't strain to be cute. A headline like "Computer Club Sets Membership Record" or "That Championship Season" are perfectly adequate.

## Layouts

Review the guidelines for magazine layout in Chapter 8; they will help you design yearbook spreads. The elements you will have to work with are photos, copy blocks, headlines and art work, laid out in double-page spreads. Copy blocks may be small (picture captions) or large (feature stories). Captions may be printed in a group called a *caption cluster*. Feature stories may be printed in any number of columns from two to six.

Your yearbook publisher will provide sample layouts which you can follow in some or all of the sections. If you don't like those, use one of the traditional layout styles: magazine/mosaic, horizontal, vertical, or modrian. These can be mixed and matched among sections but must remain consistent within each section.

Following are examples of each style.

### *Magazine/Mosaic*

This style is nearest to that described in Chapter 6. The elements are fitted around a central focus, most often a large photo. In this example, two photos are spread across the gutter.

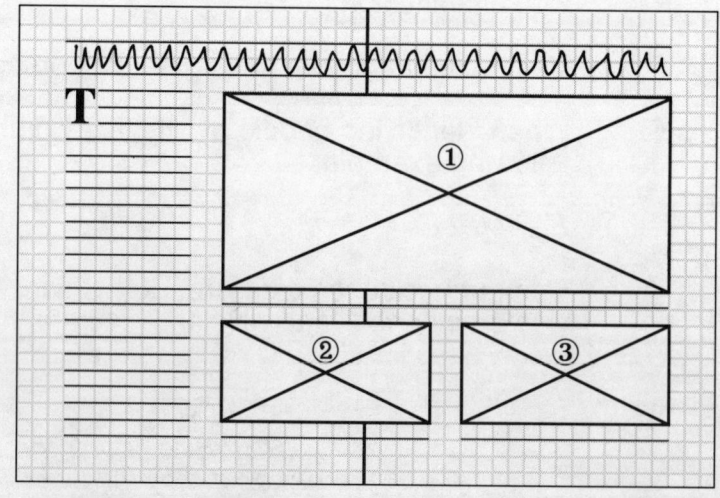

Magazine/Mosaic

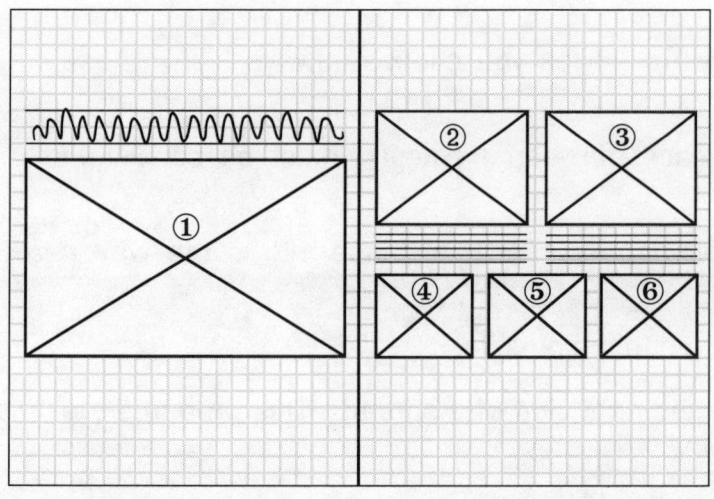

### Horizontal

Upper and lower margins are pulled in, and the design is laid out in a horizontal band across a double-page spread. Captions are grouped in two caption clusters.

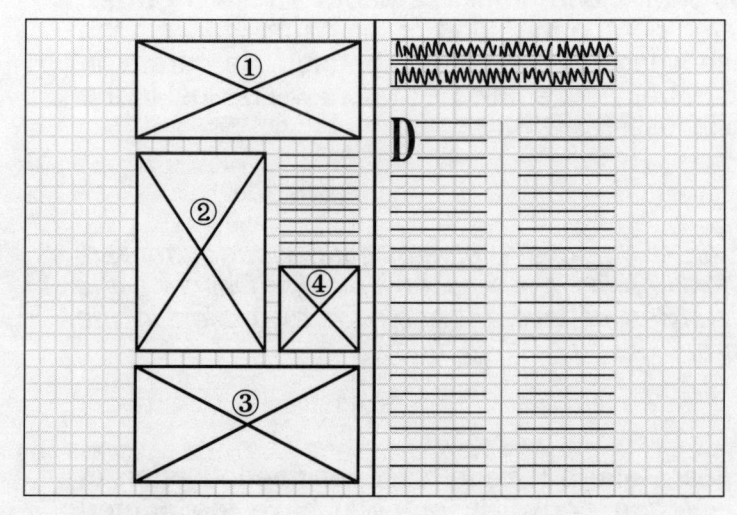

### Vertical

Right and left margins are pulled in, and the design is laid out in a vertical band across the double-page spread. All captions are grouped in one caption cluster.

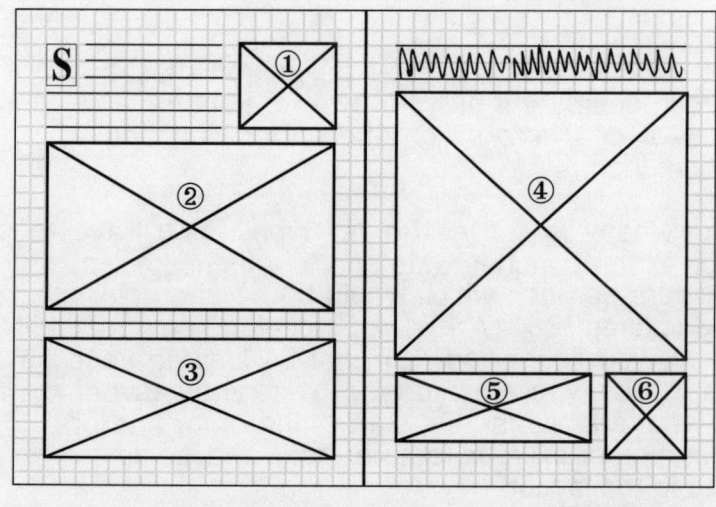

### Modrian

The space is divided into four uneven quadrants, and the elements are laid out within each quadrant. In this example, the uneven quadrants are balanced internally and with each other. Unlike the Magazine/Mosaic design, no element creates a central focus.

Horizontal

Vertical

Modrian

Regardless of which style or styles you choose, always follow these guidelines:

1. Internal margins (the space between elements) must be consistent throughout the book.

2. Design layouts in double-page spreads, because this is the way a reader will see them.

3. Keep copy and white space to the outside.

4. Place division pages on the right side of a spread. This prepares the reader for a change in section.

5. Use the same style of type throughout the yearbook.

Two special techniques are used frequently to make layouts more interesting. They are *bleeding* photos and running a photo across a *gutter*. A bleed is a picture that is printed right to the edge of the page, ignoring the margin. The gutter is the place where the pages are bound. Be careful in placing a photo across the gutter, because a little bit always will be lost in the binding. Don't use photos with faces.

> ☆ *REVIEW: Explain bleed, double-page spread, gutter, caption cluster, copy block. Describe the four styles of layout. Look for examples in the yearbooks you have to study.*

Yearbook editors must learn one additional skill not needed often in newspapers and magazines -- *fitting copy*. In order to have the printed page come out like your layout, you must know exactly how many words (or letters) it takes to fill each copy block you have drawn in. As a yearbook editor, you don't have the option of cutting a story or jumping to another page.

Your yearbook publisher should provide a copy guide that makes it easy to fit copy. However, you can compute it on your own. Each type size and style has a specific number of *characters*, or letters, per inch and a specific number of lines per column inch.

For example, the yearbook copy is set in 10-point type. You have marked on your layout a copy block three inches wide and four inches deep. This 10-point type has 17 characters per inch which would be 51 characters in each line of a three-inch wide column (3 x 17 = 51). Since you know that six lines fit into each column inch, you figure you can print 24 lines in your four-inch column. Therefore, set your typewriter to type 51 characters per line, and edit your copy until you have 24 lines. Or, start at the other end of the process by counting the characters in your feature story and deciding how large a copy block is needed in the layout.

Try this example: You have marked your layout with a block six inches wide and three inches deep. Using the same 10-point type, how many lines of copy will fit into that space? How many characters will fit in each line?

If you said, 18 lines with 102 characters per line, you are correct.

☆ REVIEW: *Define character. Explain fitting copy.*

Remember to label every photo, caption and copy block with the page number and to key each one to the layout. Copy blocks, headlines and artwork are marked with letters; photos with numbers. If you write on the backs of photos, use a felt-tip pen, not a ballpoint.

✔ *CHECK YOUR UNDERSTANDING of yearbook layout by completing Worksheet #76.*

Editing photos requires special skills. The difference between a good and bad picture often is in how it is ***cropped,*** which means how it is trimmed. Cropping means to eliminate the parts of the photo which detract from the focal point. Photos also are cropped in order to fit into a layout.

You don't actually cut off the edges of the photo. Using a grease pencil which can be rubbed off, place marks on the photo. A darkroom technician will use the marks as a guide to crop the photo by sizing it on the enlarger before printing it. Crop carefully, however, so you don't amputate any body parts or make the picture hard to understand.

Another photo editing technique is ***sizing.*** In the darkroom, photos can be enlarged or reduced. The same picture is printed in a different size but in the same proportions; the shape cannot change.

The easiest way to crop and size photos is to use the device provided by your publisher or a proportion wheel available from graphic arts supply stores. These aids help you to figure out size changes. For example, the editor wants to reduce the width of an 8 X 10 photo to fit a four-inch column in the layout. Since the width of the original is eight inches, a 50 percent reduction will bring it to four inches. Since the proportions of the photo are constant, the height must also be reduced by 50 per cent, bringing it to five inches.

After they are sized, photos are marked on the back with the amount of reduction or enlargement expressed in percentages, such as 38% or 120%.

☆ *REVIEW: Explain cropping, sizing. Look at some photos in old yearbooks and decide how they might have been cropped.*

✔ *DEMONSTRATE your understanding of fitting copy and sizing photos by completing Worksheet #77.*

The managing editor will keep track of deadlines by keeping a record for each page, either in a notebook or on a chart. It will state the page number and a checklist for when each step is completed: rough layout, final layout, copy and headlines, photos, proofreading. Your adviser must initial each completed layout before it is mailed.

## Section 5. Yearbook staff.

Following is a list of yearbook staff positions.

Managing editor:
-- Supervises and assists section editors
-- Reviews rough layouts and photo assignments
-- Keeps track of deadlines
-- Reviews each completed layout
-- Maintains futures book

Section editors:
-- Assign photos
-- Prepare layouts
-- Edit copy and photos
-- Write headlines

Writers:
-- Write captions and feature stories as assigned by section editors

Typists:
-- Type all copy, using publisher's forms according to instructions

Proofreaders:
-- Read all typed copy and mark errors
-- Read page proofs and mark errors
-- Check to be sure photos are correctly identified

Photographers:
-- Take all photos as assigned by editors

Artists:
-- Prepare line drawings of illustrations required for ads or other yearbook pages

Advertising manager:
-- Supervises and assists sales representatives
-- Makes layouts for ad pages
-- Keeps files of advertising contracts

Advertising sales representatives:
-- Prepare ad layouts for prospective buyers
-- Make sales calls
-- Complete advertising contracts

Business manager:
-- Keeps records of advertising sales and income
-- Keeps records of yearbook sales and income
-- Keeps records of all expenses

Distribution manager:
-- Promotes yearbook sales
-- Supervises and assists sales representatives

Probably some jobs will overlap. The advertising manager and managing editor may be the same person. Students may double as salespeople for ads and for yearbooks. In some schools, every staff member is required to sell advertising.

# Handbook Chapter 3
# School Magazines

Most school magazines are literary and arts magazines, collections of drawing and writing by students. The magazine staff does not write the stories; their job is to edit. All the writers are "freelance." A magazine is a showcase for all students' talent and an opportunity for the media class to be creative in layout and publication design.

## Section 1. Structure.

School magazines have these parts: cover with nameplate, table of contents, masthead, and a variety of features. If you are just starting a magazine at your school, pick a name and design a distinctive nameplate to go at the top of the cover. Examples of names are *Wordsmith* and *Magical Thoughts.* As with other magazine, the nameplate remains the same on every issue. The cover picture may be a design by the staff art director, artwork submitted by other students, or an outstanding photo.

Write the table of contents last, after the final layout is complete. List each piece by title, author, and the page number it begins on. Do not number the contents page. Be sure to include the magazine name, school name and address, volume number and date. This can be at the top of the table of contents or on a separate title page.

List names and titles of all staff (editor-in-chief, typist) and advisers on the masthead. It may appear on the inside of the front cover or at the bottom or on the back of the contents page.

The editors will look for a variety of fresh, original features. Decide what kinds of writing your magazine will have. Here are some suggestions: poetry, short story, essay, critiques, and short nonfiction. Artwork is limited to prints or charcoal or ink drawings. Paintings will not reproduce well in black and white. Don't overlook illustrations students draw for reports. If you have the printing capability, you may add artistic photos or a photo essay. This is not the place for yearbook-type photos of students.

Strive for a balance among *genre,* or types of writing and art. Look beyond language arts classes for contributors. Nonfiction articles can be reports written for history or science. Your goal should be to gather as many different types of writing from as many different students as possible. If you receive a piece that is too long to print in full, you may use an *excerpt,* a portion of it.

Early in the year, issue an announcement about the magazine and follow up with regular reminders. Encourage students to submit their original work through their teachers. Use the bulletin, posters, personal visits, the newspaper, and any other means of publicity you have to keep reminding students to submit their work.

Following is a table of contents from a school magazine.

## MAGICAL THOUGHTS
### C. W. Stanford High School
*Volume 5, No. 2*

| | |
|---|---|
| School is Out, poem by Susan Ort | 2 |
| Tornado, story by Eric Plotz | 3 |
| Drawing, by Li Fong | 5 |
| Ghost in the Attic, poem by Jan Crum | 6 |
| Photo, by Amy Leibowitz | 8 |
| To Mom, poem by Maria Martinez | 9 |
| In Time of War, story by Edward Holzent | 10 |
| Drawing, by Norman Holzent | 13 |
| Drawing, by Judith Lynn O'Conner | 14 |
| Life on the Cell Level, illustrated essay by Janine Ferrance | 15 |
| Billie Jean King, biography by Shawn White | 17 |
| Photo, by James Ngu | 19 |

☆ *REVIEW: Explain genre and excerpt. List the parts of a magazine.*

## Section 2. Editing.

Selecting work to go in the magazine is an important job. An ***editorial board*** will review all the work submitted and select the pieces to be included in the magazine. The editors and one or two adult advisers will make up the board. In your publicity, encourage everyone to submit, but make it clear that it is a competitive process. Not everyone's piece will be published.

To be sure each piece is the original work of the student, ask him/her to sign a Statement of Originality, which is attached to the manuscript or artwork. This protects the magazine from violating another author's ***copyright***. Literary and artistic work is protected by copyright, which gives the author or artist sole rights to distribute it. It means no one can reproduce any part of it without the artist's permission, which may include paying a fee. When students submit manuscripts to the editorial board, they are giving permission for publication in the magazine, but nowhere else.

You can copyright the material in your magazine by printing the word "Copyright," the date, the name of your school or your teacher, and the words "All rights reserved" on the back of the cover or title page. Then anyone who wants to reprint any of it will have to get your permission.

If you copy someone's work and pass it off as your own, you are committing ***plagiarism***. The Statement of Originality is your way of guaranteeing the work has not been plagiarized.

☆ *REVIEW: Look at the copyright in this book. Explain genre, copyright, plagiarism.*

Once you are satisfied the work is original, it must be evaluated. The editorial board establishes criteria for an objective evaluation so each piece is judged by the same standards. Poetry, fiction, nonfiction, drawing and photos each are judged differently.

Following are points to consider in evaluation. Study them before you start to review any work submitted for publication.

You must be able to state the theme or main idea of every piece. Be sure each piece is in good taste -- no offensive language or descriptions.

The foremost criterion for artwork and photos is that they must reproduce well. If photos are blurry or lack sharp contrast, you can't use them. They will only get worse when printed.

In evaluating fiction, consider if it has a logical plot and if the characters are believable. Dialog should sound natural. Nonfiction must follow a logical sequence and show that the writer has done his/her research. Both fiction and nonfiction should have an opening paragraph that gets the readers' attention and pulls them into reading more.

Read poems aloud to see if they flow smoothly. Good poetry includes figures of speech such as simile and metaphor or poetic devices such as rhyme or alliteration. However, not every poem has to rhyme.

☆ *REVIEW: Explain several points to consider when evaluating written or visual work for a school magazine.*

## Section 3. Production.

A literary/arts magazine probably will be published only once, usually in the spring. Undoubtedly, many of the magazine staff also will be on the newspaper or yearbook staff. Set the final deadline in March.

Magazine staff and their tasks include:

Editor-in-chief
-- Sets up deadlines and holds staff responsible for completing tasks on time
-- Assists in planning, layout, production
-- Makes the final decision on placement of stories and pictures
-- Serves on the editorial board

Poetry editor; story editor
-- Reads and marks all copy
-- Prepares layouts with art director
-- Serves on the editorial board

Art editor
-- Prepares layouts with poetry and story editors
-- Prepares pasteups
-- Letters titles; draws other graphics
-- Serves on the editorial board

Proofreader
-- Reads everything and marks corrections

Typesetter
-- Sets type and makes corrections as marked

Printer
-- Prints, collates and staples magazines

Advertising manager (if ads are to be sold)
-- Use the same process you learned for the yearbook

Business/distribution manager (if magazines are to be sold)
-- Plans and supervises distribution
-- Keeps financial records

As editor of a literary/artistic magazine, you will not rewrite or change the writers' work in any way, except to correct errors of spelling and grammar.

Your creativity will come out in the layout and design. Review sections in Chapter 8, on magazine layout and production, and in Handbook Chapter 2, on publishing a yearbook. Don't be afraid of bold design and unusual layout. School magazines usually are printed in a 8.5 X 11 format or 7 X 8.5 (an 8.5 X 14 sheet folded once). Follow instructions for layout in Handbook Chapter 1.

❏ *FIND IDEAS for graphics and design by completing Homework #30.*

# Handbook Chapter 4

# Advertising

Advertising can play an important part in financing your school newspaper, magazine or yearbook. If your budget depends in part on advertising, set your goal early in the year for the amount you need to sell. In this chapter you will learn to (a) identify prospects, (b) make a sales call, and (c) design ads for your customers.

## Section 1. Prospects.

*Prospects* are the businesses you think will buy an ad. Different kinds of businesses are good prospects for each of your publications. In Chapter 7 you learned that a newspaper's biggest advertisers are retailers. They can advertise sales and specials, include coupons in their ads, or feature products that will attract students into their stores. Frequent advertisers in school newspapers are fast-food restaurants, clothing stores, hair salons, and book or music shops. In yearbooks and magazines, good prospects are service businesses like banks and real estate companies. They will advertise to establish their image in the community and they know that parents read the publications.

After you have a list of prospects, it is the advertising manager's job to keep it up-to-date. Record information on each merchant, such as whether they have advertised before and the name of the person who places advertising. The advertising manager also will keep a record of what happened at each sales call. Did the prospect buy an ad, say to come back, or simply was not interested?

Concentrate on businesses within walking distance of your school but don't omit stores in other neighborhoods where your students live or visit.

☆ *REVIEW: Define product, service, prospect.*

❏ *MAKE a list of prospects for each of your school publications by completing Worksheet #78.*

Teenagers have great buying power in the U.S. Many retailers direct all of their advertising to the teenage market. Before calling on prospects, conduct *market research* in your school. Find out what items students buy most, how much money they have to spend, and what stores they spend it in. This information can be used by salespeople.

❏ *UNDERSTAND the buying power of students at your school by completing Worksheet #79.*

## Section 2. Sales.

As a salesperson, you need to be prepared before making a sales call. Visit the store and learn what its best features are. If you don't already know, call first to find out whose job it is to buy advertising. Take with you a sales kit that contains the following: a summary of your market research, a copy of your newspaper or yearbook, one or two ad layouts you've drawn for this store, and advertising contracts. Your teacher will give you copies of contracts.

The more you sound like a professional salesperson, the better chance you have to make a sale. Introduce yourself like this to a new prospect:

"Hello. My name is Denise Carlisle, and I'm a journalism student at Yarrowville High School. I'd like to show you some ideas for ads in our school newspaper." If the merchant has advertised before, have copies of their previous ads with you. Introduce yourself and say, "We'd like to run your ad in our yearbook again this year. Do you want to make any changes?"

Be prepared to tell the retailer why s/he should buy an ad. The best reason is that you can guarantee almost 100 percent readership of their message; most students read every word in their school publications. Point to information from your market research. You may have learned that students think their restaurant has the best hamburgers in the neighborhood.

If the merchant says no, find out why. That information can help you improve your next sales presentation.

Don't be a pest, but be positive. Be sure you have a chance to sell the benefits of advertising and show your layouts.

☆ REVIEW: In pairs, role-play introducing yourself to a store manager and explaining the benefits of advertising in a student newspaper, yearbook and magazine. Take turns playing each role.

## Section 3. Layout.

Prospects are much more likely to buy an ad if you can show them creative layouts. A layout is an actual size drawing of the ad. If the store has not advertised before, draw a 2 X 4 layout. Review the principles of advertising and the elements of ads explained in Chapter 7. If the store you are calling on advertises in the daily newspaper, copy that ad. There is no point in creating something new if you can use the same idea.

Use your best copywriting skills to write an attention-getting headline. Draw it on your layout in large type -- 18 point or larger.

Illustrations come from several sources. Photographs of the store or an item on sale are eye-catching. A clever angle some schools use is to picture their students as models in the ad, especially for clothing stores. If you have a skilled artist on staff, ask him/her to do a sketch for you. Other sources of illustrations are books of "clip art," which contain drawings of all kinds of people and products, as well as some headlines and buzz words. Review the ad layouts in Chapter 7.

✔ CHECK YOUR UNDERSTANDING of ad layout by completing Worksheet #80.

The prospect may like the layout you prepared but may wish to change it or substitute something else. Accept the changes; don't argue.

Some customers will have camera-ready ads ready to give you. For others, you will have to add the store name and address or change the border to make it fit your column width.

First-time advertisers may want to run a small ad once or twice as a trial. Many student newspapers use a business card as the ad copy.

Don't leave without filling out and signing a contract. Have two copies with carbon paper inserted between them. Leave the original with the merchant. Be sure you are familiar with the contract before you make a sales call.

Before the ad is printed, return with a paste-up as it will appear and have it approved. Advertising deadlines are earlier than copy deadlines to allow time for this extra step. Be sure to proofread ad copy in the same way you check all copy.

After each issue, send a *tear sheet* to the advertiser along with a bill. A tear sheet is their ad, cut out of the paper and pasted on a piece of heavy paper. It proves the ad ran as stated in the contract.

> ☆ *REVIEW: Study exchange papers and yearbooks, daily newspapers, and magazines for ideas on layouts, headlines, and advertising prospects. Collect business cards from some adults and discuss whether they could be used as ads.*

Combination ads are very effective in school publications. They run as a full- or half-page under a big headline such as "Happy Holidays From These Local Merchants" or "Congratulations, Grads!" Each retailer pays a small fee to have the business name, address and telephone listed. This is also another place where copies of business cards can be used as an ad.

Except for combination ads, most yearbooks and magazines run only full-page, half-page, or quarter-page ads. Usually, these are grouped together at the back in an advertising section.

An alternative to selling advertising in a magazine is to solicit patrons. Patrons support the arts through contributions, in this case $5 or $10 per person. In return, patrons receive a free copy of the magazine and their names listed as a patrons on a page at the back.

> ☆ *REVIEW: If you have a school magazine, list possible patrons.*

# Handbook Chapter 5
# Rights and Responsibilities of the Student Press

In Chapter 11 you learned about the rights granted to the media and to individuals under the U.S. Constitution. In this chapter you will learn what rights and responsibilities you have as student writers, editors or photographers. You will study (a) the law related to school media, (b) advertising and propaganda, and (c) editorial policy.

## Section 1. Student publications and the law.

Student publications have a problem not shared by the general mass media -- the possibility of censorship by an adviser or by the school administration. Many schools have a policy of **prior review,** which is review by an administrator before anything that might be controversial is published. Problems arise when the principal censors a story or photo s/he considers inappropriate, after the student editors and the adviser have approved it. The right to prior review has been challenged in many high schools and colleges. Most often the courts have said it is prohibited by the First Amendment unless administrators can show the material is libelous, obscene or likely to create a substantial disruption of the school environment.

Law is established by legislation and by **precedent.** Precedent means a case is tried, then often retried several times on appeal before a final decision is made which becomes the standard followed in similar cases. Some issues come to court many times, such as those regarding obscenity. The precedent the court looks at in deciding obscenity issues is *Miller v. California* (see Chapter 11).

The law regarding censorship in schools has come from numerous cases. The most important are *Tinker v. Des Moines (1969)* and *Hazelwood School District v. Kuhlmeier (1988).* In the first case, a student whose last name was Tinker, along with others, was suspended for wearing a black armband in a show of protest against the war in Vietnam. The Supreme Court ruled in favor of the students and in its decision made a statement that has served for years as a precedent for many cases of censorship in schools. The justices said ". . . students do not shed their Constitutional rights to freedom of speech or expression at the schoolhouse gate . . ."

This precedent was broadly interpreted in subsequent years to mean that students had the same guarantees to free speech in school as adults. The decision in the Hazelwood case altered that position.

In that case, the principal removed a two-page special section from the high school newspaper because he believed stories in the section to be "inappropriate, personal, sensitive and unsuitable." The section dealt with teenagers' problems. The stories in question were about teen pregnancy and teens whose parents had divorced.

The Supreme Court upheld the right of the school administration to exercise prior restraint. They said this case was different from Tinker because "the former question addresses educators' ability to silence a student's personal expression that happens to occur on the school premises. The latter question concerns educators' authority over school-sponsored publications, theatrical productions, and other expressive activities that students, parents, and members of the public might reasonably perceive to bear the imprimatur of the school."

This does not mean that school administrators must review school publications before publication, but it does give them legal authority to do so.

To avoid a confrontation, it is best to decide on a means of communication among administrators, adviser, and students that will ensure full and fair reporting of all information. Before deciding to print a controversial story or editorial, weigh the consequences of publishing against the importance of reporting the issue.

> ☆ *REVIEW: Check your School Board policies to learn what guidelines on student publications are in effect in your school district. Discuss the current practice in your school on review by school authorities.*

When students are treated like all other journalists before the law, however, it means they are not protected from suit. Advisers can be sued for what appears in student media. Because students are minors, the law allows their parents to be sued on their behalf. Legal action can be taken against the student press for obscenity, libel, invasion of privacy or ***incitement***. It is illegal to incite, or urge, others to commit illegal acts. For example, an editorial can criticize school policies, but it cannot urge students to turn over all the trash cans as a means of protest. Libel in student media is the same as in other media: publishing something that holds a person up to ridicule or that damages his/her reputation. If a court finds the school guilty as charged, administrators, adviser and students' parents could be ordered to pay ***damages*** awarded by the court. This is an amount of money which will make up for the embarrassment or harm the person has suffered.

The greatest culprits in libel cases are gossip columns in student newspapers and pictures or captions in yearbooks. For example, an item in a gossip column says, "What do John Q. and Elaine P. do when they disappear every lunch period?" John or Elaine or their parents could sue for libel, charging that this statement damages their reputations.

Since yearbooks are such an important part of a student's school year, the yearbook staff has a responsibility to be sensitive in depicting students. Don't use pictures of people taken off-guard where they look wild-eyed or silly. Don't try for a joke at someone's expense. Be careful of labeling students (Biggest Flirt, Cutest Couple, Class Clown). The students named, or their parents, may not care to be remembered in that fashion. Sarcastic or insulting predictions and comments in yearbooks have been the object of lawsuits filed by students who were humiliated and suffered emotional distress.

Follow these suggestions to avoid a libel suit:

1. Attribute a source for every quote. Check a quote with the source if it may be controversial or open to misunderstanding.

2. Don't repeat rumor as fact. Check out leads with a second source and verify the accuracy of everything you print.

3. Use careful language in reporting an incident. While you may not need to protect an accused murderer, you may have to report on an alleged cheating scandal or other rule violations.

4. Don't use labels or name-calling, even if you intended the line to be humorous. "I was only kidding" is not an acceptable defense in a libel suit.

5. Consider school and community standards in your choice of language. Profanity is not acceptable in school and is not acceptable in school publications. Omitting offensive words will not change the meaning of a story.

6. Finally, use good taste. The language you use in public speaking is the language of journalism. Slang may be written as part of a quotation, but use standard English in stories and editorials.

7. Students also can be sued for invasion of privacy. It is illegal to go into private areas (files, desks, houses) to get information. It also is an invasion of privacy to secretly record what another person says or to obtain information under false pretenses, such as by concealing that you are a reporter.

Should yearbooks only portray the good things that happened during the year? This question has been controversial in schools in which a tragedy has occurred. Some take the position that events like suicide, murder or scandal are best forgotten. Others believe it is their job to provide a record of everything that happened -- good or bad. Your staff should set a policy on this issue as part of the planning process.

Copyright laws are intended to protect the market value of an original idea. You violate a copyright if you use another's words or artwork without permission and without giving them credit.

Remember these guidelines:

1. Popular logos, slogans, ID or cartoon characters may not be used without permission. Write to the company which owns the copyright for permission.

2. Poems or song lyrics, unless they are in the ***public domain,*** may not be reprinted without permission from the publisher. Material comes into public domain and can be used without permission 50 years after the original copyright.

3. Photos from other books may not be reprinted without permission. (These never reproduce well anyway.)

☆ *REVIEW: In your own words, explain precedent, incitement, prior review, damages, public domain. Explain the significance of these Supreme Court decisions--*Tinker v. Des Moines *and* Hazelwood School District v. Kuhlmeier. *Describe techniques to avoid a libel suit and copyright violation.*

## Section 2. Advertising and propaganda.

In preparing advertising for your school media, the best overall guideline is the Golden Rule: "Do unto others as you would have others do unto you." You feel cheated and angry if you have been taken in by deceptive advertising. Don't allow any ads in your publications to deceive others.

It is an illegal invasion of privacy to use a person's name or picture in an advertisement without permission. Even if you photographed students in a public place drinking cola, you could not use that picture to advertise cola without getting their permission--in writing.

As student editors, you have the right to refuse ads that are deceptive or offensive. Decide at the first of the year what your standards will be.

☆ *REVIEW: What kinds of ads, if any, should not be accepted for student publication?*

Your newspaper will be a propaganda sheet if any of the techniques discussed in Chapter 11 are allowed to slip in -- loaded words, labels, waving the flag, slanting the news.

Guard against allowing opinions to slip into news stories. A sentence such as the following is propaganda: "The band put on a great show last night which was enjoyed by everyone there." Unless you are writing a review, your opinion does not belong in the story; and it is not accurate to say everyone enjoyed it unless you asked everyone there. Describe what you saw and heard without interpretation: "The audience applauded for five minutes and called for two encores."

The following sentence in an editorial is propaganda: "Maybe a few wimps will not stand up for their rights, but this is a free country." You won't convince your reader to change by name-calling; you persuade someone by stating solid facts and reason.

Many press releases are filled with propaganda. To rewrite a press release into a fair news story, first go through and mark The Big Six. Then you can write the lead. Cross out all slanted words and phrases and see if enough facts remain to rewrite one or two more paragraphs.

✔ *CHECK YOUR UNDERSTANDING of propaganda by completing Worksheet #81.*

## Section 3. Editorial policy.

In an editorial policy, you state your responsibilities as journalists. The policy may take the form of a goal statement that is written by the staff for its guidance, or it may be a short simple statement that appears in each issue. Sometimes longer policy statements are published once in the first issue each year.

An editorial policy contains promises on accuracy and fairness. It explains to readers how to submit letters to the editor, which insures the paper's function as a forum for free expression.

Following are examples of editorial policies for school newspapers:

**Editorial Policy**

1. Letters to the Editor will be printed as written except in the case of obscenities, libelous information, or personal attacks. All letters should be signed.

2. All editorials will be unsigned and are the majority opinion of the Editorial Board, consisting of all members of the staff, Mr. Joe Brown, history teacher, and Mr. Freeman Crawford, counselor.

3. We will make retractions of all statements made in error the following issue when they are brought to our attention.

4. We will make a clear distinction between fact and opinion in all news printed.

5. We will make an effort to be fair in covering all aspects of a controversial story.

6. We will abstain from criticism of any racial group, religion, or creed.

7. We will avoid condoning illegal activities.

8. *The Centralian* is an open-minded journal dedicated to the enrichment of education in our school and community. Our policy: If it is not in *The Centralian,* where is it?

*The Centralian*
Central Middle School
Kansas City, Kansas

## Scribe Policy

To define the extent of our obligations to the students and administration of Madison Middle School, *The Scribe* would like to take this opportunity to outline its editorial policy.

Our first concern will always be the welfare of the school, the students and the community.

We will make a clear distinction between facts and opinions, and we will verify all news published.

Our editorials will be neither "the voice of the students" nor "a rubber stamp of the administration." They will be the opinions of the staff and/or editors, and we will be held responsible for their contents.

Our comments on administrative and student body practices will be confined to those practices and will not involve the individuals who administer them.

We feel it is our responsibility to comment not only on school matters but also on community, state and national affairs when they concern the students in some vital way.

We will publish letters to the editor that meet the standards of good taste, as space permits. No anonymous letters will be printed, although names will be withheld on request.

The use of language which in our judgment is offensive or suggestive will be prohibited.

*The Scribe*
Madison Middle School
Eugene, Oregon

A simpler statement may be included in the masthead, such as the following:

Opinions expressed in *The Eagle Eye* are not necessarily those of the South student body, faculty, staff, or the Anaheim Union High School District. Letters to the editor may be turned in to room 11. They must be signed and may be edited for space, libel, incorrect spelling, grammatical errors, or poor taste.

*The Eagle Eye*
South Junior High School
Anaheim, California

☆ *REVIEW: What are the main points covered by an editorial policy?*

✔ *CHECK YOUR UNDERSTANDING of the rights and responsibilities of the student press by completing Worksheet #82.*

✔ *CHECK YOUR UNDERSTANDING of editorial policy by completing Worksheet #83.*

# INDEX

Ad lib, 123
Ads, in newspaper layout, 41, 43
Advance story, 33
Advertiser, local, 94, 97, 100, 103
Advertiser, national, 94, 96, 97, 103
Advertising, deceptive, 148, 149
Advertising, magazines, 96, 97, 116
Advertising, newspapers, 19
Advertising, newspapers, 94-96
Advertising, radio, 100-101
Advertising, school publications, 208-211
Advertising, television, 97-99
Advertising account executive, 93
Advertising agency, 93
Advertising appeals, 90, 91
Advertising campaign, 87, 90, 92, 93
Advertising drawbacks and benefits, 86
Advertising elements, 94
Advertising history, 159, 160
Advertising prospects, school publications, 208, 209
Advertising techniques, 88-89, 97
Anchor, television, 135
Beats, metropolitan newspaper, 9
Beats, school newspaper, 9
Big Six, 28
Billboard, 103, 104
Binding, 117, 118
Blurb, 113
Box, in layout, 43
Budget, 21
Bulldog edition, 23
Business section, newspaper, 16
Buzz words, 94
Byline, 11, 12
Cable channel, 137, 140
Careers in journalism, 163
Caricature, 81
Censorship, 144
Circulation, 19, 23
Classified ad, 19, 20
Classified information, 144
Column inch, 20
Comics, 17, 76, 77
Communication, 1-3
Communications satellite, 140
Computers, 21, 110, 117, 160
Consumer, 85-90, 93, 102, 104
Copy, 22, 93, 94, 96, 97, 100, 102, 103
Copyreading, 40
Copyright, 205
Copywriter, 93
Count, 49, 50
Cue, 127

Cut, 43
Cutline, 15
Dangling comparison, 149
Dateline, 10
Deadline, 21
Decks, headlines, 47, 54
Demographics, 117
Demonstration ads, 89, 98
Direct mail, 101, 102
Disc jockey, 120
Display ad, 19
Double-page spread, 115, 197-198
Dummy, 185
Editing, consumer magazine, 114
Editing, metropolitan newspaper, 41
Editing, school magazine, 205
Editing, school newspaper, 184
Editing, yearbook, 196-201
Editorial board, 205
Editorial cartoons, 12
Editorial of appreciation, 80-81, 182
Editorial of criticism, 77-80, 181
Editorial policy, student press, 216
Editorials, school newspaper, 181-183
Editorials, house, 12
Elements, advertising, 210
Emergency Broadcast System, 127
Endorsement ads, 88, 98
Facts, 26, 28, 29, 31
False endorsement, 149
FCC, 126, 127
Features, background/informative, 14
Features, historical, 14, 73, 178
Features, how-to, 14, 72, 177
Features, human interest, 14
Features, humorous, 14
Features, personality, 14, 74, 179
Filler, 22
First amendment, 212
Flag, 22
Folio line, 185
Follow-up story, 33
Formats, radio, 120-122
Freedom of the press, 150
Freelance writer, 113
Headline, 22, 92, 93, 94, 96, 102, 103, 104
ID characters, 89
Interview, focus, 57
Interview, guidelines, 55-62
Interview, questions, 55, 56, 60
Interview, steps, 55-62
Inverted pyramid, 29, 30
Journal, 112

# INDEX

Justify, 21
Ladder diagram, 191
Layout, ads, 94-96
Layout, advertising, 93-95, 209-211
Layout, consumer magazine, 115-116
Layout, magazine, 114, 115
Layout, metropolitan newspaper, 41-45
Layout, school magazine, 207
Layout, school newspaper, 185-186
Layout, yearbook, 191-192, 197-199
Leads, feature, 71
Leads, news, 9
Letters to the editor, 12, 185
Libel, 147, 148
Library research, 178
Live remote, 138
Logo, 89
Magazine categories, 107-112
Magazine elements, 113, 115, 116
Magazines, consumer, 107
Magazines, history, 156, 157
Magazines, school, 203
Market research, 87, 88, 101
Market research, schools, 209
Market, 136
Mass media, definition, 3
Mass media, introduction, 1
Masthead, magazine, 13, 113
Masthead, newspaper, 13
Medium, 3, 4
Nameplate, 113
Narrative style, 70
Networks, radio, 126
Networks, television, 136
News hole, 22
News stories, types of, 33
News writing, 26, 27
News, criteria, 26
News, levels, 8
News, slanted, 31, 150
Newspaper production, 21
Newspaper, business/economy section, 16
Newspaper, features, 8, 13, 14, 17
Newspaper, sections, 7
Newspaper, types of writing, 7
Newspapers, ethnic, 18
Newspapers, history, 154-156
Newspapers, tabloid, 19
Newspapers, weekly, 18
Obituaries, 17
Objective writing, 31
Obscenity, 144-146
Op/Ed section, newspaper, 12

Packaging, 85, 87, 90, 93, 103
Paste-up, school newspaper, 187-189
Periodical, 107
Photography, yearbook, 195
Photos, 15
Photos, bleeding, 199
Photos, cropping, 200
Photos, gutter, 199
Photos, screen, 23
Photos, sizing, 200
Plagiarism, 205
Point size, 50, 51
Point-of-purchase display, 103
Polls, 62-66
Pornography, 144-146
Presentation ads, 88, 98
Press conference, 66, 67, 176
Press release, 10
Prime time, radio, 122, 127
Prime time, television, 134, 137
Prior restraint, 144
Prior review, 212
Problem/solution ads, 88, 98
Product identification, 89, 90, 92
Product, 85-89
Proofreader, 23
Propaganda, 151, 152
Propaganda, 215
PSA, 126
Public access, 137
Public domain, 215
Purposes, mass media, 3
Purposes, school media, 4
Qualifier, 148
Quotation, attribution, 147
Quotations, 60
Radio advertising, 122, 123
Radio news, 123-126
Radio production, 126, 128
Radio, actuality, 127
Radio, AM/FM, 127
Radio, history, 158
Ratings, radio, 122
Ratings, television, 137
Reporter, 7, 9, 10, 11, 15, 17, 21, 22
Research, for stories, 68
Retraction, 148
Review, critical, 8, 14, 75, 180
Right to know, 143, 146-148
Rights and responsibilities, student press, 212
Salaries, 166
School features, 176-183
School magazine editing, 205-206

# INDEX

School magazine structure, 203-205
School news, criteria, 170
School newspaper sections, 185
School newspaper, 168
School newspaper, advertising, 189
School newspaper, editing, 184
School newspaper, headlines, 184
School newspaper, layout, 184-187
School newspaper, sports, 183
School newspaper, style book, 184
Scoop, 150
Scripts, radio, 122, 123, 125, 127
Scripts, television, 139-140
Service, 85, 86
Signature, magazine, 117, 118
Signature, yearbook, 191
Skills of journalists, 163
Slug, 169, 175
Sources of news, 9, 21
Speech story, 66, 67
Sports section, newspaper, 16
Sports writing, 82, 83
Sports, school newspaper, 172, 183, 185
Spot news story, 33
Staff, consumer magazine, 114
Staff, magazine, 113, 114
Staff, radio station, 127
Staff, radio, 127
Staff, school magazine, 206-207
Staff, school newspaper, 168-170
Staff, school newspaper, 169-170
Staff, television news, 139
Staff, yearbook, 201-202
Storyboard, 97-99
Stringer, 10
Style book, 22
Subjective writing, 31
Subscriber, 19
Syndicated columnist, 12
Table of contents, 113
Tear sheet, 211
Television advertising, 137, 138
Television documentary, 135
Television history, 159
Television production, 140, 141
Television, interactive, 160, 161
Television, program categories, 133-136
Test market, 87
Tombstone headlines, 41
Type face, 49, 50
Typography, 115
Vital statistics, newspaper, 17
Weasel words, 149
Wire service, 10

Word processor, 21
Yearbook editing, 196
Yearbook layout, 197-201
Yearbook planning, 190-192
Yearbook sections, 191
Yearbook staff, 201-202
Yearbook theme, 190
Yearbook writing, 192-195
Yellow journalism, 155

LB 3621.5 .I8 1991